CURTAIN CALL

Curtain Call's inaugural book could only have been created thanks to the trust and unparalleled access that has been afforded us by the various casts, crew, stage management teams, musicians, producers, theatres, publicists and managers, to whom we are so grateful. You know who you are.

Thank You

For Lou, my half orange.

For Tat, Jack & Sammy, stuck like glue.

Published by Curtain Call Ltd.
4th Floor, International House
Queens Road, Brighton
East Sussex BN1 3XE

First published in 2016

A catalogue record of this book is available from the British Library.

ISBN 978-0-9935050-0-3

Project Management: whitefox
Project Manager: Laura Marchant
Design by Amanda Scope/www.amandascope.com
Design Concept by Ethan Kennedy

Production by David Brimble www.davidbrimble.com
Colour reproduction by DawkinsColour Ltd, London
Printed and bound by Printer Trento

1 3 5 7 9 10 8 6 4 2

Cover image: Gemma Sutton and production crew on stage during 'Gypsy' at the Savoy Theatre.

MATT HUMPHREY
AND JOHN SCHWAB

PHOTOGRAPHY BY MATT HUMPHREY

CURTAIN CALL

A YEAR BACKSTAGE IN LONDON THEATRE

FOREWORD BY
DAVID SUCHET CBE

Mark Strong during the warm-up for 'A View From The Bridge' at the Wyndham's Theatre.

Curtain Call aims to celebrate and promote the work of all those on stage, backstage and behind the scenes.

This is our inaugural book, capturing exclusive and intimate moments through photos and interviews, from a number of productions throughout London's vibrant theatre scene in 2015. Also included in the book is an extensive credit section listing all those involved in each production when we covered it.

We aim to watch every show from the audience perspective first, before a single visit backstage during a performance, when we photograph the show and conduct interviews.

Apart from the few formal portraits, all shots in this book are unposed, capturing the authentic life of each show on stage, in the wings, and backstage.

Contents

John Schwab

From the moment I sang 'Happiness' from *You're a Good Man Charlie Brown* in front of my whole school as a second-grader in 1978, I was hooked by the allure of the stage. I spent the rest of my school years in every production in which they would allow me to appear. This addiction never ceased, carrying on through my years at Durham University where I spent countless hours working on too many plays to mention at The Assembly Rooms – at that time the only theatre in Durham.

Before attending Durham University, I remember standing outside the Criterion Theatre in London. It was 1992 and I was nineteen years old, on my first visit to England. I turned to my soon-to-be wife, Tamsin, and said, "One day, I am going to be on one of these stages." Little did I know that just over six years later I would be performing on that very stage with The Reduced Shakespeare Company (which would become my home on and off for seven years). Not only that, I would also appear on stage at The Piccadilly Theatre in my first ever professional theatre engagement as well as at the Theatre Royal Haymarket – two theatres you can actually see while standing outside the Criterion Theatre.

Nearly a quarter of a century on from that first visit, while showing my sons programmes from previous productions in which I had appeared, I didn't have any actual photographs to show them of me backstage. I realised there was nothing I could physically hold in my hand other than my headshot and a few production photos to offer them a glimpse of what actually goes on backstage during a show. An idea leapt into my head and I knew the person I had to call – Matt Humphrey.

I met Matt while doing an understudy job at the Old Vic theatre in 2008. I became aware of his keen eye and watched the portfolio of his backstage photography and portraiture grow over the years. So I was absolutely overjoyed when he agreed to accompany me on this adventure. And what an adventure it has been. When we started out, we thought that if we could cover twenty shows, it would be an absolute success. To have been able to cover nearly sixty shows was way beyond our expectations (or wildest dreams).

We visited *Urinetown* to kick the project off, and what grew out of that first show was that the cast and crew wanted to talk about their experiences backstage. That changed the direction the book was going to take and we made the decision to include quotes and interviews to accompany the photography, giving the reader yet another layer of access to a show.

I felt privileged to chat with so many cast, crew, creatives, musicians, agents and more. Having spoken to more than 400 people for the book, I feel like I have been to the drama school that I couldn't afford to go to after paying overseas fees at university. Their generosity of time, candid insight and wealth of wisdom imparted in those hours and hours I was recording them backstage is something I will never forget and for which I will always be grateful.

Although I couldn't take a theatre job in 2015 due to the Curtain Call project, it's as though I was somehow involved in each production, learning so much from the cast and crew who made us feel welcome on every visit. It couldn't have been more fun meeting everyone and I can honestly say that I love theatre even more today as a result of the year I spent in the company of the hugely talented professionals who are involved in the world-class industry that is London theatre. And I love that Matt and I, and Curtain Call, are a part of it.

I wanted the inaugural Curtain Call annual to be the book that my nineteen-year-old self would have bought to find out about London theatre. I think Matt and I have achieved that.

Matt Humphrey

Photography and theatre have – in its broadest sense – always been intertwined for me. Even before I first set foot backstage, my photography had focused on people and their lives, or the drama of a situation or landscape.

Having taken a leap of faith to leave my previous career as a modern languages teacher to 'become a photographer', my brother gave me a job on the stage crew at The Old Vic. I had never been a regular theatre-goer, and I was immediately fascinated with theatre from this alternative backstage perspective – by the processes, people and logistics involved in putting on a production.

While working on shows, I started to photograph moments between my cues from the wings, fly-floor, corridors and other areas, in an attempt to hone my skills and become more technically proficient. I recall actor Tim Pigott-Smith being impressed at how my seemingly 'magic' camera could see in the dark, and capture these unguarded moments during the show. The realisation that working with low light was more like working with no light, helped refine that area of my photography and made me become a more decisive, rounded photographer.

That was about eight years ago and around the same time that I met John, when he was acting in one of the shows I crewed on. John and I stayed in touch and I started working on more photography jobs with less crew work. One of these jobs was an exciting year-long contract to document the behind-the-scenes life of the Hackney Empire; an extraordinary opportunity to get beneath the skin of an exciting, vibrant and diverse theatre. Shortly after completing that project, John proposed the idea that has become Curtain Call – it was the perfect opportunity and complement of skills.

As we set out to capture a year in the backstage life of London theatre, we had no idea of the scale of the project we were undertaking. Not just in terms of the herculean logistical effort it has been to corral those involved and gather momentum as a new business, but also the range of shows we have covered. The access we have been granted has not only been a huge privilege, but provided unprecedented insight into an outstanding and eclectic range of productions.

Photographically, this has been the most testing, in-depth and varied project I have worked on. Each production has distinct characteristics, giving rise to widely differing circumstantial challenges in capturing the essence of the show. This year has also been a marker for me as I have shot almost the entire project with a new camera system, a Leica rangefinder – it has become part of me, and allowed me to go relatively unnoticed, as it is so unobtrusive. This, and the opportunity to watch and visually unravel the inner life of these shows, while mixing portraiture and reportage photography, have made this my dream job.

When you work on a show, you rarely, if ever, get to see it from the audience's perspective. Your experience and memories of it are so entirely different from those of the theatre-going public. What we have tried to achieve with Curtain Call is not only to provide a record of the productions for everyone who works behind the scenes, giving them the chance to take a virtual bow – but also a candid glimpse of life on the other side of the curtain – rare, normally unseen moments that only go to underline just how magical the world of theatre is.

It is also worth noting that all photographs in this book have been taken without any extra lighting – using only the spill and available light backstage. In many cases it is very dark, so the grain factor creeps in, due to high ISO.
Main equipment used:
Leica M-P Typ 240 camera body
35mm 1.4 Summilux lens

Foreword

By David Suchet CBE

I remember so well the moment when I decided that I wanted to be an actor. I was eighteen years old and a member of the National Youth Theatre. The curtain had come down on our last night of *Bartholomew Fair* at the Royal Court Theatre in London. Make-up removed and back in civvies, I wanted to go down to the auditorium to watch the striking of the set. I stood to one side and saw the scenery coming down and the bars holding the lights being lowered. And as I watched this I recalled being there on that stage, just a few moments previously, and how intensely 'real' the play had been for all of us actors. I recalled the audience sitting in their plush seats, laughing and having a really good time. The atmosphere of that same space was now quite different, but it held a unique magic of its own. It was as though all the 'tricks' were being dismantled and laid bare. It was then – at that moment of inhaling this atmosphere – that I decided I would try to become a professional actor.

I was taught photography, around the age of ten, by my grandfather James Jarché, a professional press photographer. He was passionate about his camera, a

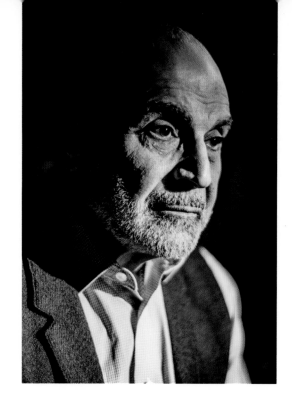

Leica M3 rangefinder, and left it to me when he died. I used the same camera in my film documentary *People I Have Shot*, in which I tried to replicate some of my grandfather's iconic photographs.

These two passions of mine, theatre and photography, have stayed with me all my life. *Curtain Call* encapsulates them both. Matt Humphrey is a most gifted and talented photographer. He too uses a Leica rangefinder camera, which enables him to photograph unobtrusively, discreetly and silently anywhere backstage in any theatre – even at the side of the stage while a play is being performed. John Schwab is also very creative and brings his experience and insights as an actor to the fore when interviewing cast and crew backstage, thus producing dramatic layouts. They're the perfect photographic journalist team.

The photographs in *Curtain Call* reveal, in an uncannily intimate way everything from the camaraderie of the actors, stage management and theatre crews, to the detail of the actors' preparation before going on stage. They even capture fascinating images

'The backstage area in a theatre is a secret place, almost a hallowed space.'

of actors standing in the wings waiting to 'go on'. There are also wonderful photographs of the theatre design sets using only the lighting provided. There is NO FLASH photography here! *Curtain Call* is, however, more than just a series of dramatic photographs. It is a book which documents a year in the theatre with some very insightful quotes from actors. It is a book, which will appeal to everyone who loves theatre – producers, directors, designers, actors and fans. It is my hope that the book might even entice new audiences into the theatre, perhaps for the first time!

There is always a 'backstage' area in places the public visit. Restaurants, hotels, art galleries and museums – they all have those areas where the public just doesn't go. The backstage area in a theatre is a secret place, almost a hallowed space. Actors, stage management and theatre crews hardly ever visit 'front of house'. Backstage is a world of its own. It is where the magic of theatre is created. *Curtain Call* reveals this world and takes me right back to that memorable moment when I decided to be an actor.

Nicole Kidman photographed in her dressing room at the Noël Coward Theatre, during the run of "Photograph 51".

Shows A–Z

A Christmas Carol

By Patrick Barlow, adapted from the Christmas story by Charles Dickens
Noël Coward Theatre

Bringing a hint of tongue-in-cheek comedic flair to Charles Dickens's most famous story, Patrick Barlow's adaptation of *A Christmas Carol* proved a festive family hit at the Noël Coward Theatre in 2015. Playing Scrooge was Jim Broadbent, with all the other roles from this Dickens's classic story played by just four other actors and two puppeteers. The swift switches of costume, accent and gender were played to great comic effect, as were the mechanics of Tom Pye's wickedly mischievous set, which combined the clever use of props with intentionally visible on-stage trickery (including a storybook-like revolve), all framed within an imposing faux theatre. Barlow's focus on the process of storytelling, leaves the actors to seemingly improvise this much loved tale with whatever they had to hand.

Jim Broadbent
(Ebenezer Scrooge)
on stage - the wooden
heads shown here, and
used in the show, were
carved by Jim himself.

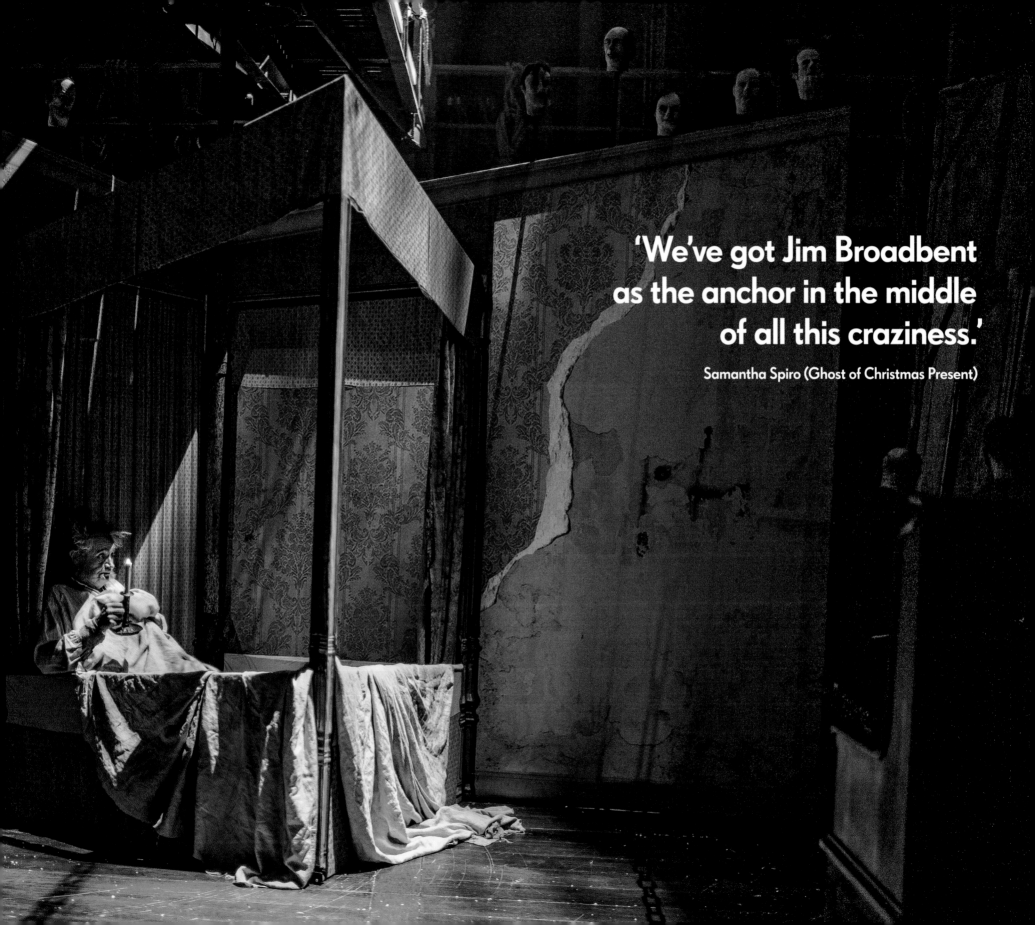

'We've got Jim Broadbent as the anchor in the middle of all this craziness.'

Samantha Spiro (Ghost of Christmas Present)

'It's sort of rough theatre, but with a budget. The stage effects are very basic on the whole. But it makes it an accessible piece of theatre.'

Jim Broadbent (Ebenezer Scrooge)

Left: Ensemble members on stage pull Marley's chains – taken from the fly floor.
Below: Samantha Spiro (Mrs Lack) during a quick change with Melody Tatania Wood (Head of Wardrobe).

Jim Broadbent (Ebenezer Scrooge) on stage.

Left: Amelia Bullmore
(Hermione Bentham)
watching from the wings.
Below: The puppet of young
Scrooge sits in the wings.

Right: Adeel Akhtar
and Keir Charles
'skating' off stage.

'It's truly manic. I don't think I've ever
played this many characters and had
this many costume changes before. I've
got fifteen quick changes in the show.'

Keir Charles (Ghost of Christmas Yet to Come)

Jim Broadbent
(Ebenezer Scrooge)
in his dressing room.

19

A Number

By Caryl Churchill
Young Vic
Transfer from Nuffield

Caryl Churchill's two-hander about cloning and identity provides unsettling source material for any director, and Michael Longhurst's revival of Nuffield's production at the Young Vic succeeded in making both the actors and the audience intensely uncomfortable. The actors, John Shrapnel and his son Lex, were confined within a mirrored box, unable to see anything but each other and endless mirrored duplications of themselves; the audience, meanwhile, looked on almost in secret, as if spying on a psychological experiment gone awry. It was a typically bold response to Churchill's intentional omission of stage directions or setting, the clinical, highly artificial design by Tom Scutt complementing the play's dark and difficult ethical questions while literally holding a mirror to a real-life father-and-son relationship. Stage actors are used to seeing and hearing their audience react; here the tables were turned upon them, and they played out their drama of greed and guilt not knowing who was listening in.

The emp
of Tom S
and clin

Curtain Call talks to John Shrapnel (Salter) and Lex Shrapnel (Sons)

Curtain Call: What's it like in the box?

Lex Shrapnel: We knew the idea and the concept, that we'd be in this mirrored box. So you try and get that in your head. But nothing can really prepare you for doing it.

John Shrapnel: It's like a police interrogation room with a two-way mirror separating us from the audience – who surround us on four sides. But we never see that audience, we only see ourselves.

LS: The people in the audience are confronted at the start of the play with their own reflection, which makes them kind of self-conscious – and seems to make them really focused on what's going on in the box.

JS: Being isolated from the audience you get no real sense of their response. It's rather like being under water – you can't see them; you only vaguely hear them, mainly when they laugh (which they do occasionally, though the play is very intense). You have to take their serious concentration on trust …

CC: You talked about intuiting an audience, but you have known your son his whole life...

JS: But I don't really know him professionally as an actor. We have been in a few things together on screen but that's a very different kettle of fish. Here, I felt a sense of wariness which might not have been the same with an actor I wasn't actually related to – that there were certain rules we were going to have to observe, and at times I must just hold back if the lines got blurred! What amazed me was how soon I got to think, "Actually, this is just an actor whom I happen to know extremely well." We were both very supportive in this, and I think we got professionally close – as we have been, obviously, as family.

LS: Mike Longhurst [director] was brilliant at knowing when it was two actors having a conversation or row between father and son. And he'd let that happen. I mean, he wouldn't step in if it was a father-and-son conversation.

CC: I was committed to the relationship straight away. I wasn't trying to figure it out – I knew it was father and son. I knew there was a strong bond already in place.

JS: Well yes – it was a great idea of Mike's to cast us together. There's a subtext there which we don't know about!

This page: John Shrapnel (Salter).
Previous double page spread:
Lee Curran's lighting design.

CC: Tell me about the tech.

LS: Getting into that box for the first time . . . It's sealed. It's extraordinarily bright in there. For you guys to see through it, it has to be extremely bright, which also makes it hot. It's impossible to concentrate. Everything is a distraction and everything makes the tension rise before you've even begun the play. It's not a calm space to be in to begin with, and it has become that. And actually everything

'The people in the audience are confronted at the start of the play with their own reflection, which makes them kind of self-conscious.'

Lex Shrapnel (Sons)

at the beginning felt like a distraction and took a long time to get used to. Actually all of those factors have led to what has become a brilliant focus once that lighting state changes and we begin. Everything about it helps us stay in that zone, which is very useful.

JS: Once that lighting change happens which puts us in the audience's view, it's the starting-gun for five intense, non-stop scenes – a five-round boxing match.

LS: No-one knew if it was going to work. They didn't know if for an audience it was going to work to be watching the performance through glass and with relayed sound. And it came pretty close to the wire where we thinking we might just do it in the round. We might just scrap all of that and just do it. And it really got quite close. Nobody knew if it was actually going to work out.

CC: I wish you guys could see the audience. Because, when that [curtain] goes back you forget that unless it's lit on the other side you're going to see yourself if there's light in the box – in our box, not in your box. So it says so much about people, audience members. There are some people who look up, look down, look at themselves.

JS: I think that's a brilliant conceit of Tom Scutt, the designer – that an audience should be looking at themselves in a rather self-conscious way, before the light suddenly switches and now they're looking at two people they'll be examining closely for an hour.

LS: Being surrounded by images of yourself to infinity, the fear of catching yourself . . . catching yourself acting badly, reflecting to infinity—

JS: Times a zillion!

LS: —is so terrifying that you really focus on the other person.

Lex Shrapnel (Sons).

This image: Lex Shrapnel (Sons)
and John Shrapnel (Salter)
doing a pre-show line-run.
Below left: Lauren Harvey
(Deputy Stage Manager).
Below right: Marina Kilby
(Company Stage Manager).

John Shrapnel (Salter).

A View From the Bridge

By Arthur Miller
Wyndham's Theatre
Transfer from Young Vic

Following a sell-out run at the Young Vic, Ivo van Hove's first Arthur Miller production transferred to the West End with a cast led by Mark Strong, Nicola Walker and Phoebe Fox. The bridge of the title being Brooklyn Bridge, it is apt that the play's runaway success in London saw it subsequently transfer to Broadway. The award-winning Ivo van Hove is known for getting to the bare bones of the plays he takes on, and in this production Jan Versweyveld's exquisite design and light stripped back scenery and props to focus on the uncomfortable family drama as it unravels into inevitable tragedy. 'It's like witnessing a car accident that you see a hundred metres before it happens', he explained. 'When I do a play, I want to do it in the most extreme way possible.' Having garnered seven Olivier Award nominations, this production won Best Actor (Mark Strong), Best Director (Ivo van Hove) and Best Revival in 2015.

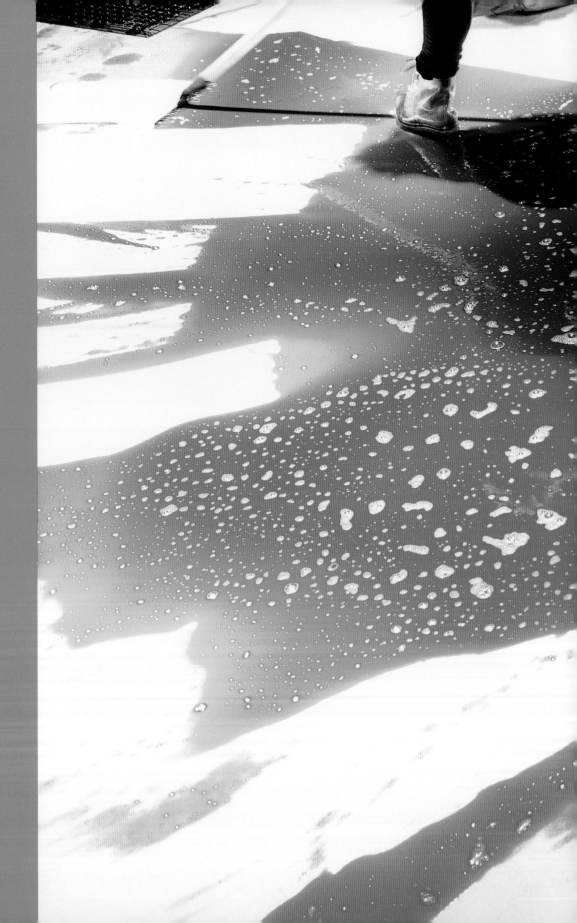

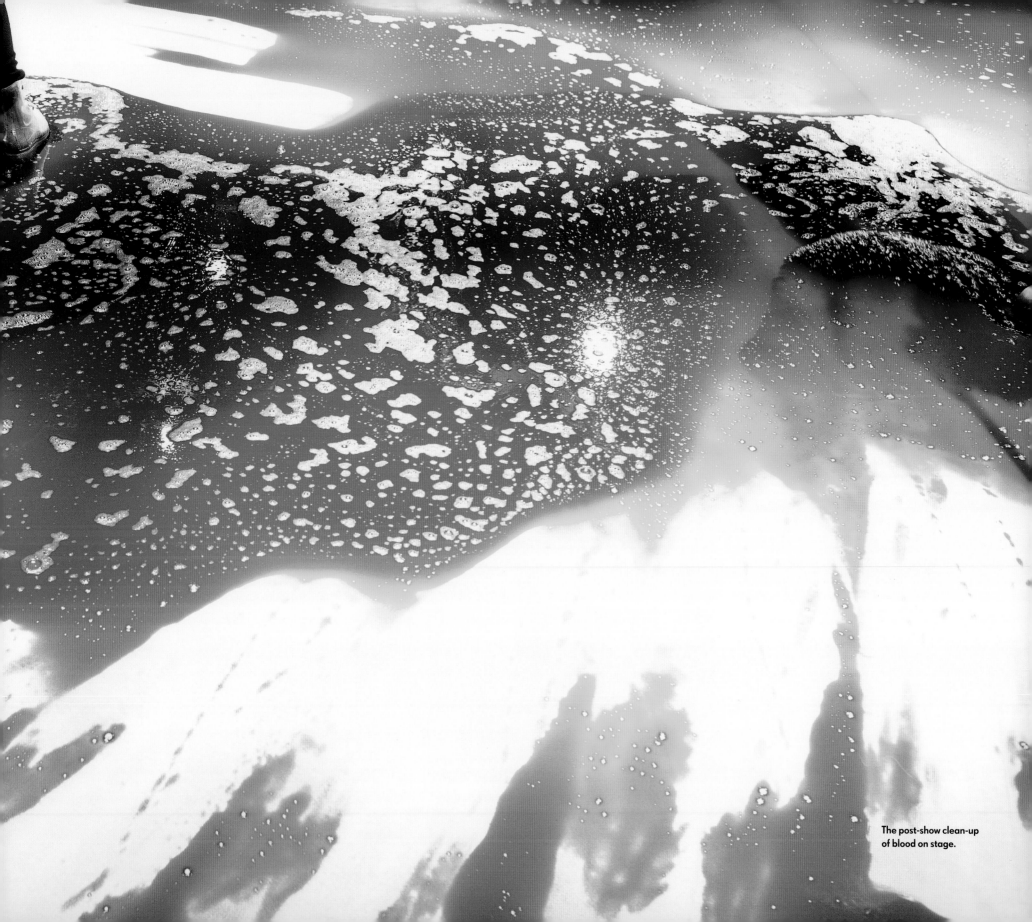

The post-show clean-up
of blood on stage.

Curtain Call talks to Mark Strong (Eddie)

Curtain Call: Could you just take me through, because this is a transfer, how different it is being here than at the Young Vic?

Mark Strong: The main issue is that the Young Vic was in the round, so we had to accommodate a proscenium arch theatre. Which meant that most of the audience would be end-on as opposed to all around. And we weren't sure if it would work. We were told that there would be seats on the stage. In fact, we were told they *are* the seats from the Young Vic.

CC: Are they?

MS: The ones on the stage, yeah. So it makes us feel at home. But it means you have to kind of adjust your performance slightly. Or we thought we would have to adjust our performances between those that are very close and those that are at the back of the stalls or the back of the circle or in the gods. In actual fact, it doesn't matter. We found a sort of playing level that seems to satisfy everywhere. Because what you get on stage, which is incredibly intense and close, from further back seems very epic.

CC: It seems a brave choice – having a character turn their back on an audience is a really brave thing. And there are moments in this where you don't get to see the actor's face. They're playing it like there is a character at the back, with the audience in the back.

MS: I realise that I spend a lot of time half-on to the audience or even three-quarters of the way, if not fully turned away, from the audience. I never even considered, really, what that would mean to an audience. What it frees us from is that terrible convention that you have to achieve when you're in a proscenium arch theatre, which is you are constantly standing three-quarters on to the audience. And should there be a lot of people on stage, you're in this semicircle. We don't have to do any of that. There's a kind of "Brownian motion" of characters and the way we move around the stage, which was conceived in rehearsals and was never adjusted in order to make it more pleasant for the audience to view our faces. Because that's not really the point. The point is what's being said – people's attitudes – and the narrative. And I don't think you always have to be able to see an actor's face in order to understand what's going on.

CC: On that point: there are no props save a chair, I think.

MS: And a cigar and a pair of heels. Those are the only three props in the play.

CC: Which really focuses the audience, I think. I have never seen a play where there haven't been props.

MS: Yeah, I think Ivo's idea was that, you know, we understand and know that theatre is artificial. Why do we work so hard in some plays and some productions to make the audience believe that they're seeing something that's real when we know it's not real? I mean, the Brechtian disassociation, which gives it too pompous a term, of having seats on the stage means that the audience actually watching the play can see the audience watching the play. So you're not bogged down in the need to convince the audience that it's real. That isn't the point. And once you've absolved yourself of that pressure, all you really need to do is deliver the story. So it's very freeing that you don't have to worry about whether what you're doing is real. There's a point where I'm asked the time by my wife. She says, "What's the time?" And I remember in rehearsals thinking I ought to have a watch. And Ivo said, "We don't care about how you know what the time is. We just want to know what the time is."

CC: You're saying it's freeing where some might think it exposing. Because you don't have anything to hide behind.

MS: I think initially it was. In rehearsals, there was nowhere to hide. And there was nothing to use to demonstrate what you were going through. But the reason the process has been freeing and that the actual performance of it has been freeing is because we have learned that it doesn't matter. There's one scene in which, after I make the phone call where I betray the boys, I'm outside. And you can tell from the lighting that I'm outside. The lighting changes. I literally take four paces across to the other side of the stage and now I'm inside and Beatrice is tidying up. And it's so obvious that one minute you're outside and one minute you're inside and nobody questions that.

'Once the show starts, you strap in and it's two hours until it crashes.'

Nicola Walker (Beatrice)

Top left: Phoebe Fox
(Catherine) during the
warm-up on stage.
Far left: Michael Gould (Alfieri)
and Richard Hansell (Louis) in
their dressing room.
Left: Phoebe Fox (Catherine)
and Nicola Walker (Beatrice)
in their dressing room.
Opposite page:
Mark Strong (Eddie).

'There were no props in rehearsals, there was nowhere to hide. But the actual performance has been freeing because we have learned that it doesn't matter.'

Ah, Wilderness!

By Eugene O'Neill
Young Vic

Eugene O'Neill once claimed that *Ah, Wilderness!*, his only foray into comedy, came to him in a dream. He frequently borrowed places and people from his own life in his works, and this play – like its darker sibling *Long Day's Journey into Night* – is set at Monte Cristo Cottage, a Connecticut beach house where he spent much of his childhood. It is a combination of these two ideas that inspired set designer Dick Bird to flood the Young Vic's stage with several tons of sand, in his own words 'the magic dust that, sprinkled in our eyes, makes us dream of creating an uncertain, shifting, interior landscape'. He also wanted to evoke the dereliction of an abandoned building, ravaged by nature and the passage of time. To enhance the effect of the surreal staging, director Natalie Abrahami edited the text to cut out the need for an interval, so that the audience felt 'swept up in the dream of O'Neill's world'.

Curtain Call talks to George MacKay (Richard Miller)

Curtain Call: The Young Vic is quite a big, open space, isn't it?

George MacKay: It was definitely the biggest venue I've worked in. You kind of realise that if you just do a completely naturalistic volume, you literally won't be heard. It was sussing out how not to shout, you know, trying to do it with the right part of your body and all of that.

CC: Following on from that, yours is a very physical performance and you spend a hell of a lot of time on stage. How was that in preparation?

GM: We all did a kind of "bums and tums" workout before each show because of the sand. Just to keep our legs strong throughout. And Ann Yee, our movement director, would begin each day of rehearsals like that.

CC: How was getting used to that sand? I mean, there's a lot of digging things out; a lot of buried treasure, as it were, for the set. How did you rehearse that? How did you get used to doing that during the technical period?

GM: We were really, really lucky because we didn't have to get used

to it in tech or anything. They built this really amazing scale rehearsal set when we were rehearsing at the National Youth Theatre on Holloway Road. And the Young Vic gave us, as close as they could, a rehearsal set.

CC: I have never heard of anything like that.

GM: It was amazing. There were subtle differences. We weren't able to get the ramp at the back, so that was new. All the curves were steeper than we had been playing on thus far. And also, the back of stage where it ramps up pretty steeply – we didn't have that in the rehearsal room. But otherwise, we were provided with amazing rehearsal facilities. And it's also very cleverly made. In the middle there's a teardrop shape, if you like, that middle kind of island down the front, that's relatively deep sand because there's that slight bowl where the water fills. But otherwise, there's a lot of trickery in the sense that it's kind of like beige carpet and a very thin layer of sand that's always there, it doesn't go, and then there's dressing on top of that. So we were working on pretty solid stuff most of the time. It wasn't a literal heap of sand, which would have been really difficult. It was amazing when we went into tech – it was overwhelming, actually – to see the back of the set with those huge doors. We'd sort of been working with door frames – we had no back of set in the rehearsal room. So you didn't really appreciate the scale and the size of the set. There was so much in the play that was an homage to O'Neill and what he had done before and what his interests were. He really liked Greek theatre and there was something really epic and Greek about the back wall, I thought, with the size of those doorways.

CC: It's almost like an amphitheatre anyway at the Young Vic, just with the "bowl" being slightly different and you guys being raised.

GM: Yeah, and I think he [O'Neill] would have quite liked that.

CC: How long did it take to gel

as a company in that space?

GM: It's funny. By the time we got into that space we were all really close anyhow. So we entered in a really good state. It wasn't like we were meeting each other and having to get used to each other. I really enjoyed the fact that we all shared

'It's weird – you get to spend fifteen minutes in a very small space next to someone, but we've not talked!'

George MacKay (Richard Miller)

dressing rooms. It's nice to have that sort of camaraderie. It's funny, for the first sort of week, two weeks of the run we all had different spots in the warm-up. Then without ever asking or saying, "This is my spot", we all ended up going to the same spot in the last three weeks, when we did our warm-up together.

CC: What was it like backstage during the show?

GM: It was cool. To be honest, I found that once we got started with the play I just got my head into that and found it very hard to concentrate on anything else, really. And so spent most of my time trying not to lose focus when I was backstage. So you try to listen, to

understand what type of audience is out there, when you're backstage. But mainly it's about trying not to lose focus. I find it so much easier being on stage. You're backstage going, "What's my next line? What's my next line?" Whereas when you're on stage, you realise that you stop thinking about it. I would kind of make an effort to just keep myself in my own head, at least in between scenes backstage. I had a bit of time off with Janie Dee. It's weird – you get to spend fifteen minutes in a very small space next to someone, but we've not talked! We've got to be listening and focusing. But it's just strange to be in a small, confined space with someone, just listening to the same thing but not really acknowledging anything.

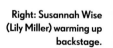

Right: Susannah Wise (Lily Miller) warming up backstage.

American Buffalo

By David Mamet
Wyndham's Theatre

Much of David Mamet's work shows a fascination
with desperation and deception, specifically
scenarios in which the former might legitimise the
latter. In this play, we are faced with a particularly
thorny ethical conundrum: which of a bunch
of dubious rogues deserves most to swindle an
innocent man. The play is ostensibly about a single
antique coin, but it encompasses so much more:
notions of value and worth, honesty and trust, and
the interplay of men conditioned to be selfish and
suspicious. For Daniel Evans' West End revival,
set designer Paul Wills wanted to create a sense of
the action taking place everywhere and nowhere
at once. He created a room full of life's junk, with
windows to the outside world, but a resolutely
inward focus, in which Mamet's questionable
characters play out their drama of self-preservation.
The production featured a stellar cast, including
Tom Sturridge as Bob, Damian Lewis as Teach and
John Goodman, in his West End debut, as Don.

John Goodman (Don).

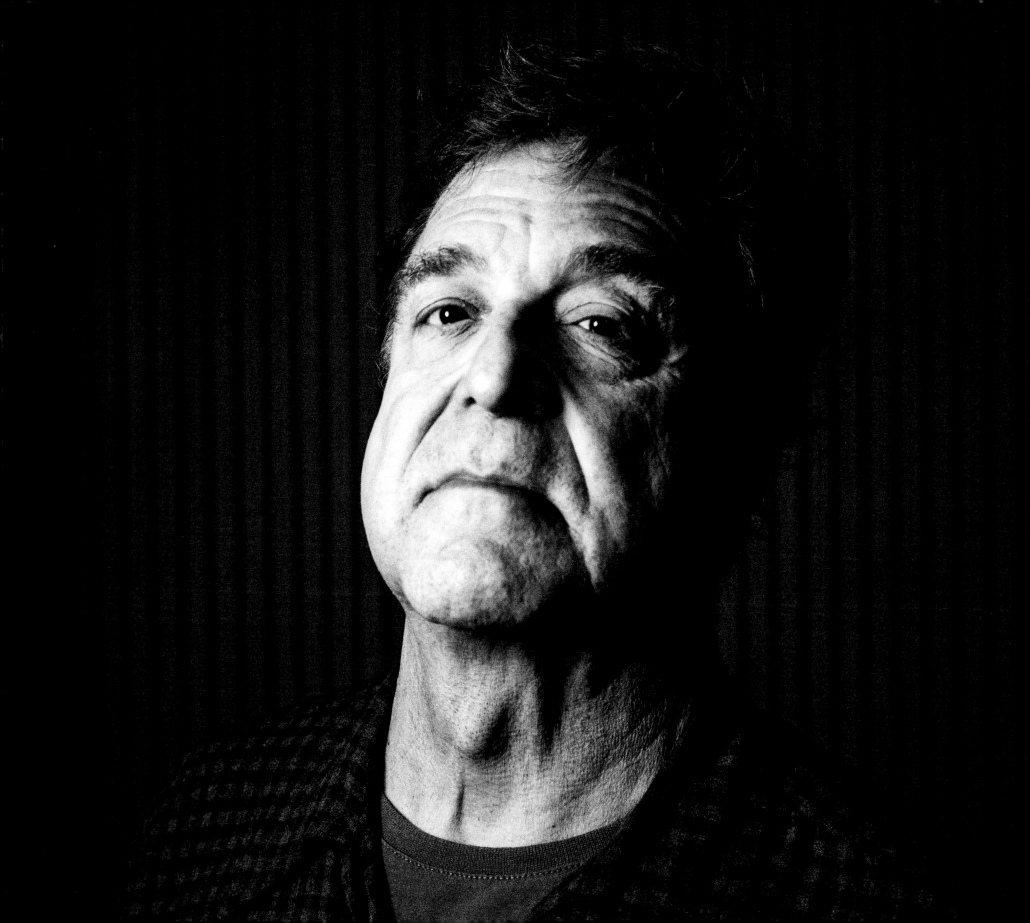

'Try to be a blank space, so
that when you come on
everything that happens feels
more like an improvisation.'

Damian Lewis (Teach)

Damian Lewis (Teach)
in his dressing room.

Paul Wills' intricate set, taken from the fly floor.

44

Left: Damian Lewis
(Teach) and Kirsty Nixon
(Deputy Stage Manager).

Right: John Goodman
(Don) on stage.

American Idiot

Music by Green Day
Lyrics by Billie Joe Armstrong
Book by Billie Joe Armstrong
and Michael Mayer
Arts Theatre

On paper, *American Idiot* is one of the more unlikely West End successes of recent years. A post-9/11 punk rock opera developed from a concept album of the same name by American rockers Green Day, it debuted in California before transferring to Broadway in 2010, where it won two Tony Awards and a Grammy. Bringing this all-American show to London was always going to be a risk for director Racky Plews, who has described it as 'an ambitious challenge', but she also recognised the global appeal of the play's air of political disenchantment. Her production was praised for its flair and frenetic energy, its intimate setting at the Arts Theatre augmenting for the audience both the in-your-face frustration inherent in the music and a feeling of genuine empathy for a troubled generation.

Lucas Rush (St Jimmy).

'When the full ensemble is on stage, it's high energy. It's quite explosive.'

Phil Massingham (Flyman)

'They say when the band started out, they were like, "Should we have a green day?" – where they would smoke weed all day. So that's what Green Day means.'

Steve Rushton (Will)

Right: Steve Rushton (Will).

Right: from left to right: Natasha Karp (Alysha), Raquel Jones (Leslie) and Robyn Mellor (Libby) in their dressing room. Far right: Aaron Sidwell (Johnny).

Left: Luke Baker (Theo).
Bottom left: Robyn Mellor (Libby) and Llandyll Gove (Gerard) taking a breather backstage.

'I think this is the first show where I don't get time to come back to the dressing room. So I just lie on the floor if I get a minute.'

Robyn Mellor (Libby / Dance Captain)

Aaron Sidwell (Johnny).

Assassins

Music & Lyrics by Stephen Sondheim
Book by John Weidman
Menier Chocolate Factory

Discomforting and powerful, *Assassins* dwells on the darker side of the American Dream, giving voice to those unfulfilled men and women who have attempted, and sometimes succeeded, to assassinate the American presidents they felt were the cause of their woes. This latest production of Stephen Sondheim's award winning musical debuted at the Menier Chocolate Factory Theatre in 2014, where director Jamie Lloyd's gift for visual sensation was well-matched by set and lighting designers Soutra Gilmour and Neil Austin. Dominated by the toppled, oversized head of a clown, the audience had to walk through an archway formed by the clown's mouth to reach their seats, and lit by a canopy of bulbs that flickered in time to the pulse of gunshots and music, the decrepit fairground shooting gallery was the perfect accompaniment to a musical that has always hovered uneasily between the macabre and festive. Catherine Tate's memorable performance as Sara Jane Moore, one of two potential killers of Gerald Ford, and Simon Lipkin as the Proprietor, along with a knockout cast including Jamie Parker, Andy Nyman and Carly Bawden, helped this production to be lauded as the definitive production of *Assassins*.

Mike McShane
(Samuel Byck) and
company on stage.

Above: Andy Nyman (Charles Guiteau) on stage at the Menier Chocolate Factory.

Right: Catherine Tate (Sara Jane Moore) and Carly Bawden (Lynette 'Squeaky' Fromme) go head to head on stage.

Above: Simon Lipkin (Proprietor) on stage.

Andy Nyman (Charles Guiteau) peeks through the curtain at the top of the show.

Right: Catherine Tate
(Sara Jane Moore) getting
ready front of house.

Right: Andy Nyman
(Charles Guiteau)
getting into his harness.
Far right: Jamie Parker
(Balladeer) on stage.

As You Like It

By William Shakespeare
National Theatre, Olivier Stage

With its cross-dressing, wise-cracking heroine and warm, witty cheer, it is no surprise that *As You Like It* is one of Shakespeare's most frequently performed comedies. Last staged at the National in 1979, director Polly Findlay reinvented the play's traditional pastoral setting, using pastel office floors complete with vibrantly clad employees and wrestling crash mats for her 2015 production on the Olivier Stage. The setting quickly morphed, thanks to Lizzie Clachan's innovative and sharp design, into the Forest of Arden in an explosive set-piece and an unforgettable scene change. Furniture floated into the ceiling to form a forest of tables and chairs, complete with actors who perched above the stage, creating the whistles and flaps of Carolyn Downing's soundscape. Aside from the set design, critics praised performances by Rosalie Craig and Patsy Ferran for their nuanced celebration of sisterly affection.

Rosalie Craig (Rosalind) in her dressing room.

Right: Fra Fee (Amiens) backstage.

'The play is magical, mystical. It's really worked itself into us without us being aware of it.'

Philip Arditti (Oliver)

Right: Jonathan Dryden Taylor (Sheep / Forest Lord) and Leo Wringer (Sheep / Duke Frederick) exiting stage.
Far right: The dramatic scene change from backstage.

Right: Leon Annor
(Charles) waiting to enter
from substage level.

'It's a wonderful and dark
set. Nothing like a festival
or, "Come hither, come
hither." A bit of danger.'

Siobhán McSweeney (Audrey)

Below: Alex Constantin (Stage
Manager) during the blackout
dramatic scene change.

Patsy Ferran
(Celia) in the wings.

'Celia is far more interesting than people sometimes give her credit for. She's a wise one. She grows.'

Patsy Ferran (Celia)

Rosalie Craig
(Rosalind) and
Patsy Ferran
(Celia) in the
wings.

As You Like It

By William Shakespeare
Shakespeare's Globe

As You Like It can be one of Shakespeare's more difficult comedies to stage well – Blanche McIntyre's production at the Globe expertly sidestepped any such problem helped by superb casting. As Rosalind, Michelle Terry was praised for her sympathetic, unflaggingly energetic performance, while Globe newcomer, Daniel Crossley, was lauded for making jester Touchstone genuinely funny for a modern audience. The production was for the most part traditionally staged, with a sparse set and Elizabethan costumes and instruments, but McIntyre was not afraid to break with tradition by adding elaborate ensemble dances and the odd anachronistic prop. As the play raced towards its denouement, its camp cross-dressing became all the more exuberant, much to the delight of the groundlings – particularly the appearance of a risqué, bearded goddess Hymen.

Ellie Piercy (Celia) at one of the front of house entrances.

Left: Gwyneth Keyworth (Phebe) and Sophie Nomvete (Audrey) waiting for cues front of house.

Above: Perri Snowdon (Le Beau) having make-up applied.
Right: Ellie Piercy (Celia) backstage.

The company curtain call.

Michelle Terry (Rosalind) front of house.

'I think the largest character in this play is the audience. And you don't really know what you've got unless they come and play with you.'

James Garnon (Jaques)

Phil Whitchurch (Adam) peering through a curtain front of house.

Left: Ellie Piercy (Celia) and Michelle Terry (Rosalind) backstage.

'I love it, because it's totally unique. There's nowhere else like it – that I know – anywhere in the world.'

David Beames
(Duke Senior / Duke Frederick)

Right: Sophie Nomvete (Audrey), Daniel Crossley (Touchstone) and Matthew North (Stage Manager). Far right: James Garnon (Jaques) in his dressing room.

Sally Greene

CC: What brought you into the theatre business?

SG: Theatre has always been a part of my life, from my grandfather to my father, Basil, who was a renowned theatre lawyer. I tried my hand at acting, but soon realised my potential lay behind the stage and not on it. My father convinced me to buy and restore Richmond Theatre and my love grew from there. The rest is history, as they say.

CC: The Criterion Theatre and The Old Vic Theatre are two very different venues. What is unique about them both to you?

SG: The Old Vic is so special to me because it was in dire need of saving when we first took it on. There is so much history rooted in The Old Vic as the birthplace of The National Theatre and Sadler's Wells, so it feels so special to have been able to put the life back into it and now see it thriving once again. The Criterion has such a fabulous position, right in the heart of Piccadilly looking down Shaftesbury Avenue. Much the same as The Old Vic, I took over at a time

when it had been dark for three years and needed saving. Critics at the time referred to it as 'the jewel in the crown of theatres'. In 2010 I turned it into a charitable trust and asked Stephen Fry to be the new Chairman.

CC: London theatre is experiencing a real boom. Actors want to be on stage, and ticket sales increase year on year. What is it about London theatre that is so attractive to the public? And professionals?

SG: London has always been the epicentre of culture in this country, and I think that is down to the sheer amount of talent we attract, and the quality of work produced. London theatre allows the public to see huge stars, incredible talents and lesser known people in an intimate space, giving them access to raw talent and quality that you can't get through a television or cinema screen. As for the professionals, I think the draw of London is performing on some of the most iconic stages in the world, and marvelling in the beauty of London's theatres. It is a

diverse city that allows an actor to work with an elaborate proscenium arch, or a black box theatre, creating something that audiences respond to. There is a huge amount of support

> 'There is so much history rooted in The Old Vic . . . so it feels so special to have been able to put the life back into it and now see it thriving once again.'

for the theatre in this country, and I think the London theatre boom is the biggest result of that.

CC: This year sees the end of an era with Kevin Spacey stepping down as Artistic Director of The Old Vic. What impact has he had on The Old Vic?

SG: Kevin has had a huge impact on this theatre. Twelve years ago it was a dark and, frankly, underwhelming place to be – I called it the 'black box'.

After Kevin's formidable eleven years as artistic director, it is now one of the best theatres in London with an eclectic mix of performances and a burgeoning list of talent. Kevin has not only revitalised this theatre, but his work at the theatre has transformed Waterloo and put the South Bank on the map as a destination to be seen.

CC: Matthew Warchus steps into Spacey's shoes. Do you think there will be a significant change of tone in the style of plays put on?

SG: Kevin and Matthew come at this job from very different angles. Kevin is an actor first and foremost, and Matthew is a director. So the way they see the theatre is completely different and I love their diversity. Their beliefs are the same, and the work with young people will continue well into Matthew's season, but I think the tone of the theatre and the plays will change. Matthew likes to challenge himself with new writing, showcasing new ideas and styles, and I think his new season really puts his varied tastes on show.

Sally Greene in Mark's Bar
at The Old Vic, in front of a
mural by Chris Martin.

Billy Elliot the Musical

Victoria Palace Theatre

Based on the 2000 film, *Billy Elliot the Musical* is often heralded as one of the greatest British musicals of the last thirty years. It follows the story of twelve-year-old Billy – a miner's son – who discovers the joy of dance and dreams of trading in his boxing gloves for ballet shoes. Set in County Durham against the dark backdrop of the 1984/'85 miners' strike, the show is both gritty and heart-warming, historical and universal; a moving exploration of the strength of a father's love and the redemptive power of art. It premiered at the Victoria Palace Theatre in 2005 and has since enjoyed a decade of success. Having won four Olivier Awards in 2006, the show went on to inspire productions across five continents, including an incredibly successful Broadway production which won ten 2009 Tony Awards including Best Musical. Directed by Stephen Daldry, the book and lyrics are by Lee Hall, who created the character of Billy Elliot and wrote the original screenplay, with music by Sir Elton John.

72

'I just want to carry on for the whole of my future – carry on what I'm doing. It's great.'

Thomas Hazelby (Billy)

Thomas Hazelby (Billy) prepares to face the audience at a special performance for Sunday Night at the Palladium.

'The Billys are like a league of superheroes and they've all got their different superpowers.'

Matthew Seadon-Young (Tony)

Right: Thomas Hazelby (Billy) on stage.
Centre right: The Ballet Girls in the wings, about to perform 'Shine'.
Far right: Ruthie Henshall (Mrs Wilkinson).

Right: George Norris (Small Boy), Lewis Elliott (Tall Boy) and Ben Robinson (Michael) await their entrance backstage.
Centre right: Thomas Hazelby (Billy) dances with James Butcher (Billy's Older Self).
Far right: Ruthie Henshall (Mrs Wilkinson) and the Ballet Girls on stage.

Far left: Ross Finnie (Ensemble), Ruthie Henshall (Mrs Wilkinson), Paul Basleigh (Ensemble) and Craig Armstrong (Ensemble) share a joke backstage.
Centre left: Thomas Hazelby (Billy) takes a well deserved drink of water backstage.
Left: James Butcher (Billy's Older Self) during warm-up for the show.

'It's the best job I have ever had, because you get to remember what it was like for you when you were that age. I think about the people I used to look up to.'

James Butcher (Billy's Older Self)

'It feels like we have made a part of theatre history. I feel very honoured to be part of it.'

Ruthie Henshall (Mrs Wilkinson)

Above: The Ballet Girls and
Thomas Hazelby (Billy) during
Billy's first 'ballet lesson.'

'I was at youth theatre with Lee Hall (Book
and Lyrics) when I was about 13. I feel very at
home in one of his plays. I feel in safe hands.'

Deka Walmsley (Dad)

Thomas Hazelby (Billy) with
Matthew Seadon-Young (Tony),
Deka Walmsley (Dad) and the
male ensemble performing
'Once We Were Kings'.

'It's just a reflection on how talented kids are in general. If you don't tell them there's a limit, and if you make them think that it's just normal, they will just keep going.'

Deka Walmsley (Dad)

Right: Peter Cork (Ensemble) and Thomas Hazelby (Billy Elliot) during the acro warm-up on stage. Centre right: Thomas Hazelby (Billy) dances at the end of Act I. Far right: Ensemble members – Mike Scott standing beside Lee Hoy as Maggie Theatre, and Kerry Washington.

Right: Ross Finnie (Ensemble) and Sharon Sexton (Ensemble) prepare to go on stage. Centre right: Thomas Hazelby (Billy) on stage at the ballet school. Far right: Thomas Hazelby (Billy) performing at the start of 'Angry Dance'.

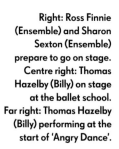

Far left: The cast perform 'Grandma's Song'.
Centre left: The Company prepare for curtain up on Act II.
Left: Thomas Hazelby (Billy) and Ruthie Henshall (Mrs Wilkinson) at ballet practice.

'If you feel like you're having a day where you can't cope, look at the boy, look what he has to do and shame on you if you don't go out and give it 150 per cent.'

Ruthie Henshall (Mrs Wilkinson)

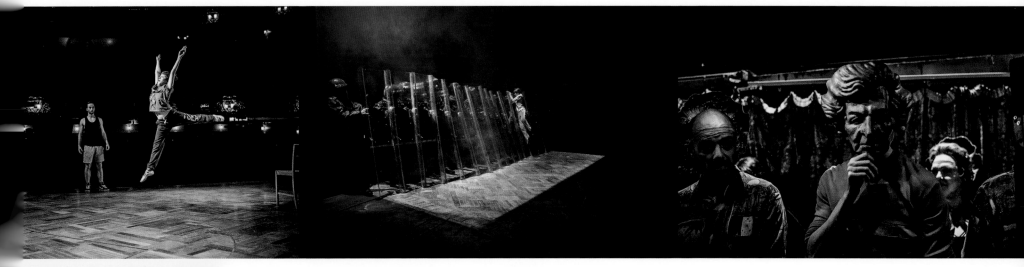

'I've worked with 20 Billys, and it's an absolute delight. It's a joy, because they're just starting and I'm at the end of my career. It's really refreshing.'

Gillian Elisa (Grandma)

Charlie and the Chocolate Factory

Book by David Greig
Music by Marc Shaiman
Lyrics by Scott Wittman and Marc Shaiman
Theatre Royal, Drury Lane

For over fifty years, Roald Dahl's *Charlie and the Chocolate Factory* has held an enduring appeal for adults and children alike. With new songs by the award winning partnership of Marc Shaiman and Scott Wittman and a book by acclaimed playwright David Greig, this 2013 adaptation presented a fresh take on Dahl's classic tale. It premiered at the Theatre Royal, Drury Lane and broke the West End box office record for weekly ticket sales twice in its first year. The musical was universally praised for Mark Thompson's sets and Olivier Award winning costume design. Sam Mendes' careful direction and Peter Darling's ingenious choreography ensured the production was as heartfelt as it was lavish, never forgetting its origins as a morality play while retaining all the magic and wonder of the original story.

The Oompa-Loompas
on stage.

'This show is a monster, this theatre is a monster. This stage is definitely the biggest stage in the West End and backstage is colossal.'

Steven Serlin (Mr Teavee/Oompa-Loompa)

Jonathan Slinger (Willy Wonka) and Toby Higgins (Musical Director) conduct the orchestra at the top of Act Two.

Emma Seabrook
(Wigs and Make-up)
and Kelly Edwards
(Oompa Loompa).

Georgia Carling
and Divine Cresswell
(Oompa Loompas)
roller-skating upstage.

'From every department, this is the most disciplined professional team I think I have ever worked with. They're extraordinary.'

Jonathan Slinger (Willy Wonka)

Murray Lane (Dresser),
Barry James (Grandpa
Joe) and Claire Carrie
(Grandma Josephine).

Jonathan Slinger
(Willy Wonka), Woody
Woodcock (Assistant
Stage Manager) and
Gavin Keenan (Dresser).

'As an Oompa-Loompa, you get to be crazy and do things that you wouldn't ordinarily be able to do on stage and get away with it.'

Dan Cooke (Oompa-Loompa)

Gregory Sims and Joe
Allen (Oompa Loompas)
waiting in the wings.

It was my childhood book – the book I grew up with. The fact that I could embrace this show, which married to my book, was just fabulous.'

Josefina Gabrielle (Mrs Teavee)

The Wonka Factory gates.

Closer

By Patrick Marber
Donmar Warehouse

Patrick Marber's third play debuted at the National in 1997, but in its 2015 revival at the Donmar Warehouse seemed to have found its natural home. An almost claustrophobically intense four-hander in which relationships are formed, betrayed, switched and abandoned, *Closer* worked brilliantly in the intimacy of the smaller theatre. For all the accolades the play had previously garnered (the Evening Standard Best Comedy Award, the Laurence Olivier Award and New York Drama Critics' Circle Award), not to mention its Hollywood incarnation starring Julia Roberts and Jude Law, Marber was reluctant to see it revived in London – a city that has been referred to as the play's fifth character – until he was confident it had the right director and the right space. This production brought together the combination he had long dreamed of: 'Back in 1999 I thought, "One day I would love this brilliant guy [David Leveaux] to do Closer." And I've always thought the Donmar would be a fantastic place to stage that play.'

The cast during
warm-up on stage.

Below, from left to right:
Rachel Redford (Alice), Nancy
Carroll (Anna), Oliver Chris
(Dan), Rufus Sewell (Larry).

'In some of the scenes I feel for the people in the front row,
people who are having a horrible scene... or going on holiday

because there's a slight feeling of being trapped in a lift with
with people at the worst time in their relationship.'

Rufus Sewell (Larry)

Dear Lupin

By Roger Mortimer & Charlie Mortimer
Adapted by Michael Simkins
Apollo Theatre

Between 1967 and his death in 1991, *The Sunday Times* racing correspondent Roger Mortimer wrote a series of witty, affectionate, exasperated letters to his wayward son, Charlie, nicknamed Lupin after an equally insubordinate son in the Grossmith brothers' *Diary of a Nobody.* Mortimer senior would surely have been astonished to see the collected correspondence became a surprise bestseller when it was published in 2012; even more so when it was then turned into a hit West End play in which he was portrayed by James Fox and Lupin by Fox's real-life son, Jack. Adapting a book of largely unanswered letters for the stage was a formidable challenge for debut playwright Michael Simkins, who found he needed to develop a greater sense of interaction between the characters than the letters themselves show. It was the casting of the Foxes that assured all involved that the Mortimers' loving, despairing father-and-son dynamic could realistically be reproduced on stage.

Jack Fox (Lupin) warming up on stage before curtain up.

'My agent said, "Why don't you read this script?" I read it on the train and it murdered me. When I was offered it, it was a no brainer.'

Jack Fox (Lupin)

James Fox (Roger) and Jack Fox (Lupin) warming up on stage.

'It's a great thing having the audience knowing that you're father and son. This is the first outing with a family member, so it's just natural. You don't have to force it.'

James Fox (Roger)

Above: James Fox (Roger) waiting in the wings for his entrance.

Right: James Fox (Roger) and Jack Fox (Lupin) on stage.

Death of a Salesman

By Arthur Miller
**Royal Shakespeare Company
at the Noël Coward Theatre**

The centenary year of Arthur Miller's birth saw
numerous revivals of his work. Among them, the
Royal Shakespeare Company's production of *Death
of a Salesman*, which debuted at the RST in Stratford-
upon-Avon before transferring to the West End.
Director Gregory Doran described it as, 'the greatest
American play of the twentieth century'. It won
both the Pulitzer Prize and the Tony Award for Best
Play in 1949, and Doran's first-rate casting certainly
lived up to that reputation. Antony Sher played the
flawed and frustrated salesman, Willy Loman, one
of modern theatre's meatiest roles, opposite Harriet
Walter as his long-suffering wife. Sher was praised
for his mastery of a character whose temper turns
on an instant. A failure of a man held together by
fantasies and memories. The set by Stephen Brimson
Lewis and lighting by Tim Mitchell, likewise, had
to switch erratically between present-day reality and
the world inside Loman's mind. The overall effect
was a touching portrait of broken love and broken
dreams, and a fitting tribute to Miller's genius.

Sam Marks (Happy Loman),
Alex Hassell (Biff Loman) and
Harriet Walter (Linda Loman)
in the green room recreating
the photo above them
featuring Noël Coward.

Left: Alex Hassell (Biff Loman) and Sam Marks (Happy Loman) in their dressing room.
Below: Guy Paul (Uncle Ben) prepares to enter.

Right: Emma King (Miss Forsyth) gets her wig fitted.
Far right: Antony Sher (Willy Loman) in his dressing room.

96

'I never imagined that
I would play this part.
Sometimes the parts that
are everything you're not
are the ones that inspire you.'

Harriet Walter (Linda Loman)

Antony Sher
(Willy Loman)
descends to stage level.

Di and Viv and Rose

By Amelia Bullmore
Vaudeville Theatre
Transfer from Hampstead Theatre

'It's a wonderful
play for women – a
beautiful exploration
of female friendship.'

Jenna Russell (Rose)

Can university friendships last a lifetime? This
is the question explored in Amelia Bullmore's
all-female three-hander, which follows three
inseparable fresher friends as they set off along
wildly disparate grown-up paths. The play debuted
at Hampstead Downstairs in 2011 and was the
first in-house production to be promoted to the
main stage. It transferred to the West End in
2015, still with director Anna Mackmin – who
also directed Bullmore's first two plays – at the
helm. The transfer to the Vaudeville Theatre
allowed for some clever script alterations, as well as
considerations and enhancements in terms of the
set and size of the stage. For a tragicomedy with a
significant cast of unseen characters, the production
was highly praised for its intimacy, drawing the
audience into a state of empathy that had them
laughing and weeping along with the characters.

Jenna Russell (Rose)
in her dressing room.

Jenna Russell
(Rose) waits to
make an entrance.

'Tamzin (Outhwaite, Di) started out great and managed, somehow or other, to get better every time.'

Amelia Bullmore (Writer)

Top right: Tamzin
Outhwaite (Di) backstage.
Right: Jenna Russell (Rose)
and Samantha Spiro (Viv).

Left: Samantha Spiro (Viv) during a quick change backstage.

'It really was like a family. And that went for everyone, right through to stage management.'

Samantha Spiro (Viv)

Right: Tamzin Outhwaite (Di) on stage.
Far right: Jenna Russell (Rose), Tamzin Outhwaite (Di) and Samantha Spiro (Viv) leave the stage after the curtain call.

'It was the third incarnation of it, but neither Tamzin Outhwaite (Di) or Anna Mackmin (Director) ever made us feel like we were the new girls.'

Samantha Spiro (Viv)

Samantha Spiro (Viv) in her dressing room.

Dirty Rotten Scoundrels

Music & Lyrics by David Yazbek
Book by Jeffrey Lane
Savoy Theatre

Paying homage to the golden age of the musical, *Dirty Rotten Scoundrels* tells the story of rival conmen Freddy Benson and Lawrence Jameson as they swindle and cheat their way across the French Riviera, determined to outwit each other as well as their marks. Based on the hit 1988 comedy film of the same name, the play premiered on Broadway in 2005 before making its way across the Atlantic a decade later to be staged at the Savoy Theatre. It was written and composed by Jeffrey Lane and David Yazbek and starred Alex Gaumond as Freddy Benson opposite Tony and Olivier Award winner Robert Lindsay who played Lawrence Jameson. The pair's highly entertaining and impeccably timed on-stage chemistry meant Jerry Mitchell's slick production received rave reviews, as did Peter McKintosh's elaborate art deco set, which reflected the theatre's own interior and effortlessly captured the impossible glamour and decadence of the Riviera.

Robert Lindsay (Lawrence Jameson) and Katherine Kingsley (Christine Colgate) on stage.

Alice Fearn
(Ensemble) backstage
in the sound booth.

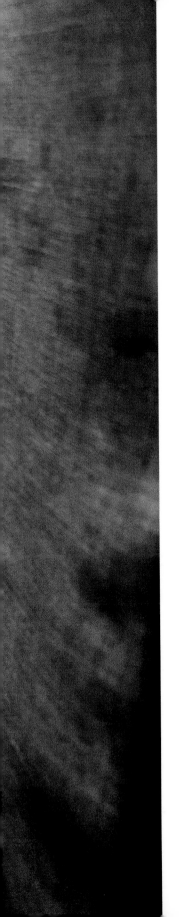

Above: Robert Lindsay
(Lawrence Jameson)
and Alex Gaumond
(Freddy Benson)
on stage during a
scene change.
Left: Selina Hamilton
(Ensemble) backstage.

Far left: Darren Carnall (Associate Choreographer) and Jason Golbourn (Stage Manager) on stage before the show.
Left: Ensemble on stage.

Bonnie Langford (Muriel Eubanks) backstage in the wings.

'There is a ritual and routine to being backstage. Watching crew and cast repetitiously do their show is a bit like observing some sort of abstract choreography.'

Katherine Kingsley (Christine Colgate)

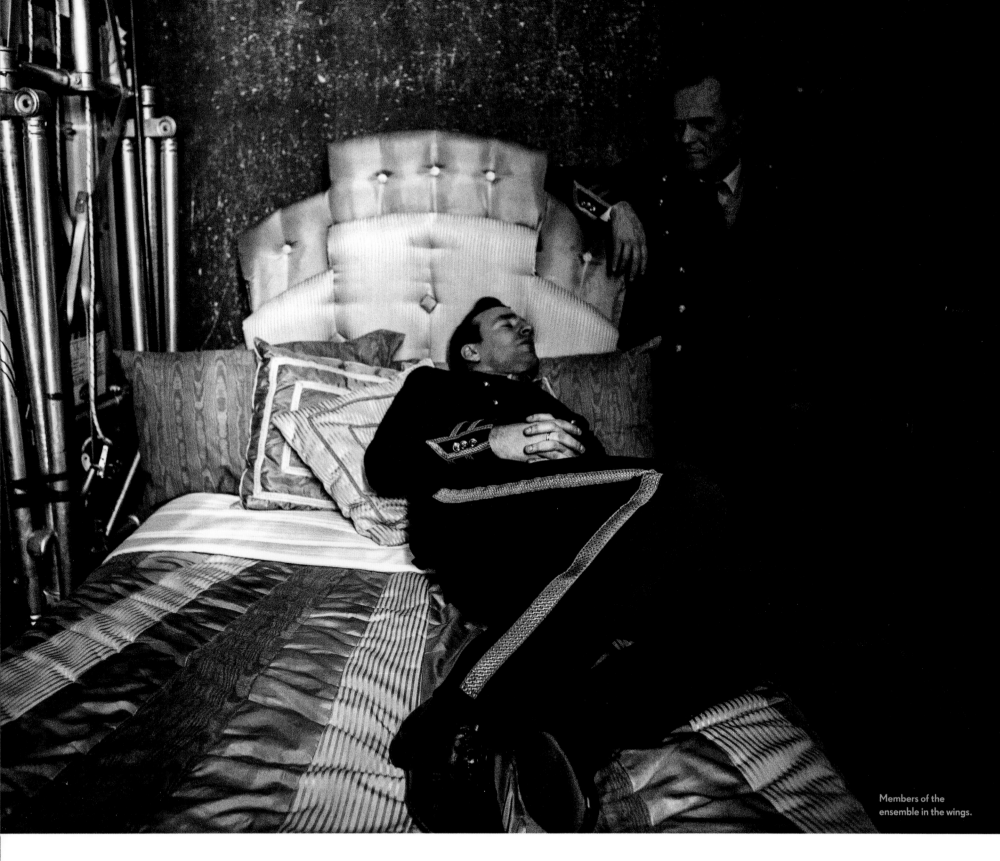

Members of the ensemble in the wings.

Elf -
The Musical

Music & Lyrics by
Matthew Sklar and Chad Beguelin
Book by Thomas Meehan and Bob Martin
Dominion Theatre

Based on the 2003 New Line Cinema film written by David Berenbaum, *Elf* sees Buddy, the orphan reared as a Christmas elf, returning once again to New York City in search of his birth father in this heart-warming seasonal musical. The show first premiered in 2010 on Broadway before transferring to the West End in 2015. It starred ITV's *Superstar* Ben Forster as Buddy the Elf, in a performance universally praised by critics for its charm and vulnerability. Girls Aloud's Kimberley Walsh played Jovie, Buddy's department-store love interest. *Elf* was the fastest selling show since the Dominion Theatre opened in 1929, with crowds drawn to its catchy, upbeat music, bright, projected backdrops, and family-friendly cheer. Director Morgan Young's production was praised for its ability to tap into the spirit of Christmas and its sense of genuine, touching innocence.

The cast on stage
in the interval.

'It's the most iconic comedy
Christmas character ever. It is
scary. I was in two minds about
doing the gig just because of that.'

Ben Forster (Buddy)

Left: Kimberley Walsh
(Jovie) and Graham
Lappin (Store Manager)
waiting to enter stage.
Bottom left: Ben Forster
(Buddy) in his dressing room.

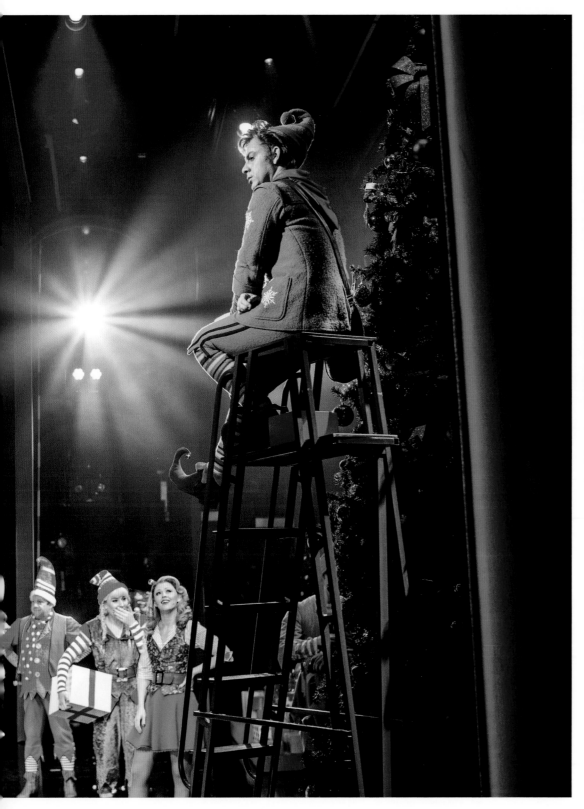

Top: The male ensemble
Santa cast fill the elevator.
Above: Jessica Martin (Emily
Hobbs) in her dressing room.

Left: Ben Forster
(Buddy) and the
Company on stage.

Mark McKerracher (Santa).

'This show gives you all of that Christmas showbiz extravaganza, but it also makes you swallow hard in places because it really touches you.'

Jennie Dale (Deb)

Above: Jennie Dale (Deb) and Julie Burnett (Deputy Wig Mistress).
Far left: Joe McGann (Walter Hobbs) in his dressing room.
Right: The Ensemble cast sing backing vocals in the wings.

Everyman

By Carol Ann Duffy
National Theatre, Olivier Stage

Rufus Norris's first production as director of the National Theatre was *Everyman*, a tale almost as old as time, and one that has reappeared in myriad incarnations since it was first written down in the fifteenth century. And the broad outline of Carol Ann Duffy's adaptation is simple: one man falling to his death is forced in his final moments to contemplate his life. In the hands of Poet Laureate Duffy and Norris, this thoroughly modern *Everyman* was anything but predictable. Her selfish, unlikeable Everyman is high on life, high on drugs and booze, pursued around the stage by pulsating music and choreographed demons; this is an *Everyman* in which God is a cleaning lady and Death a pathologist. Norris was mindful not to abandon the play's origins entirely, and the score by William Lyons melded medieval instruments with modern club beats, an intentionally unsettling device that undermined the idea of historical progression and placed Everyman's quest for meaning, for self-justification, at the heart of the human experience.

Chiwetel Ejiofor (Everyman) flies in to stage at the top of the show.

Chiwetel Ejiofor
(Everyman).

Curtain Call talks to Kate Duchêne (God) and Dermot Crowley (Death)

Kate Duchêne: I am Kate Duchêne and I am playing God.

Dermot Crowley: And I am Dermot Crowley and I am playing Death.

KD: That's the first time I have managed to say it without laughing. I've got used to it but when people say, "Are you working at the moment?" And I say, "Yes. I'm playing God." They just fall about. I think the parents at my kids' school think I'm lying.

CC: And on the flip side of that, playing Death is . . . Well, he's not as dark a character as you would expect.

DC: He's not. He's a laugh. He's got his serious points as well, of course.

KD: He's quite grim.

DC: He's grim, but I guess he sneaks up on people. I just think that Carol Ann Duffy's captured the nature of that sort of nebulous thing that we call "death" rather well. The difficulty we had in rehearsal was to try and make human these abstract entities like "God" and "Death" and "Good Deeds" and all of those traits. Which I think would have been perfectly understood in medieval times, when the play was originally done. But

it's more difficult for us today.

CC: This play can have a particular impact on how people perceive their relationship with their parents, can't it?

DC: There was one particular person who came out and tweeted, "Oh my God, I saw last night. It was so fantastic. I came straight out, called my mum and told her that I loved her."

KD: It's rather lovely, isn't it?

DC: It's rather lovely. And you think, "This show is so special." It's not like people come in and see a play, in the ordinary sense – they come and they see something and they take something away with them that stays with them for quite a while.

CC: The writing was extraordinary because you didn't realise you're being talked to in verse. But the whole production, the costumes and the lights, that dummy drop at the end, it's astonishing. Being on that stage here at the National Theatre is an amazing thing. Have either of you played it before?

KD & DC: Yes.

CC: Technically, how is it different from other theatres?

A fluorescent Everyman mask is donned backstage.

DC: You have to make sure that you're heard. And you have to make sure that you share the performance with everybody, as opposed to playing it out front. Because if you do that, the people at the sides are going to feel very cheated. Because as lovely as the back of Kate Duchene's head is, they want to see her beautiful face. That's what you have to bear in mind.

'I sat in the foyer when I was fifteen and thought, "If I ever work here, I'll be happy." And here I am playing God!'

Kate Duchêne (God)

DC: I think we're all aware of that. You have to be aware of it. Because it's got demands, the Olivier. But, God, does it pay off.

KD: It does. I have seen things at the Olivier right at the top, at the back of the circle, and felt quite detached. So I've always got that slight worry in my head about those people right at the back. Just because it's such a long way. When you're up there, we're tiny. And I do think about that quite a lot and

sometimes worry about it. And this is the first time I have played in the Olivier mic'd. And so you don't have to push so hard, which is a nice thing.

CC: This is quite a physical show as well. What was that rehearsal process like? Because there's a lot of movement.

DC: It's great for us because we don't do anything.

KD: Yeah, I sit there and go, "God, they're good."

DC: When Rufus asked me to do it, I said, "Fine, as long as you don't have any of these highfalutin ideas about bringing me in on a trapeze or anything." And I said, "I don't do any of that dancing stuff." And he said, "No, they'll all be doing it around you." And I said, "That's great!"

KD: We just come on and talk.

CC: Was it a heavy tech period? Because each show has a different framework when it comes to the teching and there are a lot of elements to this show. There's a lot of costume changes and comings and goings and lighting, cues . . .

KD: Speaking personally, I just watch

119

people doing all the hard stuff like that. For me, this was a really simple show, in that I come on and talk and go off . . . and then I come in on a trolley – I don't even have to walk! And then I come on at the end and talk. I mean everybody else, from my point of view, is doing all the hard stuff. The tech didn't feel very hard.

DC: It didn't. I think we're both the same – we have those little moments where we come on and have a scene and then we're gone. We can look at the rest of the show. It's great to be able to observe the tech. It's quite spectacular – the flying business and that amazing wall and everything. But it wasn't a fraught tech and Rufus kind of runs the rehearsals really well. One of the things that took weeks to work out was the police tent at the end, which is a great coup de théâtre – suddenly the entire company are just gone.

KD: There were all sorts of different versions of that.

DC: It took forever! But that was him trying to find the right way of doing it. And that arrived just before the tech, really. And it's fabulous. So a lot of the work was done in the rehearsal room.

KD: And a lot of the work was

done by what we call the Fellowship Company. All the movers. And they invented lots of it. They invented masses. They worked

'I would happily work out my career, such as it is, or what's left of it, at the National Theatre.'

Dermot Crowley (Death)

out the cocaine sequence on the first day of the workshop. The first day before we arrived.

CC: It's funny you say how little you guys are on stage, but your presence is felt throughout the show. I remember you being there a lot.

KD: I'm hardly there. It's very odd.

CC: Has anyone else commented on that?

KD: Yes, it must be people's notions of God and Death. You're aware of them. I'm hardly on.

DC: Well, I'm on a few silent times with that white suit that's totally

upstaging everybody – and the hat. I'm keeping the hat as a souvenir.

CC: And lastly, in regards to this theatre, what does it mean to you being here at the National?

KD: I sat in the foyer when I was fifteen and thought, "If I ever work here, I'll be happy." And I am. I just think it's the best place to work. Everything is fantastic: the best stage management, the best wardrobe . . . It's just great. For me, I didn't have the RSC in my head, or film either. I had here. And here I am playing God!

DC: I would happily work out my career, such as it is, or what's left of it, at the National Theatre. I spent an awful lot of time here when I was a young actor. I spent three and a half years here and did fourteen productions at the Olivier in the late seventies with some incredible people who are sadly no longer with us. Like Robert Stephens and Ralph Richardson, Michael Bryant and Dorothy Tutin – I mean the real greats. It was such an utter privilege as a younger actor to be part of that company and to learn from these amazing people. And I would die defending the National Theatre. I think it's fantastic. It's THE place to work.

Opposite page, clockwise from top left: Kiruna Stamell (Discretion) after warm-up. Clemmie Sveaas (Insecurity/Goods) in the Drum substage area. Itxaso Moreno, (Taste), Nick Holder (Strength) and Ira Mandela Siobhan (Sight) waiting to enter stage. Sharon D Clarke (Mother) singing on stage.

'It was such an utter privilege as a younger actor to be part of that company and to learn from these amazing people. And I would die defending the National Theatre. I think it's fantastic. It's THE place to work.'

Dermot Crowley (Death)

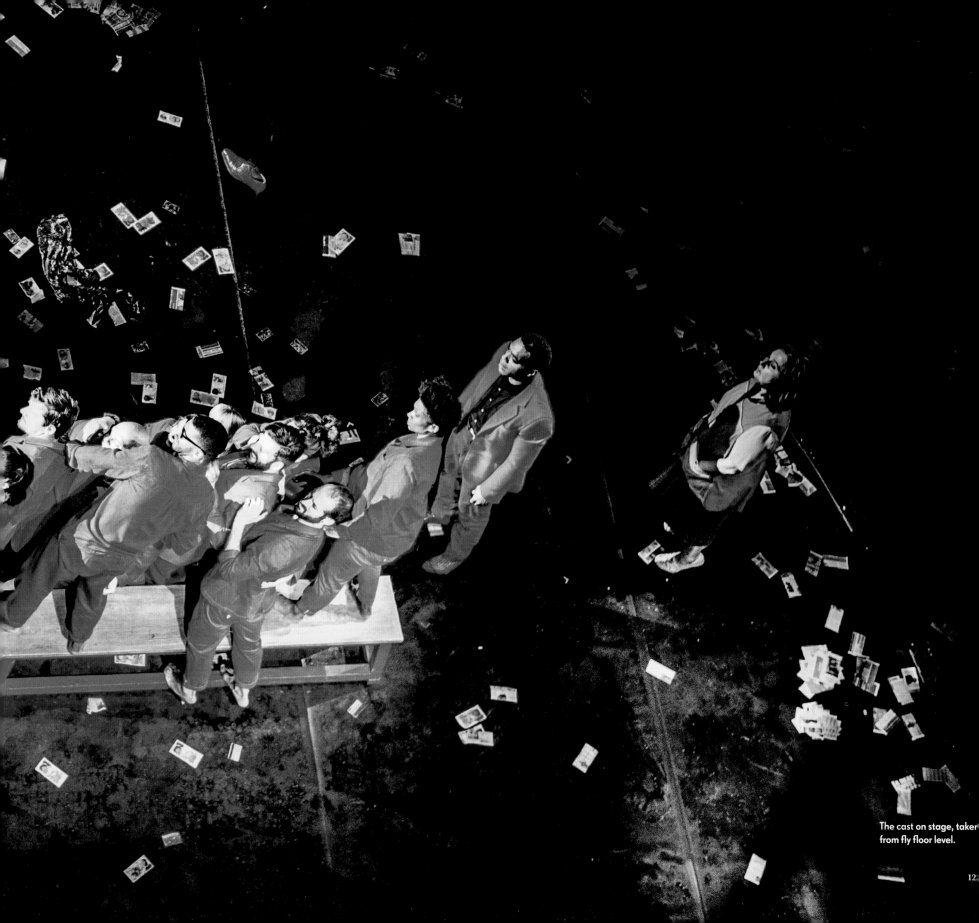

The cast on stage, taken from fly floor level.

Farinelli and the King

By Claire van Kampen
Duke of York's Theatre
Transfer from the
Sam Wanamaker Playhouse

et in eighteenth-century Spain, Claire van
Kampen's play tells the intriguing true story of
Farinelli, once the world's most famous castrato
nd one of the greatest celebrities of his time,
nd his decision to trade fame and fortune in the
pera houses of Europe for a life of servitude at the
ourt of King Philippe V, played by a mesmerising
Mark Rylance. A renowned composer and former
musical director at the Globe, van Kampen
rranged the music for this play, which included
number of arias by Handel deftly brought to life
by Iestyn Davies. Having opened at the Globe's
Sam Wanamaker Playhouse, *Farinelli and the King*
ransferred to the Duke of York's Theatre, bringing
ll of its candle-lit charm and onstage seating
o the West End for a sold-out limited run.

**Mark Rylance
(King Philippe V)
peers onto stage.**

24

James Johnstone
(Deputy Musical
Director) at the curtain
call on the final matinee.

Far left: Edward Peel (De la Cuadra) and Katherine Tippins (Candle Technician) during a swift handover backstage.

Left: Mark Rylance (King Philippe V) and Sam Crane (Farinelli) in the front of house area before entering the auditorium.

'When we first did it, we had seven weeks to rehearse. It felt like a cosy little workshop with mates and some people turned up to watch it. When it came here, that feeling continued.'

Colin Hurley (Metastasio)

Right: Mark Rylance (King Philippe V) during a quick change backstage.
Far right: Iestyn Davies (Singer) backstage.

127

Far left: Melody Grove (Isabella Farnese) backstage. Left: Iestyn Davies (Singer) is lowered on to the stage in a harness.

'Mark is a very good comic actor, a clever comedian and clown. He's a master at keeping a company happy. His generosity, open spirit and sense of fun and play really filters down to all of us.'

Melody Grove (Isabella Farnese)

Right: Becca Ridley (Deputy Stage Manager) lighting candles during the preset. Far right: Sam Crane (Farinelli) in the sub-stage area, just before entering stage.

Melody Grove
(Isabella Farnese)
backstage.

Guys
and Dolls

Music & Lyrics by Frank Loesser
Book by Abe Burrows
Savoy Theatre

Guys and Dolls is undoubtedly one of the most loved musicals of all time – on both sides of the curtain. Having premiered at the Chichester Festival Theatre in 2014 to rave reviews, Gordon Greenberg's much-anticipated revival and West End transfer eighteen months later did not disappoint. Peter McKintosh's colourful megaphone-shaped set design allowed performances by David Haig as small-time crook Nathan Detroit and Sophie Thompson as his lovelorn fiancée Miss Adelaide to take centre stage. They captivated audiences with their on-again off-again relationship that contained moments of real pathos beneath the comedy. Jamie Parker received high praise for his role as Sky Masterson, playing the New York gambler with the perfect mixture of boyish charm and sly swagger, opposite an earnest Sarah Brown deftly played by Siubhan Harrison. Dramatic choreography by Carlos Acosta and Andrew Wright was masterfully accompanied by Gareth Valentine's brassy band, ensuring a snappy, fast-paced production that looked and sounded as good as it felt.

'When I heard I got the role, I jumped up in the air because Adelaide is the one part I think I did have, somewhere in my heart, a hope of.'

Sophie Thompson (Miss Adelaide)

Sophie Thompson (Miss Adelaide) backstage.

'There's a lovely double act that Ian (Hughes, Benny) and I get to do every night. That's quite a joy.'

Gavin Spokes (Nicely-Nicely Johnson)

Right: Female ensemble
members waiting to enter stage.
Centre right: Jamie Parker
(Sky Masterson).
Far right: Siubhan Harrison
(Sarah Brown).

Right: Lucy Jane Adcock
(Mimi) and Rochelle Porter
(Wigs Assistant).
Centre right: Sophie
Thompson (Miss Adelaide)
makes her entrance.
Far right: David Haig
(Nathan Detroit) in his
dressing room.

'When I first walked into the Savoy, I got completely choked up and very emotional because it's a childhood dream to be in a West End theatre.'

Lorna Gayle (General Cartwright)

'There's a lot of intimate scenes in this show, and there's not a bad seat in the house. You get to appreciate the the intimacy as well as the big dance numbers.'

Frankie Jenna (Agatha)

'During the Havana scene, I get to be drunk and thrown around. And as a non-dancer, to be in a dance number is amazing.'

Siubhan Harrison (Sarah Brown)

Above: Siubhan Harrison (Sarah Brown) crawling on the bar in the Havana scene.
Right: Sophie Thompson (Miss Adelaide) on stage.

'The line you get all the time is, "I don't like musicals, but I love Guys and Dolls." It's like people who don't listen to jazz but love Ella Fitzgerald.'

Jamie Parker (Sky Masterson)

Below: Jamie Parker (Sky Masterson) and cast on stage.

Gypsy

Music by Jule Styne
Book by Arthur Laurents
Lyrics by Stephen Sondheim
Savoy Theatre

Inspired by the memoirs of notorious striptease artist Gypsy Rose Lee, who as a child in the 1920s was pushed into a showbiz career by her mother (played in Jonathan Kent's glorious revival by the incomparable Imelda Staunton), *Gypsy* has been described by numerous critics as one of the greatest American musicals ever written. It is a worthy accolade for a play that was devised by the musical dream team of writer Arthur Laurents, composer Jule Styne and lyricist Stephen Sondheim. This production is a success story for British theatre, having debuted at Chichester before transferring to the West End, where it earned rave reviews for its raucous evocation of the long-gone age of vaudeville theatre. But the highest praise was reserved for Staunton in the complex role of 'Momma Rose', a well-meaning bully who was as loving as she was determined to secure a glimpse of the limelight – for herself as well as her children. Critics and public alike have been unanimous in their appraisal of Imelda Staunton, in the stage role of her career.

'Acting with Imelda is…
I cannot describe it.
You don't even have to
act because you just
listen to her and you are
in that moment.'

Lauren Hall (June)

Imelda Staunton taking her bow at the curtain call.

'I have a huge advantage because I play all my scenes with Imelda. When you're working with Imelda, you simply have to keep up. And it's enormous fun to do that.'

Peter Davison (Herbie)

Right: Imelda Staunton (Rose) on stage.
Centre right: Imelda Staunton (Rose) backstage just before the start of the show.
Far right: Gemma Sutton (Louise) and Lauren Hall (June) on stage during the show.

Right: Cast members gather on stage for the curtain call.
Centre right: George Cook (Stage Manager) and Lauren Hall (June) backstage.
Far right: Gemma Sutton (Louise) and Imelda Staunton (Rose) at the end of the show.

Far left: The cast
backstage just
before curtain up.
Centre left: Imelda
Staunton (Rose)
in her dressing room.
Left: Gemma Sutton
(Louise) and crew on stage.

'It's a perfect show for this theatre with the 1920s styling. And
the design by Anthony Ward is just perfect. It fits beautifully.'

Gemma Sutton (Louise)

'In my career, I have never had a standing ovation for every
single performance. To be part of that is something I will miss.'

Dan Burton (Tulsa)

'It's the only show I have worked on where it's complimented what's going on, front and back. The nature is that on bigger shows these days automation plays such a big part – whereas on this show, you don't see a lot of that happening, and that's kind of the point. The magic is hidden.'

John Caswell (Company Stage Manager)

Left: Lauren Hall dancing at the side of the stage.
Below: Crew and Stage Management move scenery during the show.

Gemma Sutton
(Louise) and members
of the cast on stage.

Hamlet

By William Shakespeare
Barbican Theatre

One of Shakespeare's most performed and popular plays, *Hamlet*'s eponymous hero has been portrayed by some of the greatest actors, of any era. Yet none have caused such a stir as Benedict Cumberbatch, whose presence on the cast list meant Lyndsey Turner's 2015 production at the Barbican became the fastest-selling ticket in London theatre history. The latest to take on this challenging part, Cumberbatch proved himself undaunted by the intensity of interest surrounding his casting, captivating the audience with an intelligent and introspective interpretation. With critics praising Cumberbatch's skilful soliloquies and energetic command of the stage, Es Devlin's extravagant two-tiered set featured a stately hall complete with adjoining rooms, grand staircase and opulent chandelier – its sense of scale persisting even after it was reduced to rubble.

Benedict Cumberbatch (Hamlet) on the set for Act IV

Above: The Company
exiting the stage.

Right: Benedict
Cumberbatch
(Hamlet) on stage.

Above: Oliver Bagwell Purefoy (Assistant Stage Manager) talks to members of the crew.

Below: Anastasia Hille (Gertrude) has her hairpiece adjusted by Rebecca Kempton (Head of Hair and Wigs).

Benedict Cumberbatch (Hamlet) and Karl Johnson (Ghost/Gravedigger).

Right: Matthew Steer
(Rosencrantz) and
Benedict Cumberbatch
(Hamlet) backstage.

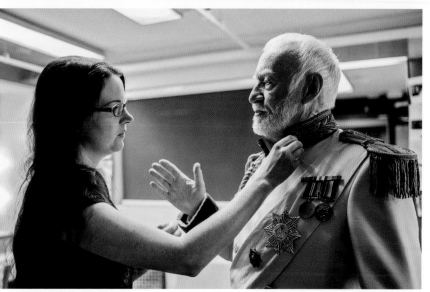

Right: Jordan Colls (Dresser)
and Jim Norton (Polonius).
Far right: Siân Brooke (Ophelia)
in her dressing room.

Above: Ellen Rey de Castro
(Dresser) and Ciarán Hinds
(Claudius) backstage.
Left: Benedict Cumberbatch
(Hamlet) on stage.

Below: Kobna
Holdbrook-Smith
(Laertes) in his
dressing room.

Karl Johnson
(Ghost/Gravedigger).

The Curtain Call Interview
Artistic Director, The Royal Court Theatre

Vicky Featherstone

CC: What got you into theatre?
VF: When I was younger my dad, who is a chemical engineer, had pictures of himself as an actor when he was at Imperial College. And I used to look at those pictures and think, "That's really weird." He would always lament, "If only I'd actually committed and become an actor." I thought, "Why didn't you do the thing that you wanted to do? Why did you do something else", and when I was about six years old we lived in India and he was directing the company review. I remember sitting at the back with the script, and I saw a character name and then a line of dialogue and I thought, "That's amazing!" They were doing the thing that I was reading on the stage. That's when I first knew about it.

CC: What brought you here to the Royal Court?
VF: I went to Manchester University and the drama course was very political. It became very clear that I really didn't want to do Classics alone, I was much more interested in work that was pushing the boundaries. So,

I became really excited about new writing and read lots of plays that were at the Royal Court. When I started out as a director, I always wanted to do new work. I worked in television for a long time as a script editor, but eventually got a job at Paines Plough as Artistic Director and that took me to The National Theatre of Scotland and that took me to here.

CC: The Royal Court has always championed new writing, hasn't it?
VF: I have only really ever directed new plays. The thing that is amazing

> 'It's always been about discovering new talent and taking risks with new talent.'

about the Royal Court is it was set up in 1956 in opposition to the West End. It was saying, "We don't want to do all that 'elite' Noel Coward stuff. We want to be putting on plays that are actually representing the world that we

live in." It also looked at the European canon which wasn't commercial – so Brecht, Ionesco, Beckett. That's always what the Royal Court has been about. Its always been about discovering new talent and taking risks with new talent. I feel really strongly that the British theatre scene now, with so much new writing, has totally been influenced by the Royal Court.

CC: Next year is the 60th year of the Royal Court. Next season is going to be scrutinised.
VF: I think the Royal Court is always scrutinised in a way. The 50th anniversary was an amazing retrospective. I am really keen that at 60 we are asking, "What is the future? Who are the writers of the future? What are the plays that we should be doing?". We have got a really exciting year coming up.

CC: Because you are championing new writing, when a play does transfer and has a huge success, like _Jerusalem_ and _Hangmen_, do you feel that more than a normal transfer?

VF: I think there's a really interesting balance about what success is at The Royal Court. It's really important that our imperative mustn't be *commercial success*. We have to be business successful. But if our imperative becomes about commercial success, we start to water down the risks that the writers need to be allowed to take to fail here. And it's really important that writers write us plays not thinking that they need to be able to transfer into the West End. Some writers have that robustness. Martin (McDonough, writer of *Hangmen*) is extraordinary and brilliant and that's part of what he is and what he does – his writing is so muscular that it works for a universal audience. But we've just had a play called *Lela & Co.* in the theatre upstairs, which is a duologue about a woman who has been sex trafficked. That writer has to believe that she can write this fragile, moving, dark, difficult play here. It's an interesting balance. In the end, it's extraordinary to have the *Jerusalem's* and the *Hangmen* and I am honoured when they're here and it's thrilling that the writers do that. More people see the work, which makes us more money and means we're able to take more risks with the other work. The whole ecosystem of that is brilliantly. But one of the things the Royal Court has to do is affect other writers, so it feeds into the symbiotic thing of, "Who wants to become a writer? And why?" Then we need to put on plays that make people say, "That has made me change the way I think about theatre."

CC: Writers getting caught up in the commercial aspect of it can be infectious in a bad way, can't it?
VF: Totally and most writers don't want to write for that because they won't achieve it, so they don't want to write for it.

CC: What goes into planning a season?
VF: It's the hardest thing. Being an artistic director and chief executive, you're responsible for the business, the HR – all of that. I have amazing teams and it's not me on my own. However, ultimately you are responsible for all those things. The most difficult thing is that programming is relentless. You come up with a programme and you think, "Brilliant! I've done a programme and that's fantastic", and then someone comes up to you and says, "The deadline for the next programme is this date", so you're never able to relax. The biggest challenge for me at the Royal Court is that if the writers haven't written it, I can't programme it and it's all original work. I have to find the writers, commission them, hope that they write the best possible plays and then I can put them on. I am totally at the mercy of the writers and the responsibility I have is to create the environment that they want to write their best plays for.

CC: Do you know how long you're going to be here?
VF: Until they chuck me out. I have the most amazing job in the world.

151

Hangmen

By Martin McDonagh
Royal Court

Gallows humour is the name of the game in Martin McDonagh's much anticipated return to the theatre after a successful Hollywood hiatus. Set in the 1960s, as the era of capital punishment gives way to a more socially liberal age, *Hangmen* centres on Harry Wade – played by David Morrissey in Matthew Dunster's production – who to his great chagrin is famed as England's second-best hangman behind the great Albert Pierrepoint. As the action moves from a brutal prologue in which we see him at the height of his power to the post-abolition world in which he struggles to find his place, Wade is forced – by the press, by pub locals, by his own conscience – to reflect on what he really achieved in a career that has suddenly been outlawed. *Hangmen* premiered at the Royal Court, where it received universal praise for its pitch-black comedy and unflinching portrait of the dark side of humanity, before transferring to Wyndham's Theatre.

David Morrissey (Harry)
shot from the substage
during the performance.

'The fact that we're going to the West End for three months is wonderful because more people will get to see it – get to see Martin's writing, get to see the play. Because it deserves to be seen.'

David Morrissey (Harry)

'It's lovely to be ahead of the audience, and they're catching up. You feel very empowered by that. It's enjoyable.'

Reece Shearsmith (Syd)

Above: David Morrissey
(Harry) in his dressing room.
Right: Johnny Flynn (Mooney)
during a scene on stage.

'Every actor at Equity would have killed to be in this show – killed two people if they had read the script.'

Simon Rouse (Arthur)

Left: Bronwyn James (Shirley)
and Sally Rogers (Alice) in
their dressing room.

'One thing I always notice is the scene with Johnny and the rope. One second it's a joke, and then the next second you can literally hear the audience go pin-drop silent.'

Bronwyn James (Shirley)

Above: Johnny Flynn (Mooney) enters stage.

Left: Ryan Pope (Charlie) during a quick change, preparing to enter stage.
Below: Simon Rouse, John Hodgkinson, David Morrissey, Reece Shearsmith and Ralph Ineson in their dressing room.

Sally Rogers (Alice) during an off-stage scene.

Happy Days

By Samuel Beckett
Young Vic

Disquieting and poignant, Samuel Beckett's *Happy Days* takes place over two acts that see Winnie attempt to maintain her veneer of calm as her imprisonment within a pile of gravel becomes increasingly extreme. Often considered a metaphor for the encroachment of the sands of time, what is most affecting is the extent to which Winnie accepts her entombment and determines to be cheerful in spite of it. The latest actress to take on this iconic and difficult role was Juliet Stevenson, who garnered universal praise for her nuanced and expressive performance at the Young Vic in 2015 while capturing the unique blend of burgeoning fear and relentless optimism that Winnie's situation demands. Expertly directed by Natalie Abrahami, Stevenson's reprisal of her 2014 performance was perfectly complemented by Vicki Mortimer's stage design, which replaced Beckett's usual setting of a low mound of scorched grass with a dramatic rocky escarpment whose harsh lines and fierce lighting underscored the lonely hopelessness of Winnie's predicament.

Juliet Stevenson (Winnie) backstage with Lauren Penfold (Dresser).

'Happy Days was like a gift from the female gods. And ultimately there aren't a large number of plays like that, and there needs to be more.'

Juliet Stevenson (Winnie)

Juliet Stevenson
(Winnie) on stage.

Curtain Call talks to Juliet Stevenson (Winnie)

CC: *Happy Days* is an incredible piece. Is that why you went back a second time to do it?

JS: I wanted to do it a second time, because I learned a huge amount in that first run last year. But when it came to the end of the run, I thought, "No, don't take this away from me yet. I just know there's so much more to discover here and I will never again have the opportunity to get inside a piece of material this demanding, complex, brilliant, profound."

CC: Is it liberating or more restricting as an actor where you can't move?

JS: Yes, it is liberating actually. In fact, she is stuck, but in some ways it felt like the most physical show I have ever done. Although I can't take a single step in the first half, in our production we felt strongly that she's a glass-half-full girl. She may think that she's stuck from the waist down, but what she focuses on is, "I'm free from the waist up. I'm going to make the most of that." Our brilliant movement director, Joseph Alford, worked hard on the arms and upper body so she never slumped and she never rested her elbows on that mound. It's a bit like being at a table where you're

not allowed to put your elbows on the table and you're not allowed to put your hands on the tablecloth.

CC: You must be exhausted, because you never stop. You're there before the audience gets in and then you really don't have an interval, do you?

JS: No, the interval was the craziest part of the whole evening because of the transformation. Last year, I raced to my dressing room and we did it all there. And we had this clock running. We literally had a clock running saying, "2 minutes, 3 minutes, 4 minutes" because we knew I had

Right: Juliet Stevenson (Winnie)
with Claudia Stoltz (Wigs, Hair
& Make-up Manager).

160

David Beames
(Willie) backstage.

to get back on stage. As soon as I got back on stage and went up through the hole, they were able to take the tent away and there I was before the audience fully assembled for the second part. If I got up too late, they would treat my appearance as a Part Two beginning and then would lose that very precious thing of just being in the room with them. So we needed to get back there in time for the audience to know, as they pottered in and out with their drinks, that I was just part of the scenery, as it were. So it was very challenging to do that.

CC: In rehearsals, did you focus on this almost being a one-act play for you, a long monologue?

JS: We didn't factor it into rehearsal. We went through it during the tech. It was a bit of a scary first preview because we hadn't been able to factor it in other than a preview situation with a full house. I was quite resistant to the idea of not leaving the set and not getting out. I thought I just have to get a break between Acts 1 and 2. In fact, I loved it almost immediately. I love the fact that I didn't break out of the zone. It was always difficult to get back under the stage and get up and then start Part Two and think, "So now I've got to go even further down into her psyche." Whereas this year, not leaving the zone meant that Act 2 flowed out of Act 1 much more fluidly and I didn't have to search for her mental state. It was hairy, because you couldn't factor it in, but it was so fascinating that when I got up

there at a certain time, the audience would just keep on chatting – I would appear, but they would just keep chatting. They knew that the second half wasn't starting. One minute later than that, when I appeared they would say, "Oh. This must be Part Two," and they'd stop talking and sit there for far too long in silence staring at my head in the semi-dark.

CC: It's funny how thirty seconds can take an audience in or out of a play.

JS: Isn't it? It's one of those miracles. It's one of those stranger wondrous things that you almost can't write about it, or talk about it. You just don't

David Beames (Willie) beneath the stage.

'Everything is minutely choreographed by Beckett – everything that she takes out of that bag and looks at and uses and puts back or lays out in front of her.'

Juliet Stevenson (Winnie)

know why there's this strange alchemy that goes on. This conversation that we can't really describe between a performer and an audience. But it was absolutely practical and clear that they were fine if I got there within a certain time frame – a minute later they were confused.

CC: This is one of the great female roles out there, and people came in droves to see you.

JS: I think it wasn't a play where only women loved it, men loved it too. All plays transcend gender. I think it

meant just as much to men as it did to women, which was wonderful.

CC: And having David there with you the whole time was great.

JS: Absolutely. In our production, it was very much a play about marriage. It's so not a one-woman show, it's a two-hander and it's about the marriage, not just about her. I had the most fantastic actor to play that with. David Beames is just the perfect partner. I think it did mean a lot, and there was a lot of discussion about Willie and about their relationship.

CC: During the curtain call there was a little flicker of a smile from you. Or there was an acknowledgement, which you can't help. It has to be so hard, that curtain call.

JS: It was quite weird. I said, "I've got to get out of that hole and be a normal actress." And Natalie said, "You can't get out of the hole." My concession to that was to smile a little tiny bit just so the audience knew that I was conscious of the curtain call.

163

Hay Fever

By Noël Coward
Duke of York's Theatre
Transfer from Theatre Royal Bath

Noël Coward paid his first visit to America in
1921, full of hope and optimism, both of which
were swiftly dashed. Unknown and unemployed,
he was on the verge of destitution when he fell in
with a set of eccentric playwrights and performers,
whose social gatherings, good-natured games and
bad-tempered arguments inspired him to write
Hay Fever upon his return to London. It was an
instant hit and has rarely been off the stage since.
In 1964 the National Theatre Company, then
in its infancy and under the artistic direction of
Laurence Olivier, selected it as its first production
by a living playwright. For all its farcical humour,
however, it is a deceptively difficult play that
requires a technically outstanding cast – or as
Coward said of the 1964 line-up, which included
Maggie Smith and Lynn Redgrave, 'a cast that
could play the Albanian telephone directory'. This
Theatre Royal Bath production has assembled
an impeccable cast – in the hands of actors
of the calibre of Felicity Kendal and Simon
Shepherd, the ghastly Blisses are as hilariously
outlandish today as they were in the 1920s.

Felicity Kendal
(Judith Bliss) on stage.

'I sit backstage every night. I have listened to two hundred performances. I find it really magical. And the fact of the matter is, I don't want to lose touch with the play.'

Mossie Smith (Clara)

Right: Felicity Kendal (Judith Bliss).
Centre right:
The company.
Far right: Celeste Dodwell (Jackie Coryton) and Alice Orr-Ewing (Sorel Bliss) backstage.

Right: Michael Simkins (Richard Greatham) and Alice Orr-Ewing (Sorel Bliss).
Centre right:
Mossie Smith (Clara).
Far right: Simon Shepherd (David Bliss).

Far left: Felicity Kendal (Judith Bliss). Centre left: Peter Christian (Master Carpenter, Duke of York's). Left: Edward Killingback (Sandy Tyrell) and Alice Orr-Ewing (Sorel Bliss).

'It's a very hot and airless theatre – you'll hear that from everybody. You see people using their fans backstage, people dropping their trousers and lifting their skirts.'

Simon Shepherd (David Bliss)

'You know, this play is a lemon meringue, and if you have to really welly it, the thing falls in on itself. It requires crispness and a certain lightness of touch.'

Michael Simkins (Richard Greatham)

'With a Coward play you have to be so accurate and on it. There's nowhere to hide and everybody gets so tired. It's very high-energy and by the end of the week we are absolutely knackered.'

Simon Shepherd (David Bliss)

Left: Alice Orr-Ewing (Sorel Bliss) and Celeste Dodwell (Jackie Coryton) in their dressing room.

Edward Killingback (Sandy Tyrell), Sara Stewart (Myra Arundel), Celeste Dodwell (Jackie Coryton) and Michael Simkins (Richard Greatham) waiting to enter stage.

Henry V

By William Shakespeare
**Royal Shakespeare Company
at the Barbican Theatre**

Gregory Doran's acclaimed production of
Shakespeare's most famous history play debuted
at Stratford-upon-Avon in 2015, the 600th
anniversary year of the Battle of Agincourt. It
then transferred to London's Barbican Centre,
where it became part of the Royal Shakespeare
Company's *King and Country* season, marking the
400th anniversary of Shakespeare's death in
January 2016. Alex Hassell, fresh from playing
Prince Hal in the RSC's productions of *Henry IV
Part I* and *Part II* the previous year, returned to
the character, reprising his role, this time as the
newly crowned King Henry. Running against a
backdrop of great international unrest, Doran's
interpretation was studiously neutral on the subject
of war, focusing instead on the hesitant young
King's gradual assumption of statesmanship.
Stephen Brimson Lewis' stripped-back set and
Tim Mitchell's subtle lighting complemented the
sense that this production was less about victory
and patriotism than about the psychological
evolution of a great man in the making.

'You have to be more
truthful in this space.
You can't lie. You have
to be more connected.'

Alex Hassell (Henry V)

Alex Hassell
(Henry V) backstage.

Stage crew with Andrew Westfield (MacMorris) just before entering stage.

Right: On stage, during
company warm-up.

'I really appreciate the support of live music
from the Royal Shakespeare Company. It really
makes a difference.'

Helen Raeburn (Soprano)

'I have never played a part that barely speaks English. That was the challenge, but it added something to the whole process.'

Jennifer Kirby (Katherine)

Above: Jennifer Kirby (Katherine) on stage.

Right: The prop horse upstage of the backcloth – elements of Stephen Brimson Lewis' beautiful design.

Christopher Middleton, Alex Hassell and Andrew Westfield wait to enter stage.

How to Hold Your Breath

By Zinnie Harris
Royal Court

Zinnie Harris' latest play is an intriguing allegory
that turns the tables on Western civilisation and
many of the most pressing political concerns of
our times. Following an encounter with a man
who claims to be a demon, Dana, played in Vicky
Featherstone's production at the Royal Court by
Maxine Peake, embarks on a journey with her
pregnant sister across Europe just as the continent is
plunged into a devastating debt crisis. Caught up in
a mass migration of Europeans desperate to reach
the shores of Africa, the sisters become beacons
of stoicism in the face of ever-increasing adversity.
Chloe Lamford's ruin-strewn set, dominated by
peeling posters that suggested Western civilisation
in tatters, enhanced the sense of a landscape that
had become entirely inhospitable to human comfort.
The production wielded a deeply sinister, unsettling
power over audiences, as wave upon wave of surreal
but prophetic catastrophe swept the characters
ever closer to a seemingly irresistible doom.

Maxine Peake (Dana)
and Christine Bottomley
(Jasmine) on stage during
the performance.

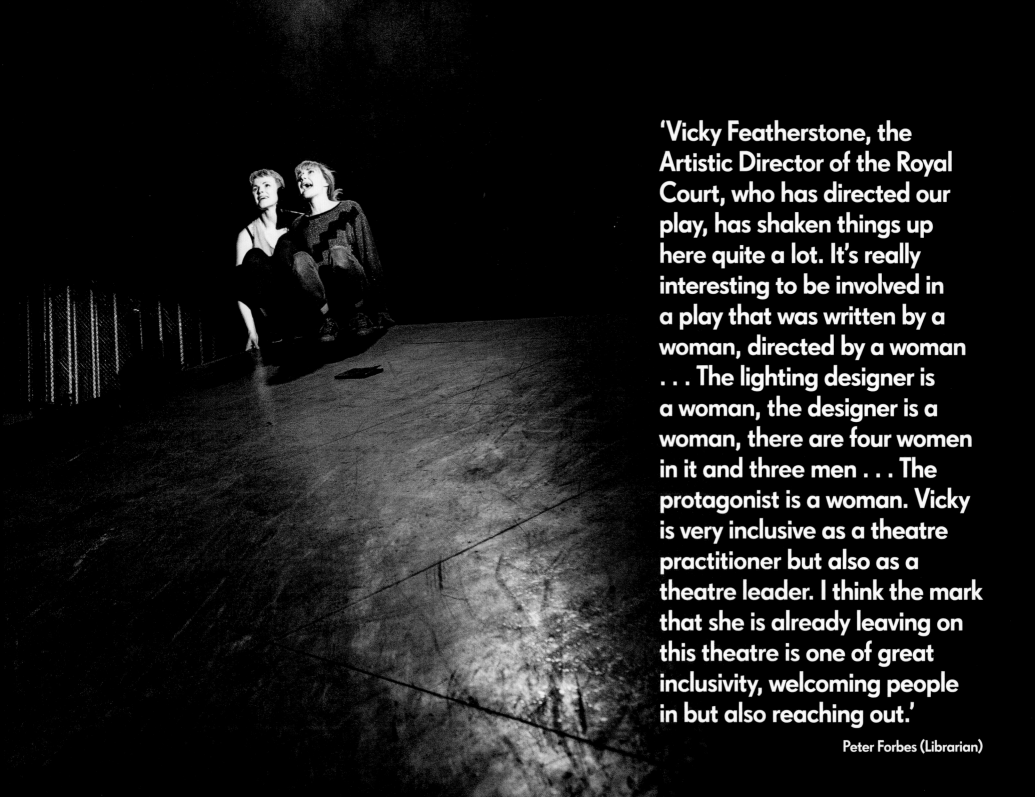

'Vicky Featherstone, the Artistic Director of the Royal Court, who has directed our play, has shaken things up here quite a lot. It's really interesting to be involved in a play that was written by a woman, directed by a woman . . . The lighting designer is a woman, the designer is a woman, there are four women in it and three men . . . The protagonist is a woman. Vicky is very inclusive as a theatre practitioner but also as a theatre leader. I think the mark that she is already leaving on this theatre is one of great inclusivity, welcoming people in but also reaching out.'

Peter Forbes (Librarian)

Michael Shaeffer (Jarron)
during warm-up before
the show.

Above: The supernumeraries make their way downstairs for their cue during the play.

Right: Maxine Peake (Dana) in her dressing room.
Below right: Michael Shaeffer (Jarron) in his dressing room.

'It's nice for the audience to come in and see not only the great sets that we can put in, but also the bare bones of what's happening around the space, so they can see the fact that, when we fly something in, there are ropes moving and stuff like that. It's great for us.'

Matt Livesey (Stage Crew)

Husbands & Sons

By D.H. Lawrence, adapted by Ben Power
National Theatre, Dorfman Stage

Husbands & Sons is an adaptation of three separate pieces, *A Collier's Friday Night*, *The Widowing of Mrs Holroyd* and *The Daughter-in-Law*, composed between 1909 and 1913 and now stitched together for the first time by playwright Ben Power and director Marianne Elliott. The melded script arose out of a day-long studio read-through at the National Theatre of all three mining plays which revealed contrasts and similarities that Power and Elliott wanted to explore. In Power's own words, 'they unlocked each other'. As their title suggests, the play is about men from the point of view of their wives and mothers; women peripheral to the mine itself but central to the working of the mining community. The play was staged in the round, with the audience looking down on Bunny Christie's exposed design: three near-identical households surrounded (or trapped) by a huge metal frame that rose and fell in noisy evocation of pit machinery. With no partition walls or doors, actors mimed entrances and exits, adding to the sense that each home was intricately woven into the lives of those surrounding them.

Lloyd Hutchison (Walter Lambert) in the backstage make-up station.

Matthew Barker
(Joe Gascoigne).

‘It's exhilarating. You're really vulnerable and exposed, but that allows you to play the rawness of it and that's exciting.’

Katherine Pearce (Gertie Coomer)

Martin Marquez (Charles Holroyd) having make-up applied backstage.

Right: Matthew Barker (Joe Gascoigne), Joe Armstrong (Luther Gascoigne) and Katie Barrett (Assistant Stage Manager).

183

Above: Cassie Bradley (Maggie Pearson), Katherine Pearce
(Gertie Coomer), Josie Walker (Clara), Tala Gouveia
(Clara) and Johnny Gibbon (Ernest Lambert) backstage.
Right: The company on stage just before the curtain call.
Below: Louise Brealey (Minnie Gascoigne) backstage.

'It doesn't feel like anything I have ever done before, because your cue might be the oven door in another household or a shout or a squeal. More often than not it's a line, but sometimes it's a sound.

Philip McGinley (Blackmore

Anne-Marie Duff
(Lizzie Holroyd) after
exiting the stage area.

King Charles III

By Mike Bartlett
Wyndham's Theatre
Transfer from Almeida Theatre

Mike Bartlett's 2014 play debuted at the Almeida Theatre before transferring to the West End and then on to Broadway with Tim Pigott-Smith as the lead (also nominated for Best Actor in the 2015 Olivier Awards). Perhaps a surprising validation for such a wickedly provocative 'future history', Rupert Goold's production opens with the funeral of Queen Elizabeth, questions the existence and role of the monarchy, and features the ghost of Princess Diana. But far from being a subversive bit of fun at the expense of the royal family, *King Charles III* examines some of the most pressing political questions of our age in a turn of events that may yet prove not to be far from reality. It is also a technically difficult play to play well, skirting as it does the easy option of farce and impression. 'It wasn't a parody or a pastiche,' Bartlett has said of the challenging writing experience. 'It was a play, telling a story the audience should care about. Anything that worked against this was swiftly cut.'

Right: Keshini Ranasinghe (Dresser).

Curtain Call talks to Tim Pigott-Smith (Charles)

Left: Tim Pigott-Smith (Charles) in his dressing room.

Curtain Call: Did you feel any kind of responsibility playing a living character?

Tim Pigott-Smith: Yes, a huge responsibility. As somebody who I have sort of grown up in parallel with – I think he's two or three years younger than me. So people say to me, "Did you do any research?" And I say, "I don't have to. I watched him grow all my life." And I quite like him. I quite like his zaniness. And, so, it was a huge thought. You know, was this a play that was fundamentally irresponsible? Was it something that we shouldn't be doing? And I felt that it was okay and you were just left

with the responsibility of honouring the person you're playing. And I didn't find that difficult, especially the way the play is written. He's written pretty much the way that he is, really. He's a slightly old-fashioned man of principal. So I think that I've put myself in pretty much the same bracket. I rather like that.

CC: Absolutely.

TPS: But it is, of course, a massive responsibility. I play it like I played Francis Crick, for example. He was one of the guys that discovered DNA, but nobody knows what he's like. I played Brendan Bracken,

who was Churchill's parliamentary private secretary during the war – nobody knows what he was like, you know? So you have a responsibility. But it's nothing like the responsibility of playing this man who's known throughout the world.

CC: It was a fantastic performance. Watching somebody where circumstances were beyond his control and those dictated which way he was facing in the wind.

TPS: I think that's one of the things I like about it. That it says, "There's nothing wrong with this guy." And particularly, in the play, somebody who the audience comes on side with. So when you first read the play, you think, "Well, this is going to be royal pastiche. It's not going to last fifteen minutes, and then it will just cease to exist as a piece of drama." But, of course, about fifteen minutes in the drama really kicks in and you realise that Mike has written a really interesting play about the way the world is changing and leaving somebody like Charles behind.

CC: Were there any ways, technically, inside the character, that you used to say that you were the heir to the throne?

TPS: I know what you're trying to say. The way I work on a script is always "the text, the text, the text". So first of all you go with absolutely what happens in the play. And then, one of the issues we were all dealing with in this production – some of the people were not real so they didn't have that concern – but I think there were five of us in the play who were playing real people. So we all looked at the issue of the level of impersonation and we decided, basically, not to do . . . I can't say "any", because that was the fundamental decision . . . that we shouldn't impersonate. But that said, I was working, at the time that I was offered the play, with a friend of mine that used to do *Spitting Image* and he's a brilliant impersonator. And I said to him, you know, what impersonators do is that they pick out, like cartoonists do, salient features. Things that make someone immediately recognisable.

And there are two or three things that Charles does which make him very recognisable. One of them is that he holds his signet ring with his other hand, and turns the hand in the signet ring – that's very specific.

'... you realise that Mike has written a really interesting play about the way the world is changing and leaving somebody like Charles behind.'

Tim Pigott-Smith (Charles)

And he does a similar gesture with his cuffs. His hands hover, often, outside the outside pockets of his jacket, as though he's going to put them in . . . but he never does. That's a slightly more detailed thing, you know? That's something I do for me rather than for the audience. But the most obvious thing, I think, is just occasionally, I pull my mouth down to the side and just make a sound . . . just because . . . And that helps the audience. I tend to do that when there's comedy around, you know? Just to punch up a bit of comedy – just to remind them who it is. And indeed, in the middle of the fifth act, when he's really under pressure, I suddenly do one line and let my mouth fall down in his voice. But it's very, very discreet, I hope.

CC: So what's it like being on stage there at the Wyndham's? You really didn't have any kind of wings. When you were on, you were on.

TPS: Nowhere to hide. It's just the most wonderful theatre. I don't know why. The Coward [Noël Coward Theatre] is a theatre that was built almost exactly at the same time by the same designer, Walter Sprague. And yet there's something about the Wyndham's that makes it an easier, more enjoyable theatre to play. It's peculiar. They're almost identical, but there's something about the Wyndham's. I don't know what it is, whether it's the ghosts of the past or just some weird relationship between the stage and the auditorium. It's just absolute heaven to play. Of course, the stage there was almost a replica of the Almeida stage. And that will be our set when we go to Broadway. I love the Coward, and it's good. But you can't explain that a theatre that is almost a twin doesn't have the same feel. It might even be something as stupid as which way the stage is pointing. The Coward stage points the other way. One points west and the other points east. The ley lines are different. It's just extraordinary. And wonderful.

CC: Have you had any chance to chat with director Rupert Goold about how it could be received differently by an American audience?

TPS: You mustn't forget that Rupert and I worked on *Enron* together. Now *Enron* went across to the States,

and having had the most amazing success here, didn't catch on at all there. So, we're keenly aware we're on the edge of a precipice, you know? And how will they take what we'll offer? Well, I've played Broadway a couple of times before and I'm sort of ready for the feel. And I suspect that they'll be less quick onto the comedy. Because they'll think that this is a play about the royal family and they'll be very respectful. And the less "sophisticated" they become the more that will be the case. So I think that might make it a bit harder. And we've already implemented a few cuts because we think it should be a bit shorter for the American audience. I think that's very wise. Beyond that, you just have to suck it and see.

Right: The cast in the wings before curtain up.

King John

By William Shakespeare
Shakespeare's Globe

Dominic Dromgoole's last season as artistic director of the Globe saw him complete what he called 'a very big jigsaw puzzle', started by Mark Rylance twenty years earlier. By staging *King John* as part of its Justice & Mercy season, the Globe finally succeeded in presenting all of Shakespeare's thirty-eight plays. The timing was perfect, coming 800 years after the 1215 signing of Magna Carta by the embattled monarch. The play was directed by James Dacre, artistic director of the Royal & Derngate in Northampton, which had initially staged this production at Northampton's Church of the Holy Sepulchre. There the candles, heavy costumes and echoing plainchant made a strikingly powerful impression, but they were no less evocative of medieval kingship in the hallowed round of the Globe. *King John* is not Shakespeare's most popular play. It is the furthest back of his English histories, with a lead who is thoroughly unlikeable – but Dacre's pacy direction and Jo Stone-Fewings' wonderfully shady John made this a triumphant celebration of the Globe's great achievement.

Aruhan Galieva (Blanche of Castile) backstage.

Tanya Moodie
(Constance) backstage.

Right: The musicians
Paul Johnson, Sarah Homer
and Phil Hopkins.
Below: Candle on stage.

'I have had 22 years playing a traditional relationship with the audience. In this space, it is spun on its head and that really shocked me. I had always held the power. Here, they own the space. They tell you what to do. They will tell you if they're not happy.'

Tanya Moodie (Constance)

Above: Stage Management (Sally Hughes and Mary O'Hanlon) listening out for cues.
Right: Jo Stone-Fewings (King John) and stage management at a front of house entrance.

'You don't get calls when you're backstage here, of course. There are no lights. Our stage management have their ears to the doors and then they throw them open.'

Jo Stone-Fewings (King John)

Various members of cast
waiting front of house
for an entrance.

Kinky Boots

Music & Lyrics by Cyndi Lauper
Book by Harvey Fierstein
Adelphi Theatre

A failing shoe factory in the Midlands proved
unexpectedly fertile source material for this
Broadway hit musical, based on a 2005 British film
that was in turn based on a true story. With six
Tony Awards to its name, including for first-time
musical theatre songwriter Cyndi Lauper, the play's
ultimate transfer to the West End was inevitable.
Announcing the move, producers Daryl Roth and
Hal Luftig said they were 'thrilled and deeply
honoured to be bringing *Kinky Boots* back home'. A
coup for director and choreographer Jerry Mitchell
was the casting of seasoned musical actor Killian
Donnelly in the role of reluctant factory owner
Charlie Price, with *The Voice* finalist Matt Henry
donning the kinky boots of the title. But critics also
praised the stellar contribution of the supporting
actors and ensemble, not to mention Gregg Barnes's
gloriously outrageous costume design, all of which
exuded colourful energy and feel-good fun.

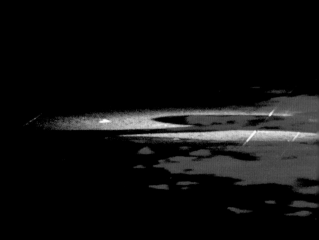

Matt Henry
(Lola) on stage.

'Once you get your wig and
your face on, you get a bit of
a sassy mouth sometimes.
We all have good banter, all in
comedy jest. It's all from love.'

Luke Jackson (Angel)

Luke Jackson at the substage Angels make-up station.

'As soon as I come out my show doesn't stop. It's like the train's arrived and only at the end of the show do I get a break.'

Matt Henry (Lola)

Above: Matt Henry (Lola) and Killian Donnelly (Charlie) on stage during the show.

Right: Angels Javier Santos, Jordan Fox and Arun Blair-Mangat backstage at the curtain call.

Matt Henry (Lola),
Amy Ross (Nicola)
and Killian Donnelly
(Charlie) on stage
during the show.

Linda

By Penelope Skinner
Royal Court

Penelope Skinner won the Charles Wintour Award
for Most Promising Playwright in 2011, for *The
Village Bike*. In her most recent play *Linda*, which
debuted at the Royal Court in 2015, that promise
was amply fulfilled. Starring Noma Dumezweni
in the title role, Linda is about a fifty-five-year-
old beauty-industry executive who falls victim to
the ageism her products are ostensibly designed
to counter. As her life and family unravel in ways
she had never anticipated, there are hints of *King
Lear* alongside starker manifestations of the sort
of casual prejudice towards older women that
suggests Linda's fate is almost her own fault. In
Michael Longhurst's acclaimed production, the
feminist theme clashed to great effect with the
showroom-perfect family kitchen in which much
of the action took place. Es Devlin's rotating set
and Lee Curran's contrasting lighting were slick,
modern, bright and clean – perfectly suited to
this brutal tale of façade versus harsh reality.

'Linda is pitching
to people at the
beginning and she's
pitching to people at
the end. Pitching for
the same thing. But the
whole world has shifted
on its axis for her.'

Noma Dumezweni (Linda)

Noma Dumezweni (Linda).

'Mike Longhurst (Director) talked about how
the stage was Linda's dollhouse and we're on it.
Once we get off, things fall apart.'   Jaz Deol (Luke)

Right: Dominic Mafham
(Neil) in the dressing room.
Centre right: The cast
upstage, on the revolve.
Far right: Dominic
Mafham (Neil) relaxed
in the dressing room.

Right: Jaz Deol (Luke)
and Amy Beth Hayes (Amy) on
stage with Noma Dumezwen
(Linda) waiting 'backstage'.
Centre right: Osnat Koblenz
(Assistant Stage Manager)
during the storm scene.
Far right: Amy Beth Hayes
(Amy) watches from the wings.

Far left: From left to right, Merriel Plummer (Stevie), Amy Beth Hayes (Amy), Imogen Byron (Bridget) and Karla Crome (Alice). Next: Noma Dumezweni (Linda) in her dressing room. Then: Merriel Plummer (Stevie) singing on the revolve. Left: Ian Redford (Dave) waits to enter.

'Some nights we get a raucous audience, some nights we get a quiet audience, but the reaction at the end is always the same.'

Ian Redford (Dave)

'There's something about the play which makes the audience have the confidence to be vocal. They just can't help themselves.'

Amy Beth Hayes (Amy)

Made in Dagenham

Music by David Arnold
Lyrics by Richard Thomas
Book by Richard Bean
Adelphi Theatre

Based on the film that was inspired by true events at Ford's Dagenham plant in 1968, *Made in Dagenham* portrays the lives of the women whose job it was to stitch seat covers and their walkout in protest at pay inequality. The cast in Rupert Goold's all-singing, all-dancing adaptation at the Adelphi was led by Gemma Arterton, who was deservedly nominated for numerous awards for her turn as Rita O'Grady. The music, by David Arnold, was praised by critics for evoking the sounds of the 1960s, with accompanying choreography by Aletta Collins. Bunny Christie's giant model-kit inspired set and period costumes came in for particular acclaim, bedecking everyone in overalls and lurid prints, against a backdrop of endless grey industrial machinery. The show was as heart-warming as it was laugh-out-loud funny, bringing a joyous West End twist to this inspirational moment in British social history.

Show Crew
backstage at the
Adelphi Theatre.

'A lot of the boys are playing more than one character, so it became very apparent that we were going to have to change their look quite a lot. They ended up with about three or four wigs each.'

Mark Marsden (Wigs)

Above: Gemma Arterton (Rita O'Grady) in her dressing room.
Left: Various cast in the wings during the show.

Right: Mark Marson (Head of Wigs) and Sophie Stanton (Beryl).

Cast and crew on stage at the end of the interval.

Below: Various cast backstage on set.
Bottom: Gemma Arterton (Rita O'Grady) backstage.

Above: Sophie Isaacs (Sandra) on stage.
Left: Gemma Arterton (Rita O'Grady) on stage.

'It's all of us together, and I have never been involved in a company like that. There's this real energy. Last night I looked around when we were singing "Stand Up" and everyone's clapping and I got a bit emotional.'

Gemma Arterton (Rita O'Grady)

Jessica Ronane CDG

CC: Have you always been in the field of casting?

JR: I trained at Elmhurst Ballet School for years. I came to London and attended The London School of Musical Theatre in a rehearsal room at the top of the Old Vic Theatre. I was a dancer but wanted to find out if I could act and to learn how to sing properly. Just before I finished the course I was cast by Bill Kenwright in *Elvis*. We toured for a year, ending up at The Piccadilly Theatre in London. At twenty-seven years old I decided to make a big career change and met with Casting Director, Jina Jay, who cast the film *Billy Elliot*. She introduced me to Jon Finn who was producing the musical of *Billy Elliot*. I met Jon and then at another interview I met Stephen Daldry. I was offered the job to cast the boys in *Billy Elliot the Musical*. Strangely enough, what had never come up was the fact that I had trained from the age of nine at Elmhurst. The pressure they were under to find a Billy was intense, because if they couldn't find the right kids then they felt they didn't have a show.

CC: How did you go about finding them?

JR: Jon Finn and I worked geographically. We had a map of the country and started in Newcastle, then worked in circles. I called every single dance school to introduce myself and the project. *Billy Elliot* at that time was not a brand – it was a small, British film that some people had heard of.

CC: And how did the search go?

JR: There remained a lot of stigma attached to boys dancing and people would say, "I do have a boy, but he would never want anyone to know he dances." So I would arrange to visit any dance school that sounded interesting or any teacher that seemed impassioned. Occasionally we would find someone very special like Liam Mower, who is now with Matthew Bourne's company. I drove to his dance school in Hull and there were all these boys, but at the end of the line there was this little ten year old who did about forty fouetté turns. I remember feeling, "I think we may have found a Billy."

CC: From there, how did you get involved with casting *Matilda the Musical*?

JR: Peter Darling, the choreographer for *Billy Elliot the Musical*, started working on *Matilda* and called me in to meet with Matthew Warchus (Director). At that time, it was referred to as this "little Christmas show" – that's how it was put to me. He was

> **'Finding good children is not easy. Mainly because you have to be unwilling to settle ...'**

very contained about it and said, "This isn't Billy. It's not a big, big thing." Just as with Billy, these girls weren't going to be the girls who pushed themselves to the front. They were going to be the girls lurking somewhere at the back, not necessarily speaking up.

CC: Do you have to handle children differently? Is it a different process or a slower process? And you must also know when you see someone special?

JR: I mean, a kid could be clearly special but there could be concerns in other ways. The funny thing is, you do have to take it more slowly and get to know them in a very detailed way. Particularly because you can see this talent so clearly and you can see what's truly unique about them. Kids are generally so unfiltered and raw at that age but they might not know their power. It's a really special time.

CC: What shows for you have been the most challenging?

JR: Finding good children is not easy. Mainly because you have to be unwilling to settle, relentless and pushy. Billy, Matilda, Charlie . . . and not necessarily just Charlie Bucket himself, but all those parts in *Charlie and the Chocolate Factory* are very, very tough.

CC: What's been the most exciting part of 2015?

JR: Beginning work at The Old Vic – it's been a totally new learning curve. We read different plays all the time

Jessica Ronane at the Stage Door of The Old Vic.

and work with different directors. And I worked on *The Hairy Ape* with Richard Jones, an extraordinary director. I found it quite daunting going into an audition room with him on the first day and I was concerned

'Kids are generally so unfiltered and raw at that age, but they might not know their power.'

and wanted to do the best job that I could. He hadn't really picked me, he had been lumbered with me. It made me even more determined to attempt to understand him quickly and deliver what he might need. In the end, the whole casting process was so thoroughly enjoyable. I gave birth to my third child during the middle of it, and he dealt with me breaking for a few weeks and coming back with a baby plonked outside the room. The day would end and he would have seen something good in each person that came in. It was inspiring. As a casting director I wanted to always

make sure that auditions were positive experiences, as much as they could be, and I wanted to make sure that I was caring for anyone who came in to meet me, because I felt it was such a privileged part of the creative process. So I found that, once I gained my confidence, working with Richard became one of the most inspirational moments this year. Also, being able to be in the room with Matthew as the seasons are being programmed, to be able to partake in those conversations – it's an education and I feel very lucky. When I first started work here, I called Alastair (Coomer, Casting Director) at the Donmar Warehouse, who is a great friend. I said, "Before I start, I feel like I have to do massive lists – cover every kind of person, every kind of role." He said, "Jessica, there's no way you can know everyone before you start a job. It just doesn't happen. You have to do it project by project. And before you know it, each little area becomes an area of mini-expertise." He was so right.

Matilda
The Musical

Book by Dennis Kelly
Music & Lyrics by Tim Minchin
**Royal Shakespeare Company
at the Cambridge Theatre**

The Royal Shakespeare Company's *Matilda The Musical*, based on Roald Dahl's novel with book by Dennis Kelly, music and lyrics by Tim Minchin and direction by Matthew Warchus, has delighted grown-ups and children alike since it transferred to the Cambridge Theatre in 2011 after premiering in Stratford-upon-Avon the year before. With four Matildas in rotation, plus dozens of other child actors sharing the roles of her classmates, the show celebrates its fifth year in the West End in 2016. The genius of Roald Dahl's *Matilda* is that it's a book about a little girl who loves books, but Kelly quickly found that it would not do simply to transfer her hobby of reading to the theatre. Instead he made Matilda a lover of all kinds of stories, and with the superb, award winning creative team including Rob Howell's design and Peter Darling's choreography, the musical began to fall into place. With subsequent productions on Broadway and on tour across the US and Australia, the show has won more than fifty awards internationally.

Matilda takes her bow.

'One of the amazing things about working on this show is that everybody cares so much about it. It's very special because of that.'

Sally Hoskins (General Manager, London)

Left: Michael Begley (Mr Wormwood) about to enter.
Below: The four Matildas. From left to right: Lara McDonnell, Lizzie Wells, Anna-Louise Knight and Evie Hone.

Elliot Harper (The Escapologist) on stage.

'You'll get children that can't sing at all, and then you say "I think they'll be able to do it." And then they go through such a journey and work so hard and become amazing. I think that's my favourite thing about it. That they don't know how good they are.'

Laura Bangay (Children's Musical Director)

Right: Craige Els (Miss Trunchbull) on stage watched by Miria Parvin (Miss Honey).
Below: Members of the cast rehearse "When I Grow Up".

McQueen

By James Phillips
**Theatre Royal Haymarket
Transfer from St James Theatre**

The genesis of James Phillips's tribute to Lee 'Alexander' McQueen was a fantasy that inspired the late fashion designer's Autumn-Winter 2008–9 show. 'I've got a 600-year-old elm tree in my garden,' McQueen explained at the time. 'I made up a story: a girl lives in it and comes out of the darkness to meet a prince and becomes a queen.' From this, Phillips dreamt up a whirlwind nocturnal adventure in which McQueen takes the girl on a tour of London – a tour of his life and career. For the most part the material is dark, foreshadowing as it does his suicide at the age of forty. But its lighter moments presented an immense creative opportunity for Set Designer David Farley and Choreographer Christopher Marney. Indulging sporadically in McQueen-style catwalk theatrics, it featured mannequin dancers parading across the stage to a soundtrack of songs used in the designer's iconic fashion shows. In the title role of the troubled genius, Stephen Wight was universally acclaimed.

'Dealing with that man's legacy, portraying him with an original piece of theatre – it was a challenge like no other.'

Stephen Wight (Lee)

Stephen Wight
(Lee) on stage at
the end of the play.

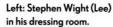

Left: Stephen Wight (Lee)
in his dressing room.

'I met Stephen (Wight) for the audition over Skype when he was
in Los Angeles, and even over that very fuzzy connection it was
extraordinary how much the physical resemblance was there.'

James Phillips (Playwright)

Carly Bawden (Dahlia) in her dressing room.

Above: The ensemble on stage.

Tracy-Ann Oberman (Isabella) in her dressing room.

'You feel so satisfied to see the man himself, in the play, create something on stage. It's such a wonderful moment.'

Carly Bawden (Dahlia)

227

Medea

By Euripides. A new version by Rachel Cusk
Almeida Theatre

The Almeida's 2015 festival of Greek drama
showcased new adaptations of *Bakkhai* and *Oresteia*,
culminating in a thoroughly modern reinvention of
Euripides' *Medea*. In selecting *Medea* for the season,
Artistic Director Rupert Goold was particularly
keen to explore theatre's perennial fixation with
glamorously violent female characters – who have,
of course, traditionally been written, portrayed
and watched almost exclusively by men. Hoping
instead to present the story in a way that was 'truly
honest about the wars waged by men and women
in the name of freedom', he turned to award
winning novelist Rachel Cusk, who has written
disarmingly openly about gender politics in the
past, to adapt *Medea* for the twenty-first century.
The production was universally praised for its
raw, ferocious energy and frighteningly realistic
domestic disputes, with Kate Fleetwood in the
title role drawing acclaim for her mastery of the
vengeance and vulnerability of a woman scorned.

Kate Fleetwood
(Medea) on stage.

Left: The chorus backstage with their babies.

Right: Kate Fleetwood (Medea) backstage.

'It's a lovely thing for a performer to know that there's going to be a challenge that's unexpected. You know that you've got that coming and the audience really don't expect it.'

Kate Fleetwood (Medea)

Above left: The baby
dolls on the props table.
Left: Charlotte Randle
(Messenger/Chorus)
applying her make-up
backstage.

'Rachel (Cusk) writes a character so well.
It's just a joy to play. I hope she'll do lots
more theatre because this is her first play.'

Richard Cant (Aegeus)

The Curtain Call Interview
Playing the role of Tracy Lord, High Society
The Old Vic

Kate Fleetwood

CC: What's it like playing on this set, because it's quite unique, isn't it?

KF: It's beautiful. I think it makes the stage feel more intimate because you're thrust out more into the room, as it were, than if you were on a proscenium arch. You're further into the auditorium, so it feels less intimidating. It's really magical being in the round. What you gain is an intimacy with the people behind you. You can turn and interact with the audience and it's almost like the people on the back, or the stage stalls, are kind of the naughty devil on your shoulder that you can turn to and have a little dialogue with. They're almost like your subconscious. Particularly in the party scene, they feel like they're actually at the party, which is just bliss to play with. You can see them getting more and more excited throughout and you want to say to

them, "You wait! You haven't even seen the two pianos yet! And then there's going to be someone dancing on the top! And then, then . . ."

CC: How did you rehearse that? (Because you have things that come up from the stage?)

KF: The footprint is very small. And the main thing of being in the round is that you've always got to be on the move so you're not blocking sight lines – something is always moving. It's very rarely static. The pool, which is the video projection pool, is moving. For the ball scene, the ensemble rehearsed in a different space while we were doing text work. Every three or four days we would add another layer to the ball – another section, another section, another section. It just builds, doesn't it? It took weeks and we had to have faith that it would all come together.

CC: There is always something to watch. People coming off stage, people going on stage. Even the scene changes are beautifully choreographed.
KF: With a show like this, which is very story heavy, with lots of characters and back stories, you just have to keep it snappy and upbeat. The interaction with the musicians is interesting for that, as well. They're so present. Of course, they even come on stage at some points.

CC: Have you started rehearsals for *Medea* yet?
KF: Yes. I started this week.

'It's beautiful being here. There's something absolutely magical about this place.'

CC: Could there be more polar opposite characters to play?
KF: I know! The funny thing is I didn't come to Tracy Lord thinking that she was some sort of great tragic heroine. You approach the characters in the same way. Why is she unhappy? What has she lost? Why is she lonely? What is she yearning for? What's she grieving for? What will change things? What do you regret about your past? *Medea* is about what went wrong. "How dare he? We had this wonderful thing." Tracy is the same in some way. "Why am I making the wrong decisions?".

It's the same place in my heart that I go to discover what that reality is, even though the outcomes are really different. Of course they're different. It's darker. I'm not going to have the same amount of fun, but I approach the part from the same part of my life, my own emotional landscape. Both stories are about love and loss and loneliness – making the wrong decisions and choosing a different path or wanting to be autonomous. Or not wanting to be misunderstood. Tracy is totally misunderstood and Medea is totally misunderstood.

CC: You're putting on two mics. Why is that?
KF: Just in case one goes down, because I am not off stage enough to change the mic. In the hat that I wear I have another microphone. So I actually have three mics on my head in the middle of the show. They're not light, but I've got used to them.

CC: And lastly, what's it like being at The Old Vic?
KF: It's beautiful being here. There's something absolutely magical about this space.

Memphis

Music by David Bryan
Lyrics by David Bryan & Joe DiPietro
Book by Joe DiPietro
Shaftesbury Theatre

Joe DiPietro's infectiously jaunty musical about great music amid racial tension in 1950s *Memphis* won four Tony Awards following its 2010 Broadway debut, including Best Original Score for composer and lyricist David Bryan of Bon Jovi. Although the character of Huey Calhoun is modelled in part on such visionary 1950s radio DJs as Alan Freed and Dewey Phillips, DiPietro intended him to be a sort of rock 'n' roll Everyman – a guide to, and product of, the revolutionary musical scene of those politically troubled times. Memphis opened in the West End for a year-long run in 2014, picking up Olivier Awards for choreographer Sergio Trujillo and sound designer Gareth Owen. In a casting coup, director Christopher Ashley secured West End leading man Killian Donnelly (followed by *X Factor* winner Matt Cardle) as Huey, opposite British soul legend Beverley Knight as Felicia. Knight in particular proved to be a revelation; it was only her second role in musical theatre, following a star turn in *The Bodyguard*.

The company in full swing.

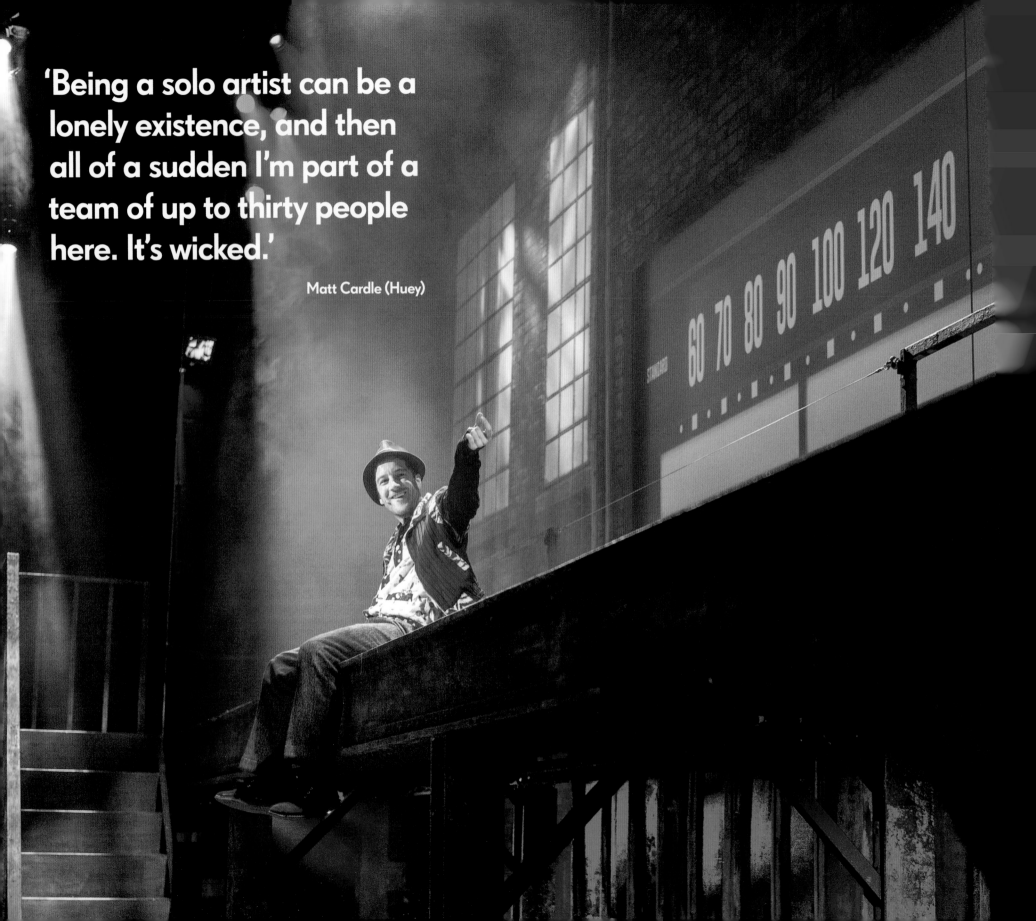

'Being a solo artist can be a lonely existence, and then all of a sudden I'm part of a team of up to thirty people here. It's wicked.'

Matt Cardle (Huey)

Left: Matt Cardle (Huey) on stage during the show.

Right: Beverley Knight (Felicia), in her dressing room.

'When you're at the helm of something, it's up to you to ensure everybody feels special. You want to be the one to provide the glue to knit everything together.' Beverly Knight (Felicia)

'This show is crazy — high impact and high energy. If you're not quite feeling it that night, you have to properly give yourself a kick up the arse to manage, especially the dance numbers.'

John Robyns (Ensemble / Alternate Huey)

Above: Rolan Bell (Delray), Jason Pennycooke (Bobby) and Harry Gabriel (Stage Door Keeper), in an after-show ritual.

Far left: The ensemble on stage during the show. Left: Tim Sutton (Musical Director) on stage.

Beverley Knight (Felicia), Matt Cardle (Huey) and the cast on stage during the show.

Mr Foote's Other Leg

By Ian Kelly
Hampstead Theatre

Mr Foote's Other Leg is a history, a biography and a tragedy, but above all it is enormous fun for actors and audience alike. It is a play about the stage – the London stage in particular – featuring as characters some of the most famous theatrical luminaries of the eighteenth century, from David Garrick to Peg Woffington. And of course there is Samuel Foote himself, a flamboyant one-legged eccentric who enjoyed enormous success followed by a dramatic fall into obscurity after becoming embroiled in a high-profile sex scandal. It is entirely fitting that this first production of Ian Kelly's play, which he adapted from his own biography of Foote, should bring together some of the biggest names from modern-day London's theatre scene, among them director Richard Eyre and actors Simon Russell Beale and Dervla Kirwan. Kelly also took a leading role in this bright, brash production, as the future King George III. The play's transfer to its own and Samuel Foote's spiritual home at the Theatre Royal Haymarket, where the play is set, heralds another Hampstead Theatre success story.

Rosy Emmerich (Wardrobe Mistress) helps Simon Russell Beale (Samuel Foote) with his leg brace backstage.

Left: Dervla Kirwan (Peg Woffington) in her dressing room before the show.

Below: Ian Kelly (Writer / Prince George) applauds in the wings during the curtain call.

'To be back there, putting him back on his stage 240 years after he was pretty much kicked off it in disgrace is something I will always feel proud of, no matter what anybody thought about this play.'

Ian Kelly (Writer / Prince George)

'Simon being in it was the "sine qua non" of me doing the play.'

Richard Eyre (Director)

Joseph Millson (David Garrick) and Dervla Kirwan (Peg Woffington) during the show.

245

The amputation scene,
taken from the wings.

'In the amputation scene when the line comes, "Then I pulled the skin up from the knee to the groin", you have to react to that in some way, and it's not pleasant.'

Simon Russell Beale (Samuel Foote)

My Night with Reg

By Kevin Elyot
Apollo Theatre
Transfer from Donmar Warehouse

By turns hauntingly evocative and hilariously funny,
My Night with Reg follows the highs and lows of a
group of gay friends in the 1980s as they struggle to
come to terms with the reality of their relationships
with the eponymous Reg – an unseen character who
hangs over the play like a dark spectre, representing
the looming threat of Aids. Over the course of
its history the play won numerous awards, before
making its transfer to the West End in 2014 for
its twentieth-year anniversary revival. This 2015
production at the Apollo Theatre retained all of
the wit and charm of the original while stellar
performances and a reimagined set brought Kevin
Elyot's tale of infidelity and friendship into a fresh,
new light. In a landscape where tired stereotypes
of gay men not only manage to survive, but
somehow to thrive, this comedy is a refreshingly
sensitive and nuanced portrayal that is as relevant
today as it was when it was first performed.

Richard Cant
(Bernie) waits to
enter backstage.

'This play is written for this sort of theatre. The comedy plays a lot faster. It's quicker off the bat and I think it's a bit clearer somehow.'

Jonathan Broadbent (Guy)

Right: Julian Ovenden (John) in his dressing room.
Below: Jonathan Broadbent (Guy) in his dressing room.

Above: Lewis Reeves (Eric)
and Matt Bardock (Benny)
waiting backstage.

Left: Geoffrey Streatfeild
(Daniel) in his dressing room.

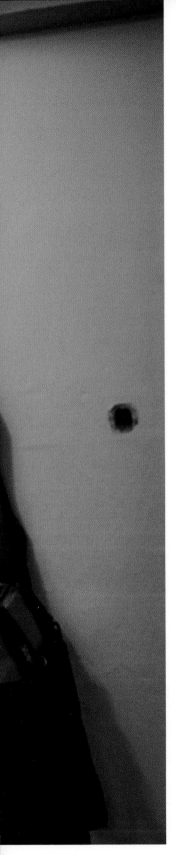

Right: The cast backstage.

'I have ten minutes off stage, which is my darts break.' Julian Ovenden (John)

Right: Geoffrey Streatfeild (Daniel) waiting backstage. Far right: The cast at the curtain call.

Left: Julian Ovenden (John) backstage.

Oresteia

By Euripides, adapted by Robert Icke
Trafalgar Studios 1
Transfer from Almeida Theatre

Aeschylus's *Oresteia* was the opening play in the Almeida's 2015 festival of Greek drama, which also presented new adaptations of *The Bacchae* and *Medea*. Originally written for an annual theatrical competition, the City Dionysia, at which it won first prize in 458 BC, *Oresteia* is a trilogy of plays that follow the fortunes of Orestes as he avenges the murder of his father, King Agamemnon. Billed as 'part *The Godfather*, part *Breaking Bad*', this production was a radically reimagined version of the plays, written and directed by Robert Icke. Gone was the chorus, traditionally the backbone of Greek drama, and in its place visceral scenes that showed (rather than told) the terrible machinations of this dysfunctional, frighteningly recognisable family. Lia Williams's vengeful Klytemnestra took centre-stage, while Hildegard Bechtler's simple but unsettling stage design, including sliding screens that made ghostly figures out of the characters behind them, heightened the atmosphere of impending tragedy.

'I think the structure of Greek theatre is very good for tension. Very early it tells you that a thing is either going to happen or not happen. And that's what tension is. You're waiting to see whether that thing happens or doesn't happen.'

Robert Icke (Director)

Lia Williams (Klytemnestra)
waiting to enter backstage.

Lia Williams (Klytemnestra)
on stage during the show.

Jessica Brown Findlay
(Electra) backstage.

'I can't be tired or bored when it's so challenging. It's six months in and there's still room to play and explore. It terrifies me and that makes it really exciting.'

Jessica Brown Findlay (Electra)

Left: Angus Wright (Agamemnon) backstage.

Left: Backstage crew moving set during a scene change.

'Robert has written a psychologically accurate piece of contemporary theatre. Okay, there are gods and child murder, but it's so rationalised in his writing.'

Neil Stewart (Walking Cover)

Annie Firbank backstage during a quick change.

Seven Brides for Seven Brothers

Book by Lawrence Kasha and David S. Landay
Music by Gene de Paul
Lyrics by Johnny Mercer
Additional score by Al Kasha
and Joel Hirschhorn
Regent's Park Open Air Theatre

From *Hello, Dolly!* to *Porgy and Bess*, Regent's Park Open
Air Theatre has in recent years been the vanguard of
classic musical revival. As if to prove the point, its 2015
season took on one of the most iconic screen musicals
of them all, transporting thigh-slapping, barn-raising
Oregon to a quiet London park. Director Rachel
Kavanaugh, fresh from directing *The Sound of Music*
on the same stage, recognised that familiarity plays an
enormous part in bringing audiences to an adaptation
of a much-loved musical, but also knew there would be
little value or enjoyment in simply replicating a tried-
and-tested sequence. She was convinced from the start
that she had to present the story as if it were new. It
was a calculated risk, and it paid off. Critics praised her
production for its outstanding new orchestration and
choreography, specially developed for this cast and stage.

James Leece (Benjamin) and
Charlene Ford (Dorcas) backstage,

Laura Pitt-Pulford
(Milly) and Rosanna
Bates (Liza) at a front
of house entrance.

'I think being outdoors does half the work for you. It just doesn't feel like we're on stage. It feels like we're inside some sort of playground.'

Alex Gaumond (Adam)

Top: Alex Gaumond
(Adam) during the show.
Right: Adam Rhys-Charles
(Frank) backstage.

'Laura and Alex are great. When you've got two leads that are very inclusive of the whole company, there's no "them" and "us" – everyone goes into each other's dressing rooms. You just see everyone work together.'

Claire Hartley (Wardrobe Manager)

Left: Laura Pitt-Pulford (Milly) in her dressing room.
Below: Rosanna Bates (Liza), Karli Vale (Ruth) and Bethany Huckle (Alice) in their dressing room.

The company
on stage during
The Harvest Social.

Sinatra: The Man and His Music

Orchestrations by David Pierce
& Don Sebesky
London Palladium

In the centenary year of his birth, it was as if Sinatra himself had returned to the London Palladium sixty-five years after his first appearance there. In a larger than life production, directed by David Gilmore, *Sinatra: The Man and His Music* featured the man himself, using Sinatra's original recordings to accompany the live band and dancers that formed the rest of this extravagant display. It featured a twenty-four piece orchestra conducted by Richard John, faithfully recreating the brassy big band sound of Sinatra's original performances, as well as a talented troupe of dancers, choreographed by Glenn Wilkinson. The centrepiece of the show was rare restored footage of Frank Sinatra performing and talking about his life. A multimedia extravaganza, critics praised the show for its sense of spectacle and the respect with which it handled Sinatra's legacy; in Nancy Sinatra's words, 'It's Frank doing Frank.'

The cast on stage at the
London Palladium.

'We have an amazing team backstage and everything works like clockwork. The changes are quite exciting.'

Bryony Whitfield (Dancer)

The ensemble
cast on stage.

'We've now found a routine where you can actually breathe. It's such a physical show, you need those stop points. When we first opened, people were running on adrenaline. Just crazy.'

Ashley Nottingham (Dance Captain)

Below: The orchestra on stage.
Top right: The cast warm up on stage at the London Palladium.
Right: Lucy Banfield (Dancer) at the make-up station backstage.

Splendour

By Abi Morgan
Donmar Warehouse

Abi Morgan is best known for her screenplays, among them *Suffragette* and *The Iron Lady*, but her early works were all for the stage. Her play *Splendour* debuted at Edinburgh in 2000 and finally made its deserved journey to the West End in 2015. An all-female four-hander set in an unidentified dictator's besieged palace, the play examines the frailty of power and the ambiguity of what we take to be fact. A translator wilfully mistranslates and best friends despise each other behind masking smiles. Against a chorus of mounting gunfire, the perfectly coiffed dictator's wife – played in Robert Hastie's production by a formidable Sinéad Cusack – insists that everything will soon be back to normal. Designer Peter McKintosh's opulent but fracturing set revealed the truth: a lavish picture window showed only darkness, while shards of glass were beginning to gather around the actors. The characters may have been lying to themselves about the danger they were in, but for the audience it was clear that the revolution had already arrived.

Due to the fact this was an entirely closed set and that all four members of cast were on stage for the entire play, we have approached this spread differently – taking inspiration from a line in the play. Each actor was photographed before and after their ritual of getting ready for the show; as they arrived at the theatre, and then just before entering the stage. The accompanying quotes reflect this transformation and process.

Clockwise from top left:
Sinéad Cusack (Micheline).
Michelle Fairley (Genevieve).
Zawe Ashton (Gilma).
Genevieve O'Reilly (Kathryn).

'When I see myself in the mirror in
the suit, and the bling, and the hair
. . . I see a woman that I don't really
recognise except as Micheleine.'

Sinéad Cusack (Micheleine)

'For me, I only really become
Kathryn once I've taken a deep
breath and walk on stage. She's going
to do a job, so I'm going to do a job.'

Genevieve O'Reilly (Kathryn)

'I have a routine where I do a warm-up, then come into the dressing room. I like to keep quiet, but once I get wet [the character enters drenched in rain] and I go and stand in the paint room, I really start to feel the layers of my character gradually coming together.'

Michelle Fairley (Genevieve)

'A lot of times I have been affected by the character. Or I suddenly feel a vulnerability that feels really akin to her. I didn't realise how vulnerable I was, walking around. I'll see an old lady eating on her own and I will suddenly feel very tearful or burst into tears. And I'll realise, "Oh my God! That's part of Gilma that I'm carrying around."'

Zawe Ashton (Gilma)

273

Temple

By Steve Waters
Donmar Warehouse

Steve Waters' *Temple* is a fictionalised account of
an event in very recent memory: the 2011 Occupy
London protest on the steps of St Paul's Cathedral.
Hoping to force change upon what they saw as
an increasingly unjust capitalist system, hundreds
of protesters set up camp outside the cathedral,
ultimately prompting its closure by the Dean for the
first time since the Blitz. There are few theatres that
could adequately stand in for such a vast, imposing
space as St Paul's, perhaps least of all the Donmar
Warehouse. But the staging of such a complex
story within the intimate confines of the Donmar
pushed the focus from the building itself onto the
conflicts – both human and spiritual – that were
played out behind the scenes during those dramatic
days in 2011. 'I wanted to go into the heads of those
who found themselves battled and beleaguered,'
Waters has explained. Behind the façade of great
buildings and titles, 'we're fragile people'.

The full company at the curtain call.

Left: Rebecca
Humphries (The PA)
waiting to enter stage.

Right: Malcolm Sinclair
(The Bishop of London) in
his dressing room.
Far right: Anna Calder-
Marshall (The Virger)
listening from backstage.

'Most theatres you can be intimate in – even in the Olivier Theatre, you can be intimate. It just requires taking the audience with you, doesn't it? Technically saying, take them down, take them down . . . silence . . . You can actually be quite soft.'

Simon Russell Beale (The Dean)

'Here people have to get on with each other, especially when you're putting a show together. It's a high-pressure environment and everyone's on top of each other.'

Linsey Hall (Company Stage Manager)

Shereen Martin (The City Lawyer), Simon Russell Beale (The Dean), Rebecca Humphries (The PA) and Linsey Hall (Company Stage Manager) share a laugh during the warm-up.

The 39 Steps

By John Buchan,
adapted by Patrick Barlow
Criterion Theatre

With a cast of only four actors and a hundred and
thirty roles to fill, performing *The 39 Steps* might
seem like an impossible challenge. But what results
is a high-energy spoof of Alfred Hitchcock's 1935
hit film, filled with lightning quick changes and
coups de théâtre. Based on John Buchan's 1915
classic adventure novel, the play was originally
adapted for the theatre by Simon Corble and
Nobby Dimon in 1995, before being rewritten in
2005 by Patrick Barlow. It debuted at the West
Yorkshire Playhouse and transferred to London's
Tricycle Theatre in 2006, before making its West
End premiere at the Criterion later that year. In
director Maria Aitken's capable hands, the play
went on to enjoy unmitigated success, winning
an Olivier Award for Best Comedy in 2007, and
became the fifth longest running play in West End
history. Critics praised its self-conscious and highly
amusing awareness of the difficulty of staging
Buchan's epic tale of espionage and deceit.

The cast on stage during a
scene (Richard Galazka,
Alix Dunmore, Tim Frances,
Daniel Tuite).

'It's pretty damn frantic backstage! But everyone knows where they're going, so you slide past each other.'

Alix Dunmore (Pamela / Annabella / Margaret)

Above: Jasper Fox (Company Stage Manager), Tim Frances (Man 2) and Daniel Tuite (Man 1) in the wings. Right: Richard Galazka (Richard Hannay), Tim Frances (Man 2) and Daniel Tuite (Man 1) on stage.

Right: Elizabeth Patrick (Assistant Stage Manager) and Daniel Tuite (Man 1) share an on-off-stage moment.

Left: Daniel Tuite, Richard Galazka and Alix Dunmore leave stage at the curtain call, Bex Harding (Assistant Stage Manager).

Right: Tim Frances (Man 2) on stage.

Below: The cast on stage during warm-up at the Criterion Theatre.

Above: Understudies Matthew Bancroft and Paul Critoph hang out in the green room with Duty Fireman Greg.

'Including all the inanimate objects, I think I play twenty-one characters. So that's fourteen people and seven inanimate objects.'

Daniel Tuite (Man 1)

The Audience

By Peter Morgan
Apollo Theatre

Few plays are successful enough to warrant being
updated and revived just two years after their
debut, but Peter Morgan's The Audience (2013)
is a justifiable exception. Featuring a sizeable
cast of still-living characters – not least among
them the incumbent British monarch and prime
minister – it is a play that is able to evolve with
British politics. Stephen Daldry's 2015 revival
with Kristin Scott Thomas was played out against
the backdrop of the general election period, and
swift rewrites were directed into the production
to respond to the surprise result during the run.
Critics praised the cast's mastery of familiar figures
whom it would have been easier simply to mimic,
as well as Morgan's insightful, often touching
speculation about how personal and political
dramas have unfolded behind closed palace doors.

Kristin Scott Thomas
(The Queen) and
various cast and
crew during the
Photoshoot scene.

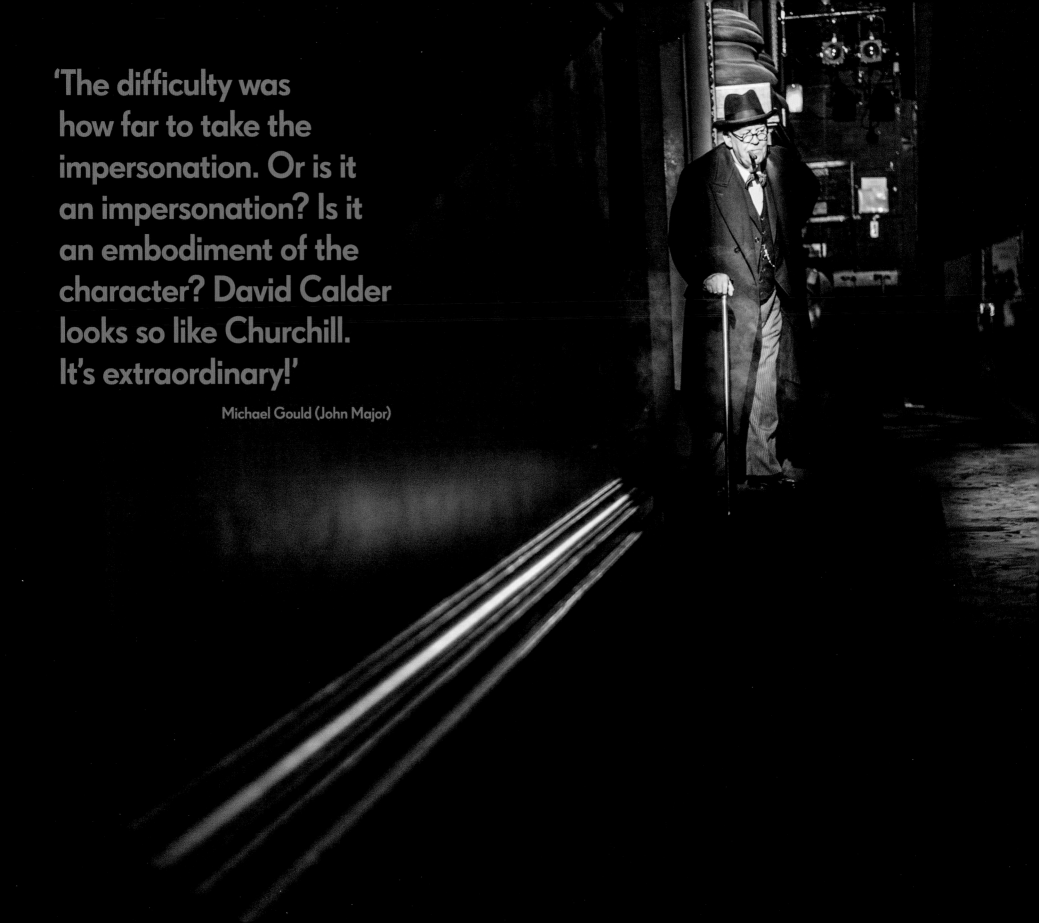

'The difficulty was how far to take the impersonation. Or is it an impersonation? Is it an embodiment of the character? David Calder looks so like Churchill. It's extraordinary!'

Michael Gould (John Major)

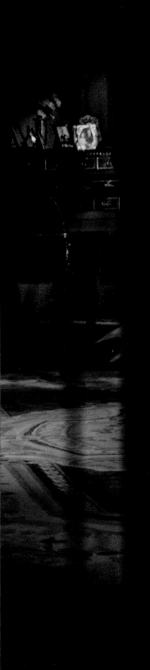

'Churchill's got such historical gravitas that the audience kind of have to work out their relationship with him. I think they're also much more interested, not in their own relationship with him, but how he can relate to the Queen in that way.'

David Calder (Winston Churchill)

Right: Stage Management and Wardrobe with Kristin Scott Thomas (The Queen) during a scene change.

Above left: Kristin Scott Thomas (The Queen) in her dressing room with Sarah Spears (Wigs Manager).
Left: Gordon Kennedy (Gordon Brown) and others in the wings.

'Blair comes on 'cos they're talking about him and then all of a sudden he appears in this beautiful light and the audience find it hysterical every single night because he does really look like him! It's brilliant!'

Georgia Bird (Deputy Stage Manager)

290

The Beaux' Stratagem

By George Farquhar
National Theatre, Olivier Stage

An updated script and tongue-in-cheek song sequences ensured the National Theatre's 2015 revival of *The Beaux' Stratagem*, written by George Farquhar in 1707, felt fresh and exuberant. Samuel Barnett and Geoffrey Streatfeild starred in this Restoration romp as charming, dissolute gentlemen Aimwell and Archer, who seek advantageous matches to mend their broken fortunes by masquerading as a viscount and his loyal servant. Meanwhile, in a role inherited from the peerless Maggie Smith, Susannah Fielding found the perfect balance between light-hearted gaiety and serious comment as Mrs Sullen, a woman trapped in a deeply unhappy marriage, looking for a way out. Critics praised Lizzie Clachan's ingenious multilevel set, which utilised sliding panels and a triple staircase to seamlessly transition between the production's two locations, and Michael Bruce's irresistibly foot-tapping music.

'My first job was here on the Olivier Stage. It was daunting, but equally exciting because I had been an usher here for three years. So it was mad to go from selling programmes to taking tickets and selling ice creams to suddenly being on stage six months later. A dream come true.'

Susannah Fielding (Mrs Sullen)

Susannah Fielding
(Mrs Sullen) just
before entering stage.

The cast playing charades backstage.

Right: Molly Gromadzki (Gipsy), Chris Kelham (Footman) and Abbie Procter (Assistant Stage Manager) backstage.

'You're surrounded by great people, the infrastructure is fantastic, the actors are always brilliant – it's like working in a Premiership football team, or something.'

Chook Sibtain (Gibbet)

Left: Alison Rankin (Stage Manager), Samuel Barnett (Aimwell) during a quick change backstage.

'Oh it's brilliant! It's a hoot. There's a lot of games being played backstage and a lot of fun going on.'

Amy Morgan (Cherry)

Nicholas Khan, Esh Alladi, Chris Kelham, Mark Rose and Samuel Barnett playing the crossword on a tablet backstage.

The Curtain Call Feature
Royal Opera House, April 2015

Backstage at the Olivier Awards

The Olivier Awards are presented annually by the Society of London Theatre to recognise excellence in professional theatre and in 2016 celebrate their 40th anniversary. The awards are given to those involved in West End shows and other leading non-commercial theatres based in London. The Olivier Awards are recognised internationally as the highest honour in British theatre. The Olivier Awards 2015 with MasterCard was a remarkable evening packed with stunning performances and stirring speeches as theatre's great and good gathered at the Royal Opera House for the unforgettable ceremony hosted by Lenny Henry. The big winners on the night included new musical *Sunny Afternoon* and the Young Vic Theatre. Former Pussycat Doll Nicole Scherzinger took to the stage to perform 'Memory' from *Cats*, and *Sunny Afternoon*, *Memphis The Musical* and *Miss Saigon* also entertained the Oliviers audience. Special Award winner, Kevin Spacey stole the show with a duet of 'Bridge Over Troubled Water' with Beverly Knight, while Angela Lansbury made Olivier history by becoming a first-time award winner at the age of eighty-nine.

Dame Judi Dench about to go on stage to present the Special Award to Kevin Spacey.

298

Chiwetel Ejiofor in
the auditorium of the
Royal Opera House.

Mark Gatiss, Angela Lansbury and Amanda Abbington pose with the Olivier statuette.

Russell Tovey and Anne-Marie Duff share a laugh backstage.

Katie Brayben and Lorna Want with their Olivier Awards for their roles in "Beautiful".

George Maguire, Ray Davies, Joe Penhall, John Dagleish pose with their Olivier Awards for "Sunny Afternoon".

The Father

By Florian Zeller
Wyndham's Theatre

A French play about Alzheimer's disease is perhaps an unlikely choice for the West End. However, Florian Zeller's Molière award winning *The Father*, translated by Christopher Hampton, captivated everyone lucky enough to see it on its journey from the Theatre Royal Bath to the Tricycle to Wyndham's. The story centres on André, played in James Macdonald's production by Kenneth Cranham, who is slowly losing his hold on reality, and whose own family is becoming a source of ever-increasing confusion. Zeller wanted the play to act as a mirror for the audience – to unsettle them as much as it unsettles its main character. Rather than watch a man decline into dementia, they seem to experience it first-hand themselves: things go missing from the stage, characters blur and shift, and nothing is quite what it seems. The effect is as terrifying as it is distressing – a sort of *King Lear* as imagined by Kafka. Ultimately it is a play that forces us to confront, in Zeller's own words, 'that fragility to life that makes us all equal'.

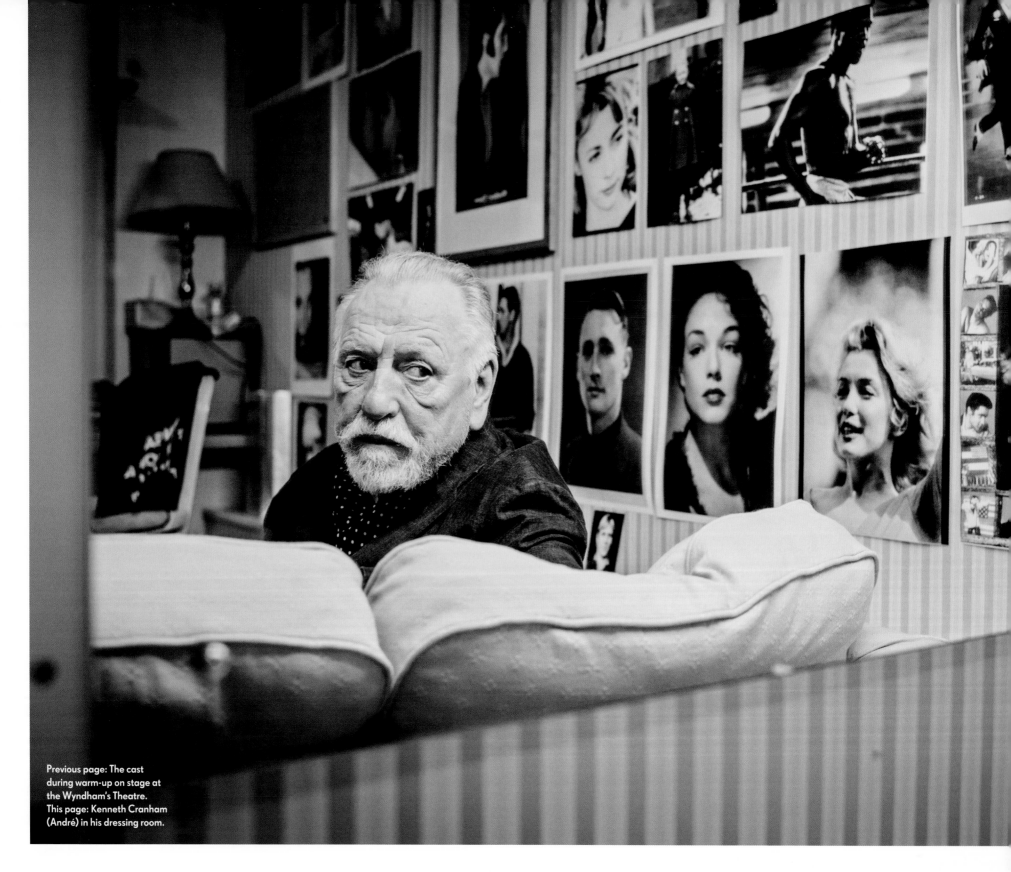

Previous page: The cast
during warm-up on stage at
the Wyndham's Theatre.
This page: Kenneth Cranham
(André) in his dressing room.

Above: The crosswords backstage.

'You're meant to enjoy it. He (Florian Zeller, Writer) calls it a tragic farce. It has to hit those two bases and get some really good laughs along the way. And it does.'

Kenneth Cranham (André)

'It was written as a black comedy in order to be surprised and not know exactly where you are. The trick was to make people feel as though they were in his mind.' Florian Zeller (Writer)

Below: Kirsty Oswald (Laura).

'It's one of those plays where you can't hug the furniture for support, because it keeps on disappearing. You've got to be brave enough to stand alone.'

Claire Skinner (Anne)

Claire Skinner (Anne)
waiting backstage to enter.

The Homecoming

By Harold Pinter
Trafalgar Studios 1

To celebrate the fiftieth anniversary of what is
widely considered Harold Pinter's finest play, the
Jamie Lloyd Company staged a gritty revival of *The
Homecoming* to open the third season of Trafalgar
Transformed. Featuring a stellar cast, including
Keith Allen, John Simm and Gary Kemp as
members of the same coolly sinister family, and
Gemma Chan as the object of all their dubious
affections, the production was widely praised for
ramping up the already-visceral aggression and
despair to which Pinter subjects his characters.
The Homecoming is no stranger to the London stage,
but Lloyd (celebrated as a leading interpreter of
Pinter's work) broke with tradition by showing the
audience snapshots of the characters' moments of
real anguish behind the dagger-sharp dialogue.
A psychologically deft interpretation of the play's
controversial ending made Gemma Chan's Ruth
the master, rather than victim, of her fate.

John Simm (Lenny) on
stage during the show.

'Francis Bacon used to do those red lines in his paintings, that's where it comes from. Because the stage and the script is so spare, every single word and gesture means something. Which is quite challenging in a way.'

Ron Cook (Max)

Left: Gemma Chan
(Ruth) backstage.

Above: John Simm
(Lenny) in his dressing
room before the show.

'I have loved doing this. Ruth is such a
fascinating character. She has a lot of power,
and rediscovers that power through the play.'

Gemma Chan (Ruth)

'I've never been in a play that has required so much concentration. I think we've all found that. It's like there's a million tiny little cogs all turning.'

John Macmillan (Joey)

Opposite, clockwise from top
left: Keith Allen (Sam), John
Macmillan (Joey), Ron Cook
(Max) and Gary Kemp (Teddy)
in their dressing rooms.
This page: The cast on stage.

The Importance of Being Earnest

By Oscar Wilde
Vaudeville Theatre

Oscar Wilde's *The Importance of Being Earnest* is one of the best-known and best-loved plays in the history of British theatre. Its quotability and wit seem to never go out of fashion. But with great popularity comes a great conundrum: how to stage the play and make it stand out from the thousands of productions that have gone before? Directed by Adrian Noble, this latest production of *The Importance of Being Earnest*, produced by Kim Poster and Nica Burns at the Vaudeville, distinguished itself by dint of excellent casting – notably David Suchet as the haughty and indomitable Lady Bracknell. Undaunted by the calibre of his predecessors in the role, Dames Judi Dench and Maggie Smith, Suchet received universal praise for his performance, which expertly navigated the fine line between comedic flamboyance and traditional farce.

David Suchet
(Lady Bracknell) in his
dressing room pre-show.

'David will be sitting in the wings watching and will say, "Your aura is smaller today. Just bring it out. The brightness in the eyes."'

Emily Barber (Gwendolen Fairfax)

Left: Philip Cumbus (Algernon Moncrieff) and Imogen Doel (Cecily Cardew) on stage during the show.

'The characters all have a fire in their bellies that fuels them to get whatever it is that they want. Whether that's love or sex or marriage or truth that another person may be hiding.'

Philip Cumbus (Algernon Moncrieff)

Emily Barber (Gwendolen Fairfax) warming up her voice backstage.

'It's incredible to think, "This is what I do for a living." A classical theatre actor ends up playing Lady B. This is great fun.' David Suchet (Lady Bracknell)

Right: Imogen Doel (Cecily Cardew) backstage in her dressing room.
Far right: Michelle Dotrice (Miss Prism) in her dressing room before the show.

The Merchant of Venice

By William Shakespeare
Shakespeare's Globe

The Merchant of Venice is a play that often vexes directors and audiences alike, thanks to the problematic character of Shylock. For his production at the Globe, director Jonathan Munby found that the best way to confront the spectre of Shylock was to put him centre stage – to make the play as much about him as it is about love and marriage and family duty. And with Jonathan Pryce in the role, with his real-life daughter, Phoebe, playing his on-stage daughter, Jessica, it was impossible not to see Shylock as a flawed man and father rather than just a caricature. In a new end scene, he is shown to be vulnerable but resilient – albeit finally broken – at the hands of his tormentors. It was a shrewd way to stage what artistic director Dominic Dromgoole described as the 'improvised, very human moral labyrinth' that is the titular merchant.

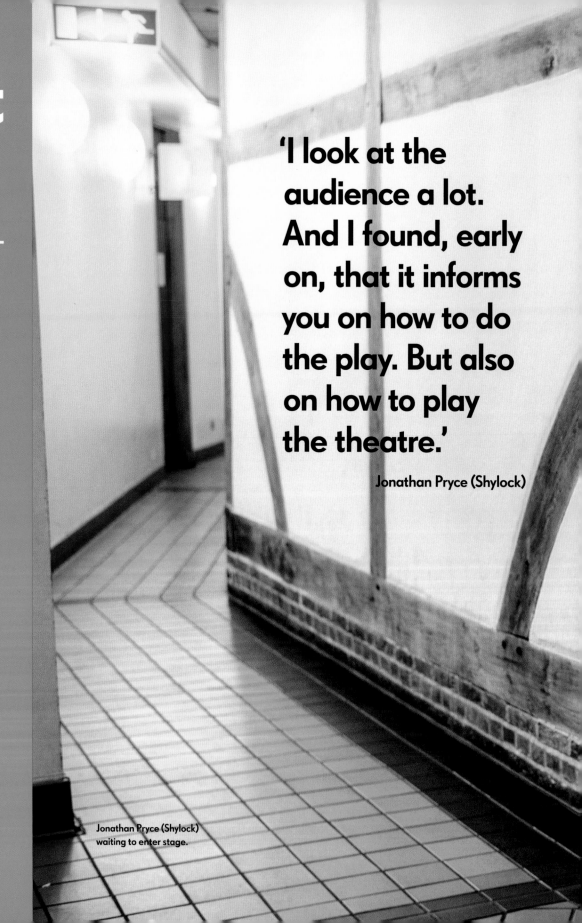

'I look at the audience a lot. And I found, early on, that it informs you on how to do the play. But also on how to play the theatre.'

Jonathan Pryce (Shylock)

Jonathan Pryce (Shylock) waiting to enter stage.

Jonathan Pryce (Shylock)
and Brian Martin (Salarino)
in the green room.

'There are simple things, like people walking through the yard where the groundlings stand, that instantly pull you together. You feel that you are part of something bigger, not just actors on the stage.'

Phoebe Pryce (Jessica)

Top: Daniel Lapaine (Bassanio) and Phoebe Pryce (Jessica) backstage. Right: Heather Bull (Wardrobe Assistant).

Left: Michael Bertenshaw
(Duke of Venice) waiting to enter
from a front of house entrance.

Left: Dorothea Myer-Bennett
(Nerissa) and Rachel Pickup
(Portia) preparing to enter stage.

'You see everything.
There's nowhere to hide.
I think, more than any other
space, the Globe is the
most vulnerable-making.'

Rachel Pickup (Portia)

A member of cast
waiting to enter stage.

The Ruling Class

By Peter Barnes
Trafalgar Studios 1

For the second season of Trafalgar Transformed,
a run of politically charged plays performed in the
shadow of London's government buildings, artistic
director Jamie Lloyd addressed the question: What
does it mean to be British? *The Ruling Class*, as
relevant today as it was amid the social rebellions
of the late 1960s, was a natural choice for inclusion.
The play, which Peter Barnes described as 'an anti-
boss drama for the shorn not the shearers', examines
class conflict and abuse of power, two themes
recurrent in his work. Barnes himself was the son
of Jewish amusement-arcade workers who had gone
on to serve his country both in the Royal Air Force
and as a civil servant; by the time he produced *The
Ruling Class*, he had honed 'an extraordinary gift for
composing dialogue in which you can smell the filth
and cruelties of the past'. This production earned
James McAvoy an Olivier Award nomination for
Best Actor for his portrayal of Jack Gurney.

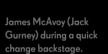

James McAvoy (Jack
Gurney) during a quick
change backstage.

Kathryn Drysdale (Grace
Shelley) about to enter stage.

Right: Anthony O'Donnell (Daniel Tucker) and Serena Evans (Lady Claire) during a quick change backstage.

'It's tight and it's hectic and it's a big technical show, so it's all hidden in a very tiny wing space. So we're all kind of squished in.'

James McAvoy (Jack Gurney)

Left: Paul Leonard (13th Earl/Detective Inspector Brockett) and James McAvoy (Jack Gurney) backstage.

Above: Anthony O'Donnell (Daniel Tucker) in the wings backstage.

Left: Emma Banwell-Knight (Company Stage Manager) and Annie Kalinauckas (Assistant Stage Manager) holding a door open during a scene.
Below: James McAvoy (Jack Gurney) in the wings.

Right: Michael Cronin (Bishop Lampton) and Ron Cook (Sir Charles Gurney) in the wings during a scene change.

'The stage
management
are amazing. I
call them the
backstage
ninjas. They wear
black hoods.
And backstage
is actually like
a ballet. It's
extraordinary
how people just
glide by each
other and they
know to stand out
of the way.'

Ron Cook (Sir Charles Gurney)

331

The Trial

By Franz Kafka
Adapted by Nick Gill
Young Vic

Franz Kafka's *The Trial*, a novel in which the main
character has no idea what is happening and in
which very little happens at all, is surprisingly
well suited to the stage. An eerie evocation of both
paranoia and authoritarianism is vividly accentuated
in this radical, almost Joycean adaptation by Nick
Gill, directed by Richard Jones. The audience
were drawn ever further into the terrifyingly vague
ordeal: a jury helpless to dispense any much-
needed justice to the anti-hero Josef K. The muted
costumes and pared back sets – save for the unique
use of a travelator – an inspired design by Miriam
Buether that periodically conveyed Kinnear as if
on a production line – augmented the unsettling
sense that K is a sort of Everyman, the victim of
a dystopian fate that could befall any one of us.

**Rory Kinnear (Josef K)
as he exits stage.**

Weruche Opia (Clerk) and Kate O'Flynn (Rosa) in the wardrobe department with Jenny Glynn (Hair, Wigs and Make-up).

Right: Sally Inch (Assistant Stage Manager), Hugh Skinner (Kyle/Block), Rory Kinnear (Josef K) and Heather Bull (Wardrobe Manager) backstage. Below: Daniel Gammon (Stage Manager) controlling the conveyor belt.

'It's like a ballet back there because it has to be perfectly choreographed in terms of the backstage team. If one thing is out of place then everything else will be out of place.'

Daniel Gammon (Stage Manager)

Hugh Skinner (Kyle/Block) entering stage on the conveyor belt.

Katie Bazell (Stage Crew) backstage before a scene change.

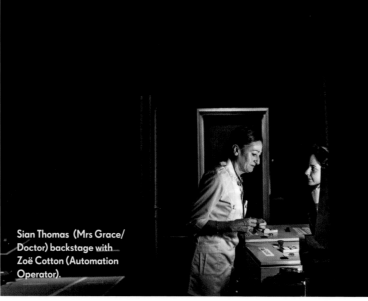

Sian Thomas (Mrs Grace/Doctor) backstage with Zoë Cotton (Automation Operator).

'There was so much to catch up on in previews in regards to the tech, so it wasn't until the fourth or fifth preview when you were aware of what the show might actually be.'

Rory Kinnear (Josef K)

Rory Kinnear (Josef K) and
Hugh Skinner (Kyle/Block)
during the warm-up on the set
designed by Miriam Buether.

The Twits

By Roald Dahl, adapted by Enda Walsh
Royal Court

Enda Walsh's adaptation of Roald Dahl's childhood
classic, *The Twits*, added a whole new twist to the
well-known story of the hideous couple, whose
mean-spirited pranks have delighted and horrified
readers for over thirty years. While audiences
would have recognised the bowl of worms served
as breakfast and glue-covered bird, this 2015 Royal
Court Theatre production revelled in pushing the
limits of the Twits' cruelty and darkness without
losing their comic grotesqueness. Walsh wanted
there to be 'nothing cute' about the production,
to create something that was 'dark and scary and
terrifying'. The torturing of monkeys and shooting
of dogs is countered, but never overwritten,
by Morris dancing set pieces and Mrs Twit's
impressions of the Queen. Directed by John
Tiffany, critics praised Monica Dolan's gleefully
malicious portrayal of Mrs Twit, as well as rising
star Chloe Lamford's inspired circular-shaped
set, a revolving brown drum littered with trash.

Monica Dolan (Mrs Twit)
and Jason Watkins (Mr Twit)
in the lift backstage.

From right to far right: Glyn Pritchard (Monkey Dad) in his dressing room. Aimée-Ffion Edwards (Monkey Daughter), Oliver Llewellyn-Jenkins (Monkey Son), Cait Davis (Monkey Mum) and Glyn Pritchard (Monkey Dad) in their cage. Monica Dolan (Mrs Twit) and Jason Watkins (Mr Twit) onstage. Cait Davis (Monkey Mum) backstage at the Royal Court.

From far left to left: Oliver Llewellyn-Jenkins (Monkey Son) on stage. Cait Davis (Monkey Mum), Oliver Llewellyn-Jenkins (Monkey Son), Jason Watkins (Mr Twit) and Monica Dolan (Mrs Twit). Aimée-Ffion Edwards (Monkey Daughter), Oliver Llewellyn-Jenkins (Monkey Son), Cait Davis (Monkey Mum) and Glyn Pritchard (Monkey Dad) in their cage. Monica Dolan (Mrs Twit) backstage on her phone.

Three Days in the Country

By Patrick Marber, after Turgenev
National Theatre, Lyttelton Stage

Patrick Marber directed his own adaptation of Ivan Turgenev's comedy of manners, *A Month in the Country* at the National Theatre. At four hours uncut, Turgenev's play is an unwieldy one to stage; the drama in Marber's version, as the title indicates, unfolds at more of a whirlwind pace. Like its parent play, this is a comedy filled with personal tragedies, mostly arising from heartbreak and jealousy. It is a play about love in its many guises, and about high society and the constraints it places on passion. But above all it is a play about people, with all the desires they surrender to and the secrets they hide. As Turgenev once explained in a letter to a friend: 'I have never taken ideas but always characters as a starting point.' Indeed, many of the characters in this play were based on real people, notably the unsuccessful lover Rakitin – played in Marber's production by John Simm – whom Turgenev supposedly modelled on himself. The stellar cast included National Theatre veteran Gawn Grainger, Sherlock creator Mark Gatiss and knockout performances from Amanda Drew and John Light.

'Everything's stripped back. Nothing to hide behind. It's like a sort of workshop.'

Lily Sacofsky (Vera)

Cherrelle Skeete (Katya)
and Joel Thomas (Kolya) on
stage just before curtain up.

Debra Gillett (Lizaveta) and Mark Gatiss (Shpigelsky) backstage.

Above: Stage Manager David Marsland backstage.

Left: John Simm (Rakitin) and John Light (Arkady) during a quick change.

The company of
Three Days In The Country.

'Sitting on those chairs, you feel so much more a part of the piece. I get to watch the whole of the last act and it's pretty amazing.'

Gawn Grainger (Schaaf)

'Beginners is called and we are all there. And everyone hugs and kisses everyone else. And I have never known that happen before in a company.'

Lynn Farleigh (Anna)

Right: The cast hug before the show.
Below: Lynn Farleigh (Anna) in the wings backstage.

Above: Mark Gatiss (Shpigelsky)
in his dressing room.

'I think the set mirrors the steppes of Russia.
The spareness of the plain, the spareness of
all that. And by the time we get to the end,
we've crept a little closer in the transparency
and everything. I think it's beautiful.'

Mark Gatiss (Shpigelsky)

To Kill a Mockingbird

Adapted for the stage by Christopher Sergel
Based on the novel by Harper Lee
**Presented at the Barbican Theatre
Transfer from Regent's Park Theatre**

Harper Lee's novel about race, rights and dignity is one of the most popular books ever written; the 1962 film adaptation won three Academy Awards. So when Christopher Sergel set about re-imagining it for the theatre, he was faced with quite a conundrum: how to tell a familiar story in a way that is challenging and new? His answer was to go back to the novel itself: in a rare inversion of 'show, don't tell', his play mixes live action with narration by members of the cast. Director Tim Sheader went one step further in this acclaimed production by having the actors narrate directly from copies of the book. It was an adaptation of a much-told tale that put the disappearing art of storytelling in the spotlight. Sheader even auditioned the actors by asking them to read prose rather than lines from the script. 'It's not actors on stage and us in the audience,' he said. 'The idea is that we all collectively listen to the story.'

Tommy Rodger
(Jem) backstage.

'It just became a question about how much I was going to channel Gregory Peck. I didn't want to mess with it. But I'm free to dance and I found things that I like that Peck didn't do.'

Robert Sean Leonard (Atticus Finch)

Right: Geoff Aymer
and Natasha Magigi
during warm-up.

Robert Sean Leonard
(Atticus) backstage.

Right: Connie Walker
(Mrs Dubose) in her
dressing room.

Left: The stage from the wings.
Below: Connor Brundish (Dill).
Bottom: Connor Brundish
(Dill), Matt Russell (Sound)
and Tommy Rodger (Jem)
backstage.

'The Park was like a big event. People would come with picnic baskets before the show and sit outside on the grass. Inside, it's a whole different dynamic, but it's still just as magical.'

Zackary Momoh (Tom Robinson)

Ava Potter (Scout) and
Matt Russell (Sound).

Urinetown: The Musical

Music & Lyrics by Mark Hollmann
Book & Lyrics by Greg Kotis
Apollo Theatre
Transfer from St James' Theatre

Setting a high bar for the most unexpected premise for a smashhit musical, *Urinetown* imagines a world in which water shortages necessitate draconian peeing regulations, with a terrible punishment awaiting anyone who dares flaunt them. The show debuted in 2001 on Broadway, where it won three Tony Awards, including for Best Original Score (by Mark Hollmann and Greg Kotis). It crossed the Atlantic in 2014, with a run at the St James Theatre before transferring to the Apollo. A dark satire on the meeting of ecology and big business, *Urinetown*'s greatest draw is its unashamed sendingup of the clichés of the musical form, parodying both the optimistic endings and big ensemble numbers exemplified by the likes of *Les Misérables*. Jamie Lloyd's London production, which featured RSC and West End star Jonathan Slinger in the role of Officer Lockstock, was complemented by Soutra Gilmour's extraordinary set, a subterranean sewer-realm that served as a fittingly gloomy microcosm for our own ecologically troubled world.

This was the first production that Curtain Call covered.

Jonathan Slinger (Officer Lockstock) on stage during warm up.

'I've never had as much fun on a show. These actors are up for absolutely anything. Even prancing around to gospel music in their Y-fronts covered in fake blood and wearing sweaty, rubber rabbit masks. Unforgettable.'

Cast and crew backstage.

Right: Simon Paisley Day (Caldwell B. Cladwell) in his dressing room.

Right: Matthew Seadon-Young (Bobby Strong) in his dressing room.

357

Left: Jenna Russell (Penelope Pennywise) and Julie Jupp (Old Woman) by the stage door of the Apollo Theatre.

'I'm so glad I got to do it because I have never been that ridiculous.'

Jenna Russell (Penelope Pennywise)

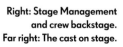

Right: Stage Management and crew backstage.
Far right: The cast on stage.

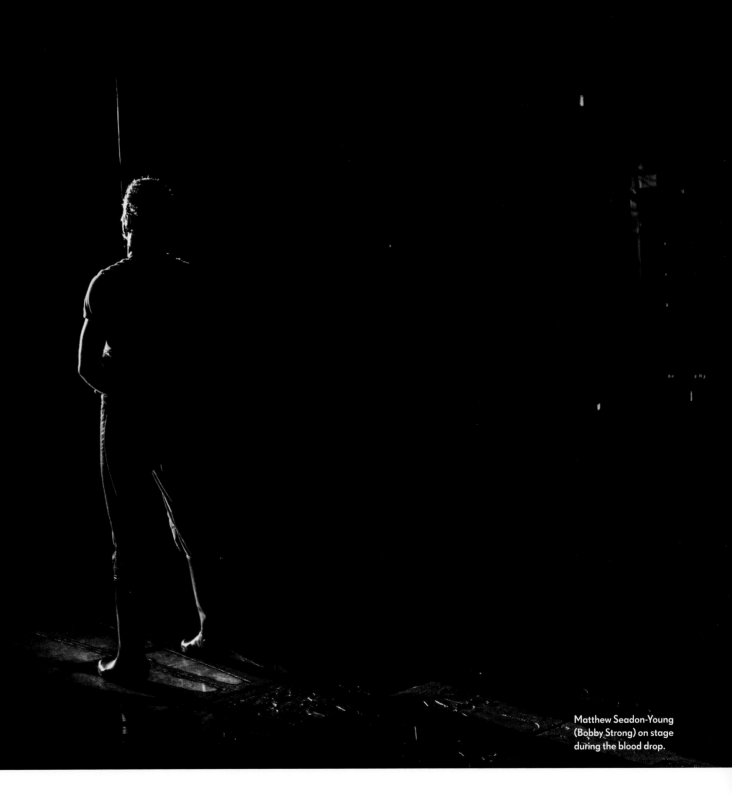

Matthew Seadon-Young
(Bobby Strong) on stage
during the blood drop.

Women on the Verge of a Nervous Breakdown

Music & Lyrics by David Yazbek
Book by Jeffrey Lane
Playhouse Theatre

Adapted from Pedro Almodóvar's Oscar-winning film of 1988, *Women on the Verge of a Nervous Breakdown* is a celebration of the power and strength of women, bringing its distinctly Spanish flavour to the West End stage. Featuring songs written and composed by dynamic duo Jeffrey Lane and David Yazbek of *Dirty Rotten Scoundrels* fame, the Playhouse Theatre's 2014 production was a radically trimmed and refocused version of the play's 2010 Broadway debut. Olivier Award winning actress Tamsin Greig played Pepa, an actress and voice actor whose world begins to unravel after she is abandoned by her lover, and Haydn Gwynne was cast as scorned wife Lucia, her rival in love.

Tamsin Greig (Pepa) in her dressing room.

Haydn Gwynne (Lucia)
about to enter stage.

Above: Wyn Williams
(Company Stage
Manager) on stage during
the pre-show checks.

Below: John Pemberton
(Technical Stage Manager)
operates the smoke machine.

Wardrobe waiting
for a quick change.

Haydn Gwynne
(Lucia) about to
enter stage.

wonder.land

Music by Damon Albarn
Book & Lyrics by Moira Buffini
National Theatre, Olivier Stage

This thoroughly twenty-first century adaptation of
Lewis Carroll's story debuted at the Manchester
International Festival before transferring to the
National. Written by Moira Buffini with a score by
Damon Albarn, and directed by Rufus Norris, the
play sees Aly, a bullied, neglected mixed-race teen
seeking sanctuary in an online game, wonder.land.
Her avatar is the blonde, doll-like Alice of Carroll's
story, and the other familiar characters have been
vibrantly reinvented through inspired design. Rae
Smith's superb set and Katrina Lindsay's costumes
made the real world relentlessly grey and gloomy,
while psychedelically vibrant graphics designed
by 59 Productions were projected temptingly in
the background. Albarn's score was an equally
psychedelic mash-up of music hall and modern
styles, all of which combined to create a spectacle for
the senses that revolutionised this much-loved classic.

Carly Bawden (Alice)
in her dressing room.

Ensemble cast members
enter stage dressed as
playing cards.

Above: Lisa Ritchie (Ensemble), Cydney Uffindell-Phillips (Mock Turtle) and Stephanie Rojas (Mary Ann).
Right: Carly Bawden (Alice) at the backstage make-up station.

Below: Ivan de Freitas (Dodo), Carly Bawden (Alice) and Joshua Lacey (White Rabbit).

'It was a big challenge. How to move. How to look after myself in this costume.'

Carly Bawden (Alice)

Right: Joshua Lacey (White Rabbit) prepping to go on stage. Far right: Abigail Rose (Kitty) at the backstage make-up station. Below: Hal Fowler (MC) being helped into his caterpillar costume.

'As the MC, you get to set the tone of the whole play. There's a sense of representing the whole craziness that is Alice in Wonderland.'

Hal Fowler (MC)

Sam Archer (Dum)
and Leon Cooke
(Dee) backstage.

The fly-floor of the
Vaudeville Theatre.

Show Credits

Show Credits

Show credits are as they appear in the official programmes from when Curtain Call visited the show. Best endeavours have been made to ensure these listings are correct. Apologies for any omissions. For these show credits, and more, please visit our website: www.curtaincallonline.com.

All cast listings are alphabetical

A Christmas Carol

Sonia Friedman Productions present
A Christmas Carol
by Patrick Barlow
adapted from the Christmas story
by Charles Dickens
at the Noël Coward Theatre

Running dates:
30/11/15 – 30/1/16

Cast
Adeel Akhtar – Bob Cratchit /
    Marley / Young Scrooge
Jim Broadbent – Ebenezer Scrooge
Amelia Bullmore – Hermione
    Bentham / Ghost of Christmas
    Past / Constance / Mrs
    Cratchit / Mother
Keir Charles – Frederick / Mr
    Grimes / Mr Fezziwig / George /
    Ghost of Christmas Yet to Come
Samantha Spiro – Mrs Lack /
    Lavinia Bentham / Mrs Grimes
    / Fran / Isabella / Ghost of
    Christmas Present / Maid

Jack Parker – Ensemble Puppeteer
Kim Scopes – Ensemble Puppeteer
Daphne Kouma – Understudy
    Hermione Bentham / Ghost of
    Christmas Past / Constance /
    Mrs Cratchit / Mother / Mrs
    Lack / Lavinia Bentham /
    Mrs Grimes / Fran / Isabella
    / Ghost of Christmas Present /
    Maid / Ensemble Puppeteer
Andrew London – Understudy
    Bob Cratchit / Marley / Young
    Scrooge / Frederick / Mr
    Grimes / Mr Fezziwig / George
    / Ghost of Christmas Yet to
    Come / Ensemble Puppeteer
Simon Stanhope – Understudy
    Ebenezer Scrooge
All other roles played by
    members of the company.

Creatives and Production Team
Writer – Patrick Barlow
Director – Phelim McDermott
Designer – Tom Pye
Movement Director – Toby Sedgwick
Lighting Designer – Peter Mumford
Sound Designer – Gareth Fry
Music Supervisor and
    Arranger – Steven Edis
Casting Director – Sam Jones CDG
Associate Director – Dan Ayling
Irish Jig Choreographer
    – Angela Clerkin
Production Manager – Paul Hennessy
Costume Supervisor – Jackie Orton
Props Supervisor – Lizzie Frankl
Hair, Wigs and Make-up
    – Carole Hancock
Puppet Maker – Lyndie Wright

Casting Associate – Lucy Taylor
Company Stage Manager
    – Matthew Cullum
Deputy Stage Manager – Maddy Grant
Assistant Stage Manager
    – Genna Hill
Head of Wardrobe – Melody
    Tatania Wood
Deputy Head of Wardrobe
    – Katy Adeney
Head of Hair, Wigs and
    Make-up – Hayley Gittins
General Management
Sonia Friedman Productions
**Marketing, Advertising
and Promotions**
Dewynters
Press
The Corner Shop PR

A Number

by Caryl Churchill
A Young Vic and Nuffield
co-production
at the Young Vic

Running dates:
3/7/15 – 15/8/15

Cast
John Shrapnel – Salter
Lex Shrapnel – His Sons
Creatives
Writer – Caryl Churchill
Direction – Michael Longhurst
Design – Tom Scutt
Light – Lee Curran

Sound – Richard Hammarton
Casting – Anna Cooper
Associate Director – Jack Lowe
Associate Designer – James Donnelly
Stage Management
Stage Manager – Marina Kilby
Deputy Stage Manager
    – Lauren Harvey
Production
Production Manager – Felix Davies
Lighting Operator – Nick
    Slater / Nicole Smith
For Nuffield
Director – Sam Hodges
Producer – Annie Reilly
Assistant Producer – Aidan Grounds

A View from the Bridge

Young Vic present
A View from the Bridge
by Arthur Miller
at the Wyndham's Theatre

Running dates:
10/2/15 – 11/4/15

Cast
Emun Elliott – Marco
Phoebe Fox – Catherine
Michael Gould – Alfieri
Richard Hansell – Louis
Pádraig Lynch – Officer
Luke Norris – Rodolpho
Mark Strong – Eddie
Nicola Walker – Beatrice
Samantha Coughlan –
    Understudy Beatrice

Cary Crankson – Understudy Marco
   / Rodolpho / Louis / Officer
Samantha Dakin –
   Understudy Catherine
Richard Hansell – Understudy Alfieri
Pádraig Lynch – Understudy Eddie
Creatives
Writer – Arthur Miller
Direction – Ivo van Hove
Design and Light – Jan Versweyveld
Costumes – An D'Huys
Sound – Tom Gibbons
Dramaturg – Bart Van den Eynde
UK Casting – Julia Horan CDG
US Casting – Jim Carnahan CSA
Associate Director – Jeff James
Associate Designer – James Turner
Associate Lighting Designer
   – Nicki Brown
Associate Sound Designer
   – Alex Twiselton
Stage Management
Company Stage Manager
   – Alex Constantin
Deputy Stage Manager –
   Ruthie Philip-Smith
Assistant Stage Manager (Book
   Cover) – George Pavelková
   / Rachel Williams
Production
Production Manager – Igor
Costume Supervisor –
   Catherine Kodicek
Associate Production Manager
   – Lloyd Thomas
Sound Operator – Gareth Tucker
Automation Operator – David
   Leigh-Pemberton
Wardrobe Manager – Caroline McCall

Wardrobe Technician – Serica
   Kavaz / Traipsy Drake
General Management
Young Vic

Ah, Wilderness!
at the Young Vic

Running dates:
14/4/15 – 23/5/15

Cast
David Annen – David
   McComber / George
Georgia Bourke – Muriel McComber
Janie Dee – Essie Miller
George MacKay – Richard Miller
Martin Marquez – Nat Miller
Eleanor McLoughlin – Norah
Yasmin Paige – Belle
Lucas Pinto – Tommy Miller
Dominic Rowan – Sid Davis
Rory Stroud – Tommy Miller
Susannah Wise – Lily Miller
Ashley Zhangazha – Arthur Miller
Creatives
Writer – Eugene O'Neill
Direction – Natalie Abrahami
Set – Dick Bird
Costumes – Sussie Juhlin-Wallén
Light – Charles Balfour
Music & Sound – Ben & Max Ringham
Movement – Ann Yee
Casting – Julie Horan CDG
Voice and Dialect – Richard Ryder
Jerwood Assistant Director
   – Craig Gilbert

Boris Karloff – Trainee Assistant
   Director – Mona Khalili
Stage Management
Stage Manager – Maris Sharp
Deputy Stage Manager –
   Sophie Rubenstein
Assistant Stage Manager
   – Emma Ryan
Production
Production Manager – Bernd Fauler
Costume Supervisor – Holly White
Lighting Operator – Nell Allen
Sound Operator – Bryony Blacker
Stage Crew – Sam Shuck
Dresser – Nicole Ashwood
Wardrobe Assistant – Melissa Cooke
Hair and Make-up – Abbie Bridgman
Hair Design – Madlen Mierzwiak
Dyeing and Breaking Down
   – Gabrielle Firth
Chaperone – Valerie Joyce
Chaperone – Julie Colbert

American Buffalo
Matthew Byam Shaw, Nia Janis and
Nick Salmon for Playful Productions
Jeffrey Richards, Jerry Frankel, Steve
Traxler, Will Trice
Tulchin Bartner Productions and
Georgia Gatti
present
American Buffalo
by David Mamet
at the Wyndham's Theatre

Running Dates:
16/4/15 – 27/6/15

Cast
Damian Lewis – Walter Cole ('Teach')
John Goodman – Don Dubrow
Tom Sturridge – Bob
George Evans – Understudy Bob
Edward Wolstenholme – Understudy
   Walter Cole ('Teach') / Don
Creatives
Writer – David Mamet
Director – Daniel Evans
Set and Costume Designer – Paul Wills
Lighting Designer – Mark Henderson
Casting Consultant – Alastair Coomer
Associate Director – Lisa Blair
Dialect Coach – Jill McCullough
Fight Director – Bret Yount
Stage Management
Company Stage Manager
   – Rosie Gilbert
Deputy Stage Manager
   – Kirsty Nixon
Assistant Stage Manager
   – Becca Ridley
Production
Production Manager – Patrick Molony
Associate Production
   Manager – Kate West
Costume Supervisor – Joan Hughes
Props Supervisor – Marcus Hall
Wardrobe Manager – Emma Ntinas
Producers
Playful Productions
Tulchin Bartner Productions
General Management
Playful Productions
Press
The Corner Shop PR
Marketing
Joe Public

American Idiot

Hutchinson Rowntree Ltd present
American Idiot
at the Arts Theatre

Running dates:
17/7/15 – 22/11/15

Cast:

Amy Anzel – Newsreader
Natasha J Barnes – Heather
Luke Baker – Theo
Davis Brooks – Newsreader
Alexis Gerred – Tunny
Llandyll Gove – Gerard
Raquel Jones – Extraordinary
   Girl / Leslie
Natasha Karp – Alysha
Amelia Lily – Whatsername
Robyn Mellor – Libby /
   Dance Captain
Lucas Rush – St Jimmy
Steve Rushton – Will
Aaron Sidwell – Johnny
Ross William Wild – Favourite Son
   / Rock and Roll Boyfriend

Creatives

Book and Lyrics – Billie
   Joe Armstrong
Book – Michael Mayer
Music – Green Day
Director / Choreographer
   – Racky Plews
Designer – Sara Perks
Lighting Designer – Tim Deiling
Sound Designer – Chris Whybrow
Musical Supervisor – Richard Morris
Musical Director – Mark Crossland
Digital Director – Ashley Joiner
Costume Supervisor – Sarah Mercade
Casting Director – Debbie O'Brien

Associate Casting Director
   – Harry Blumenau
Associate Director and Resident
   Director – Simon Kane
Associate Choreographer and
   Resident Choreographer
   – Ryan Lee Seager
Assistant Choreographer
   – Katie Bradley
Associate Musical Director
   – Dan Glover
Assistant Lighting Designer
   – Sam H Waddington
Music Production and Assistant to
   Richard Morris – Gary Hickeson
Accent Coach – Marj McDaid

Stage Management

Company Stage Manager
   –Siân Wiggins
Deputy Stage Manager
   – Kerry Sullivan

Production

Production Manager –
   James Henshaw
Assistant to the Production
   Manager – Heather Walton
General Manager – Naomi Symeou
Assistant General Manager
   – Victoria Roe
Production Electrician – Dave Stone
Production Electrician – Chris May
Production Electrician – Jon Nichols
Production Carpenter – Tim Highman
Production Carpenter – Elliot Dawes
Production Carpenter – James Ashby
Production Carpenter – Michael Shaw
Wardrobe Mistress – Sonia Hogg
Sound No. 1 – Rob Summers
Sound No. 2 – Ollie Clemerson
Props Buyer – Angela Riddell
Wardrobe Assistant – Fiona Lockton
Costume Assistant – Ashleigh Gill

Set Electrics – Mike Atkinson
Production Sound Engineer
   – Andy Hedges
KD Productions – Fit Up Crew
Scenic Artist – Fern Blevins
Scenic Art Assistant – Adam Boon

Musicians

Musical Director / Keys /
   Guitar 2 – Mark Crossland
Drums – Alex Marchisone
Bass – Brock Eddowes
Guitar 1 – Tommaso Varvello

General Management

Hutchinson Rowntree Ltd

Producers

Producer – David Hutchinson
Producer – Phillip Rowntree
Producer – Stephen McGill
Associate Producer – Hartshorn
   – Hook Productions
Associate Producers – Nathan
   Gardner, Danny Brooke, Bradley
   Bredeweg, Kate Pazakis
Associate Producer – London
   Contemporary Theatre

Press

Emma Holland PR

Marketing

JHI Marketing

Assassins

at the Menier Chocolate Factory

Running dates:
21/11/14 – 7/3/15

Cast

Marc Akinfolarin – Bystander
   / Understudy (Proprietor /
   Samuel Byck / Leon Czolgosz)

Carly Bawden – Lynette
   'Squeaky' Fromme
Adam Bayjou – Bystander
   / Understudy (Giuseppe
   Zangara / Charles Guiteau)
Stewart Clarke – Giuseppe Zangara
   / Understudy (John Wilkes Booth)
Anna Francolini – Sara Jane Moore
   (Performances 8–22 Feb only)
Simon Lipkin – Proprietor
Mike McShane – Samuel Byck
Greg Miller Burns – Bystander /
   Understudy (Balladeer / Lee
   Harvey Oswald / John Hinckley)
Harry Morrison – John Hinckley
Aoife Nally – Bystander /
   Understudy (Emma Goldman)
Andy Nyman – Charles Guiteau
Jamie Parker – Balladeer /
   Lee Harvey Oswald
David Roberts – Leon Czolgosz
Melle Stewart – Emma Goldman
   / Bystander / Understudy
   (Lynette 'Squeaky' Fromme
   / Sara Jane Moore)
Catherine Tate – Sara Jane Moore
Michael Xavier – John Wilkes Booth

Creatives

Music and Lyrics – Stephen Sondheim
Book – John Weidman
Director – Jamie Lloyd
Set and Costume Designer
   – Soutra Gilmour
Lighting Designer – Neil Austin
Sound Designer – Gregory Clarke
Choreographer – Chris Bailey
Musical Supervision and
   Direction – Alan Williams
Orchestrations – Bruce Coughlin
Voice and Dialect Coach – Penny Dyer
Hair and Make-up Design – Richard
   Mawbey for Wig Specialities

Associate Director – Richard Fitch
Associate Choreographer – Ben Clare
Assistant Musical Director
   – Huw Evans
Assistant Director – Rupert Hands
Stage Management
Company Stage Manager
   – Rebecca Ridley
Deputy Stage Manager –
   Katherine Tippins
Production
Production Manager – Simon Sturgess
Wardrobe Mistress – Corrie Darling
Wigs Mistress – Laura Richardson
Sound No. 1 – Alexander Broad
Sound No. 2 – Neil McKeown
Costume Supervisor –
   Binnie Bowerman
Production Electrician – Michael Scott
Production Sound Engineer
   – Jem Kitchen
Scenic Artist – James Rowse
Set Construction – RK Resource
Sound Equipment – Blitz
Lighting Equipment – Sparks
   Theatrical Hire
Music Copyist – Richard Lhnatovic
Props – Marcushall Props
Costumes Provider – Angels
   the Costumiers
Make-up Supplier – Mac
Specialist Hanging Effects
   – Freedom Flying
Orchestra
Musical Director / Piano
   – Alan Williams
Violin / Viola – Will Hillman
Cello – Nerys Richards
Bass – Stephen Warner
Piccolo / Clarinet / Soprano Sax /
   Alto Sax – Hannah Lawrance
Clarinet / Bass Clarinet / Tenor Sax

/ Baritone Sax – Katie Samways
Trumpet / Cornet / Flugelhorn
   – Sebastian Philpott
Drums / Percussion – Dominic Sales
For the Menier Chocolate Factory
Artistic Director – David Babani
General Manager – Tom Siracusa

As You Like It
at the National Theatre,
Olivier Stage

Running dates:
26/10/15 – 5/3/16

Cast
Leon Annor – Charles / Understudy
   (Forest Lord / William)
Philip Arditti – Oliver
Joe Bannister – Orlando
Mark Benton – Touchstone
Paul Chahidi – Jaques
Jonathan Coote – Court Lord /
   Understudy (Adam / Corin / Jaques)
Rosalie Craig – Rosalind
Jonathan Dryden Taylor – Dennis
   / Forest Lord / Understudy
   (Touchstone / Duke Frederick
   / Duke Senior / Amiens)
Fra Fee – Amiens
Patsy Ferran – Celia
Hazel Gardner – Ensemble / Singer /
   Understudy (Rosalind / Le Beau)
Patrick Godfrey – Adam
Nathan Ives-Moiba – Jaques de Bois /
   Understudy (Silvius / Forest Lord)
Ellie Kirk – Ensemble / Singer /
   Understudy (Celia / Audrey / Phebe)
Gemma Lawrence – Phebe
Siobhán McSweeney – Audrey

Ken Nwosu – Silvius /
   Understudy (Orlando)
Ekow Quartey – William /
   Forest Lord / Understudy
   (Charles / Jaques de Bois)
John Ramm – Duke Senior
Jay Saighal – Le Beau /
   Understudy (Oliver)
Alan Williams – Corin
Leo Wringer – Duke Frederick
Rebecca Askew, Jeremy Avis, Lea
   Cornthwaite, Jonathan Glew, Hazel
   Holder, Sterre Maier, Catherine
   May, Elaine Mitchener, Simon
   Prag, Osnat Schmool, Belinda
   Sykes, Rebecca Thorn – Choir
Creatives
Writer – William Shakespeare
Director – Polly Findlay
Set Designer – Lizzie Clachan
Costume Designer – Christina
   Cunningham
Lighting Designer – Jon Clark
Music – Orlando Gough
Movement Director –
   Jonathan Goddard
Sound Designer – Carolyn Downing
Fight Director – Kate Waters
Music Director – Marc Tritschler
Associate Lighting Designer
   – Peter Harrison
Artistic Collaborator – Clive Mendus
Company Voice Work –
   Jeannette Nelson
Casting – Juliet Horsley
Stage Management
Stage Manager – Alex Constantin
Deputy Stage Manager
   – Nik Haffenden
Assistant Stage Manager
   – Abbie Procter
Assistant Stage Manager – Emma Tooze

Production
Staff Director – Laura Keefe
Production Manager –
   Richard Norton
Deputy Production Manager
   – Richard Eustace
Costume Supervisor – Peter Todd
Costume Buyer – Charlotte McGarrie
Wigs, Hair and Make-up
   Supervisor – Adele Brandman
Prop Supervisor – Chris Lake
Prop Buyer – Sian Willis
Lighting Supervisor – Jeremy Turnbull
Lighting Programmer –
   Henri Charlton
Video Production Engineer
   – Richard Moores
Video Programmer –
   Matthew Morgans
Production Sound Engineer
   – Ed Ferguson
Sound Operator – Mary Stone
Stage Supervisor – Cory Evje
Rigging Supervisor – Neill Shimmens
Automation – Duncan Weir
Armourer – Paul Wanklin
Construction Supervisor
   – David Cotton
Scenic Art Supervisor – Cass Kirchner
Dingemans Bursary ASM – Eve Keer
Project Draughting – Paul Halter
Digital Art – Daniel Radley-Bennett
Assistant to the Designer –
   Charlotte Espiner

As You Like It
at Shakespeare's Globe

Running dates:
15/5/15 – 5/9/15

Cast

David Beames – Duke Senior
  / Duke Frederick
Daniel Crossley – Touchstone
James Donovan, Stefan Trout – Lords
Patrick Driver – Corin
James Garnon – Jaques
Simon Harrison – Orlando
Gwyneth Keyworth – Phebe
William Mannering – Oliver / Amiens
Jack Monaghan – Silvius
Sophia Nomvete – Audrey
Ellie Piercy – Celia
Gary Shelford – Charles / Hymen
Perri Snowdon – Le Beau
  / Jaques de Boys
Michelle Terry – Rosalind
Phil Whitchurch – Adam

Creatives

Writer – William Shakespeare
Director – Blanche McIntyre
Designer – Andrew D Edwards
Composer – Johnny Flynn
Choreographer – Siân Williams
Artistic Director – Dominic
  Dromgoole
Music Director – Bill Barclay
Casting Director – Matilda James
Fight Director – Kevin McCurdy
Globe Associate – Text – Giles Block
Globe Associate – Movement
  – Glynn Macdonald
Voice and Dialect – Martin McKellan
Assistant Director – Jack Lowe
Executive Producer – Tom Bird

Stage Management

Stage Manager – Matthew North
Deputy Stage Manager
  – Bonnie Morris
Assistant Stage Manager – Liz Isaac
Technical Stage Manager
  – Bryan Paterson

Production

Executive Producer – Tom Bird
Production Manager – Wills
Production Manager – Paul Russell
Company Manager – Marion Marrs
Assistant Company Manager
  – Harry Niland
Assistant Production Manager
  – Fay Powell-Thomas
Costume Supervisor –
  Sabrina Cuniberto
Text Assistant – Hannah
  Boland Moore
Wardrobe Manager – Megan Cassidy
Wardrobe Deputy – Emma Seychell
Wardrobe Assistant – Ruby
  Antonowicz Behnan
Wardrobe Assistant –
  Felicity Langthorne
Wardrobe Assistant – Hanna Randall
Wardrobe Assistant – Rachel Thomas
Wigs, Hair and Make-up
  Manager – Pam Humpage
Wigs, Hair and Make-up Deputy
  – Hayley Thompson
Wigs, Hair and Make-up
  Assistant – Lee Appleton
Wigs, Hair and Make-up
  Assistant – Victoria Young
Props Manager – Katy Brooks
Production Assistant – Lottie Newth
Carpenter – Jon Batt
Carpenter – Kes Hayter
Carpenter – Rupert Mead
Carpenter – Simeon Tachev
Casting, Creative and Filming
  Associate – Karishma Balani
Artistic Coordinator – Jessica Lusk
Music Coordinator – James Maloney
Music Trainee (Supported
  by Andrew Lloyd Webber
  Foundation) – Aleks Giersz

Tiring House – Josh Reeves

Orchestra

Musical Director / Cornett /
  Natural Trumpet / Hurdy-
  gurdy / Natural Horn /
  Recorders – Adrian Woodward
Bass Sackbut / Drum – Andrew
  Harwood-White
Lute / Hurdy-gurdy / Drum
  – Arngeir Hauksson
Cornett / Natural Trumpet / Bagpipe
  / Recorders / Drum – Sam Goble
Nyckleharpa / Hardanger Fiddle
  / Drum – Griselda Sanderson

Billy Elliot the Musical

Universal Stage Productions,
Working Title Films and Old Vic
Productions
In Association with Tiger Aspect
present
Billy Elliot the Musical
Based on the Universal Pictures /
Studio Canal Film
at the Victoria Palace Theatre

Running dates:
11/3/05 – 9/4/16

Cast

David Bardsley – Alternate Dad
Beatrice Bartl – Debbie
Claudia Bradley – Dead Mum
James Butcher – Billy's Older Self
Howard Crossley – George
Brodie Donougher – Billy
Gillian Elisa – Grandma
Lewis Elliott – Tall Boy
Connie Fisher – Debbie

Jack Forino – Small Boy
Euan Garrett – Billy
Thomas Hazelby – Billy
Ruthie Henshall – Mrs Wilkinson
Hollie Jayne Creighton – Debbie
Nathan Jones – Michael
Bradley Mayfield – Michael
Caspar Meurisse
Noah Miller – Tall Boy
George Morgan – Small Boy
George Norris – Small Boy
Ben Robinson – Michael
Sonny James Scott – Small Boy
Matthew Seadon-Young – Tony
Phil Snowden – Mr Braithwaite
Wendy Somerville – Alternate
  Mrs Wilkinson
Nat Sweeney – Billy
Deka Walmsley – Dad
Craig Armstrong, Richard Ashton,
  James Ballanger, Paul Basleigh,
  Rachel Bingham, Lucinda Collins,
  Peter Cork, Scott Cripps, Robbie
  Durham, Ross Finnie, Lee Hoy,
  Ruri James, Ben Redfern (Ballet
  Girls' Dance Captain Maternity
  Cover), Charlotte Riby (Ballet
  Girls' Dance Captain), Mike
  Scott (Dance Captain), Sharon
  Sexton, Wendy Somerville,
  Spencer Stafford, David Stoller,
  Kerry Washington – Ensemble
Olivia Anson, Amélie Olivia Bardsley,
  Maiya Beazley, Lucy Cheesman,
  Lydia Rose Coghlan, Rebecca
  Cogodi, Katie-Mae Collins,
  Ruby Cunningham, Brogan
  Fleming, Sammy Foster, Eleanor
  Fox, Millie Green, Pollyanna
  Charlotte Hawkes, Lauren Joyce,
  Cara McCabe, Elle Nash, Laveda
  Ogbebor, Kacy O'Sullivan,

Charlotte Pourret Wythe, Aimee Quirke, Amelia Riley, Niamh Savage, Demi Tullulah Scott, Lilly Stanion, Lillie-Mae Stewart, Amelia Stratton, Aimee Tutt, Bryony Way, Scarlett Wennink, Shanice Williams – Ballet Girls

Understudies
Charlotte Riby, Claudia Bradley – Understudy Mrs Wilkinson
David Stoller – Understudy Dad
Robbie Durham, Ruri James – Understudy Tony
Kerry Washington, Lucinda Collins – Understudy Grandma
David Bardsley, Craig Armstrong, Ross Finnie – Understudy George
Ross Finnie, Spencer Stafford – Understudy Mr Braithwaite
Rachel Bingham, Charlotte Riby, Sharon Sexton – Understudy Dead Mum
Lee Hoy, Peter Cork – Understudy Billy's Older Self

Creatives
Book and Lyrics – Lee Hall
Music – Sir Elton John
Director – Stephen Daldry
Set Design – Ian MacNeil
Choreography – Peter Darling
Costume Design – Nicky Gillibrand
Lighting Design – Rick Fisher
Sound Design – Paul Arditti
Hair, Wig and Make-up Designer – Campbell Young
Musical Supervision and Orchestrations – Martin Koch
Original Musical Director – Philip Bateman
Musical Director – Chris Hatt
Fight Director – Terry King

Temporary Resident Director – Ed Goggin
Resident Choreographer – Nikki Belsher
Resident Choreographer ('Dream Ballet' and 'Electricity') – Damian Jackson
Choreographic Supervision – Ellen Kane
Adult Casting Director – Pippa Ailion CDG
Children's Casting Director – Jessica Ronane CDG
Associate Director – Julian Webber
Children's Casting Assistant – Verity Naughton
Children's Casting Assistant – Abby Galvin
Marketing Director – Susan Butterly (for Working Title)

Stage Management
Stage Manager – James-Paul Hayden
Deputy Stage Manager – Tiffany Horton
Deputy Stage Manager – Ian Baigrie
Assistant Stage Manager – Sara Lee
Assistant Stage Manager – Sebastien Matthews
Assistant Stage Manager – Ben Stevens
Assistant Stage Manager – Hannah Swindell
Assistant Stage Manager – Hannah Wing

Production
Production Manager – Matt Towell
Original Production Manager – Stephen Rebbeck
Company General Manager – David Massey
Head of Automation – Adam Morley
Head of Sound – Chris Reid
Sound No. 2 – Sam Palmer

Sound No. 3 – Laura Caplin
Sound No. 4 – Jaymee Hayes
Head of Lighting – James Nowell
Head of Wardrobe – Marny Clulow
Deputy Head of Wardrobe – Shona McCallum
Head of Wigs – Samara Hulley
Head of Wigs Maternity Cover – Karleigh Williams
Wigs Assistant – Mags Pattinson
Assistant to the Resident Director – Craig Armstrong
Assistant Costume Supervisor – Hannah Bell
Props Supervisor – Kathy Anders
Props Supervisor – Lisa Buckley

Orchestra
Musical Director / Keyboard 1 – Chris Hatt
Assistant Musical Director / Keyboard 2 – Mark Collins
2nd Assistant Conductor – Andy Massey
Woodwind 1 – Bradley Grant
Woodwind 2 – Ben Woodgate
Trumpet – Paul Newton
Horn – Richard Ashton
Guitar – Andy Holdsworth
Bass Guitar – Phil Laughlin
Drums – Tim Weller
Orchestral Management – Musical Coordination Services Ltd
Original Musical Director – Philip Bateman

Producers
Executive Producer – David Furnish
Executive Producer – Angela Morrison
Producer – Tim Bevan
Producer – Eric Fellner
Producer – Jon Finn
Producer – Sally Greene
Associate Producer – Marieke Spencer

General Manager – Jess Wright
General Manager (Maternity Cover) – Marlaina Darmody

Press
Premier PR

Marketing
AKA

Charlie and the Chocolate Factory
Warner Bros. Theatre Ventures, Langley Park Productions and Neal Street Productions present Roald Dahl's
Charlie and the Chocolate Factory at the Theatre Royal, Drury Lane

Running dates:
25/6/13 – present

Cast
Ellie Benge – Veruca Salt
Joe Butler-Smith – Charlie Bucket
Logan Cripps – Augustus Gloop
Noah Crump – Charlie Bucket
Connor Davies – Augustus Gloop
Ross Dawes – Mr Salt
Lara Denning – Mrs Bucket
Archie Durrant – Mike Teavee
Johnny Evans-Hutchison – Charlie Bucket
Josefina Gabrielle – Mrs Teavee
Stella Haden – Veruca Salt
Derek Hagen – Mr Bucket
Freddie Haggerty – Mike Teavee
Jasna Ivir – Mrs Gloop
Barry James – Grandpa Joe
Lucinda Lawrence – Cherry
Benjamin Lewis – Augustus Gloop
Zachary Loonie – Charlie Bucket

377

Paul J Medford – Mr Beauregarde
Psalms-Nissi Myers-Reid –
    Violet Beauregarde
Shaniquah Notice-Morris –
    Violet Beauregarde
Miriam Nyarko –
    Violet Beauregarde
Mark Oxtoby – Jerry
Roni Page – Grandma Josephine
Scarlet Roche – Veruca Salt
Myra Sands – Grandma Georgina
Rebecca Seale – Mrs Pratchett
Jonathan Slinger – Willy Wonka
Kraig Thornber – Grandpa George
Harry Vallance – Mike Teavee
Joe Allen, Joel Baylis, Andy Brady,
    Georgia Carling, Dan Cooke,
    Divine Cresswell, Billy Cullum,
    Connor Dowling, Kelly Edwards,
    Lucinda Lawrence, Mark Oxtoby,
    Matthew Rowland, Rebecca Seale,
    Steven Serlin, Gregory Sims,
    Tara Verloop, Michelle White –
    Oompa-Loompas / Ensemble
Meg Astin, Simon Campbell,
    Andrew Carthy, Collette
    Coleman, Gemma Fuller, Sam
    Lathwood, Robert Tregoning,
    Mark Williamson – Swings

Understudies

Ross Dawes, Derek Hagen
    – Willy Wonka
Kraig Thornber, Mark
    Oxtoby – Grandpa Joe
Mark Oxtoby, Steven
    Serlin – Mr Salt
Lucinda Lawrence, Tara
    Verloop – Mrs Teavee
Rebecca Seale, Kelly
    Edwards – Mrs Gloop
Steven Serlin, Matthew Rowland
    – Mr Beauregarde

Rebecca Seale, Gemma
    Fuller – Mrs Bucket
Andy Brady, Robert
    Tregoning – Mr Bucket
Lucinda Lawrence, Tara Verloop
    – Grandma Josephine
Kelly Edwards, Rebecca Seale
    – Grandma Georgina
Mark Oxtoby, Andy Brady
    – Grandpa George

Creatives

Based on the novel by – Roald Dahl
Book – David Greig
Music – Marc Shaiman
Lyrics – Scott Wittman
    and Marc Shaiman
Director – Sam Mendes
Choreographer – Peter Darling
Set and Costume Designer
    – Mark Thompson
Musical Supervisor –
    Nicholas Skilbeck
Lighting Designer – Paul Pyant
Sound Designer – Paul Arditti
Video and Projection Designer
    – John Driscoll
Puppet and Illusion Designer
    – Jamie Harrison
Orchestrations – Doug Besterman
Casting – Pippa Ailion CDG
Children's Casting – Jessica
    Ronane CDG
Associate Director – Kate Hewitt
Associate Choreographer
    – Ellen Kane
Associate Set Designer – Ben Davies
Associate Lighting Designer
    – David Howe
Associate Sound Designer
    – John Owens
Associate Projection Designer
    – Gemma Carrington

Resident Director – Alexandra
    Sumner-Hughes
Resident Choreographer – Chris Piper
Dance Captain – Gemma Fuller
Assistant Dance Captain –
    Robert Tregoning
Assistant Children's Director
    – Matthew Rowland
Skating Captain – Ross Dawes

Stage Management

Production Stage Manager
    – Chris Hesketh
Deputy Stage Manager –
    Sarah Seymour
Assistant Stage Manager
    – James Barwick
Assistant Stage Manager
    – Benjamin Eddon
Assistant Stage Manager –
    Lisa Mellor
Assistant Stage Manager –
    Woody Woodcock

Production

Production Manager – Patrick Molony
Company Manager – Wyn Williams
Assistant Company Manager
    – Rory Neal-McKenzie
Head of Sound – Digby Shaw
Sound No. 2 – Seeta Mistry
Sound No. 3 – Zoe Blackford
Sound No. 4 – Tess Dacre
Sound Assistant – Tasha Turan
Head of Automation – Ben Phillips
Automation No. 2 – Danny Garth
Automation No. 3 – Dave Corrin
Automation No. 4 – Martin Wade
Head of Wardrobe – Nicky Leach
Wardrobe Deputy – Jackie Young
Wardrobe Assistant – Rachel Eastop
Wardrobe Assistant – Marine Wan
Head of Hair and Make-up
    – Lucy Mullen

Hair and Make-up Deputy
    – Laura Pyburn
Hair and Make-up Assistant
    – Fiona Middlehurst
Hair and Make-up Assistant
    – Emma Seabrook
Natalie Young

Orchestra

Musical Director – Toby Higgins
Assistant Musical Director
    – Danny Whitby
Keyboards – John G Smith, Jill
    Farrow, Danny Whitby
Guitars, Banjo – Dave Holmes
Bass Guitar, Double Bass
    – Rory Dempsey
Drums, Percussion –
    Dave Elliott
Percussion – Corrine Silvester
Alto Saxophone, Flute, Piccolo,
    Clarinet – Nick Moss
Soprano & Tenor Saxophone,
    Clarinet, Flute – Jamie Talbot
Bassoon, Baritone Saxophone, Bass
    Clarinet, Clarinet – Colin Skinner
French Horn, Cover Conductor
    – Matt Gunner
Trumpet, Flugel Horn, Piccolo
    Trumpet – John Barclay
Trombone – Phil Judge
Violin, Cover Conductor
    – Michael Keelan
Violin – Clare Taylor
Cello – Hannah Ashenden
Orchestral Management – Andy
    Barnwell/ Pete Harrison for
    Musical Co-ordination Service Ltd
Music Technology – Phij Adams

General Management

Playful Productions

Press

The Corner Shop PR

Marketing

Dewynters

Marketing Directors – Joe Public

Closer

at the Donmar Warehouse

Running Dates:
12/2/15 – 4/4/15

Cast
Nancy Carroll – Anna
Oliver Chris – Dan
Rachel Redford – Alice
Rufus Sewell – Larry

Creatives
Writer – Patrick Marber
Director – David Leveaux
Designer – Bunny Christie
Lighting Designer – Hugh Vanstone
Sound Designer – Fergus O'Hare
Video Designer – Finn Ross
Composer – Corin Buckeridge
Movement – Wayne McGregor
Casting Director – Alastair
   Coomer CDG
Resident Assistant Director – Zoé Ford

Stage Management
Company Stage Manager
   – Claire Sibley
Deputy Stage Manager –
   Mary O'Hanlon
Assistant Stage Manager –
   Catherine Pewsey

Production
Production Manager – Kate West
Costume Supervisor –
   Deborah Andrews
Video Programmer and Interactive
   Content – Jonathon Lyle

Dear Lupin

Kenny Wax Ltd presents
Dear Lupin
at the Apollo Theatre

Running dates:
30/7/15 – 19/9/15

Cast
Jack Fox – Lupin
James Fox – Roger
Ian Christie – Understudy Roger
Nick Ricketts – Understudy Lupin

Creatives
Writer – Roger Mortimer
Writer – Charlie Mortimer
Stage Adaptation – Michael Simkins
Director – Philip Franks
Set and Costume Designer
   – Adrian Linford
Lighting Designer – Johanna Town
Composer and Sound Designer
   – Matthew Bugg
Choreographer – Simeon John-Wake

Stage Management
Company Stage Manager –
   Christopher Rooney
Deputy Stage Manager –
   Julie Whitcombe
Assistant Stage Manager –
   Woody Woodcock

Production
Production Manager –
   Digby Robinson
Props Supervisor – Claire Auvache
Costume Supervisor – Katie Higgins
Wigs – Kelly Poulter
Voice Coach – Holly Hayes
Pre-production Electrician and
   Programmer – Gareth Clowes
Production Electrician – Tim Bray
Production Carpenter –
   James Whitwell
Production Sound Engineer
   – Andrew Johnson
Promotions – Georgia Edmonds
National Press – Kate Morley
Media Buying – Sold Out
Scenery – Splinter Scenery Ltd
Scenery – The Scenery Shop Ltd
Stage Hires – Meridian Staging Ltd
Digital Scenic Printing –
   Promptside Ltd
Sound Equipment –
   Dimension Audio Ltd
Lighting Equipment – White Light Ltd
Hair Styling – Paul Edmonds

Producers
Producer – Martyn Hayes
Producer – Kenny Wax
Co-Producer – TC Beech Ltd
Co-Producer – Michael Watt

Marketing
JHI Marketing Ltd

Press
Rebecca Pitt

Death of a Salesman

The Royal Shakespeare Company's
production of
Arthur Miller's
Death of a Salesman
at the Noël Coward Theatre

Running dates:
9/5/15 – 18/7/15

Cast
Tobias Beer – Howard Wagner
Paul Birchard – Older Waiter
Helen Grady – Jenny
Ross Green – Stanley
Alex Hassell – Biff Loman
Emma King – Miss Forsythe
Sam Marks – Happy Loman
Miranda Nolan – Letta
Sarah Parks – The Woman
Guy Paul – Uncle Ben
Joshua Richards – Charley
Brodie Ross – Bernard
Antony Sher – Willy Loman
Harriet Walter – Linda Loman

Creative Team
Writer – Arthur Miller
Director – Gregory Doran
Designer – Stephen Brimson Lewis
Lighting Designer – Tim Mitchell
Music Director – Malcolm Newton
Sound Designer – Jonathan Ruddick
Company Text and Voice
   Work – Michael Elliott
Dialect Coach – Rick Lipton
Assistant Director – Josh Roche
Casting – Helena Palmer CDG

Stage Management
Company Stage Manager
   – Ben Tyreman
Deputy Stage Manager – Klare Roger
Assistant Stage Manager
   – Angela Garrick
Assistant Stage Manager
   – Osnat Koblenz

Production
Production Manager – Pete Griffin
Production Manager – Richard Norton
Costume Supervisor – Laura Hunt
Sound Operator – Matthew McCarthy
Lighting and Sound Technician
   – Oliver Quintrell
Wardrobe Mistress – Thea Kay
Assistant Wardrobe Mistress
   – Emma Sheppard
Wig Mistress – Maxine Hughes

Dresser – Claire Harrison
Dresser – Louisa Reece
Musicians
Saxophones / Clarinet / Alto
 Flute – Andrew Isherwood
Trumpet / Flugelhorn –
 Kevin Wedrynchowski
Double Bass – Mat Heighway
Drums / Percussion – Jon Hooper
Piano – Malcolm Newton

Dirty Rotten Scoundrels

Ambassador Theatre Group and
Jerry Mitchell Productions
present
Dirty Rotten Scoundrels
at the Savoy Theatre

Running dates:
10/3/14 – 7/3/15

Cast
Lizzy Connolly – Jolene Oakes
Ben Fox – Andre Thibault
Alex Gaumond – Freddy Benson
Katherine Kingsley –
 Christine Colgate
Bonnie Langford – Muriel Eubanks
Robert Lindsay – Lawrence Jameson
Gavin Alex, Darren Bennett,
 Niamh Bracken, Lisa Bridge,
 Andy Conaghan, Lizzy Connolly,
 Claire Doyle, Alice Fearn, Selina
 Hamilton, Ian Knauer, Zak
 Nemorin, Genevieve Nicole, Javier
 Santos, Todd Talbot, Dominic
 Tribuzio, Zara Warren – Ensemble
Darren Carnall, Phoebe Coupe,
 Lisa Mathieson, John Tsouras
 (Dance Captain) – Swings

Understudies
Darren Bennett, Ian Knauer
 – Lawrence Jameson
Andy Conaghan, Gavin
 Alex – Freddy Benson
Alice Fearn, Lisa Bridge –
 Christine Colgate
Alice Fearn, Genevieve Nicole
 – Muriel Eubanks
Darren Bennett, Ian Knauer
 – Andre Thibault
Zara Warren, Genevieve
 Nicole – Jolene Oakes

Creatives
Book – Jeffrey Lane
Music and Lyrics – David Yazbek
Director and Choreographer
 – Jerry Mitchell
Set and Costume Designer
 – Peter McKintosh
Lighting Designer –
 Howard Harrison
Musical Supervisor – Matthew Brind
Sound Designer – Paul Groothuis
Wigs Designer – Linda McKnight
Original Dance Music – Zane Mark
Associate Director – Dominic Shaw
Associate Choreographer
 – Darren Carnall
Props Supervisor – Mandy Burnett
Costume Supervisor – Angie Burns
Associate Set Designer
 – Simons Wells
Associate Lighting Designer
 – James Smith
Associate Sound Designer
 – Tom Marshall

Stage Management
Company Manager – Mike Mansfield
Stage Manager – Jason Golbourn
Deputy Stage Manager
 – Kirsty Nixon

Assistant Stage Manager
 – Dave Armstrong
Assistant Stage Manager
 – Kate Williams

Production
Production Manager – Ben Arkell
Wardrobe Master – David Stringer
Deputy Wardrobe Mistress
 – Laura Watkins
Wardrobe Assistant –
 Rachael Higham
Principal Dresser – Sabina Paccini
Wigs Master – Sam Cox
Wigs Deputy – Alice Townes
Wigs Assistant – Katie Oropallo
Sound No. 1 – Becky Stockting
Sound No. 2 – Dan Evans
Sound No. 3 – Michaela O'Brien
Automation No. 1 – Josh Peters
Automation No. 2 – Tom McKenzie

Musicians
Musical Director / Piano
 – Richard John
Keyboards / Associate Musical
 Director – Torquil Munro
Drums – James Powell
Bass Guitar – Andy Pask
Percussion – Dan Ellis
Violin – Shelley Britton
Reeds – Andy Panayi
Reeds – Claire McInerney
Reeds – Gemma Moore
Trumpet – Andy Gathercole
Trumpet – Mike Lovatt
Trombone – Pete Beachill
Orchestral Management – Musical
 Coordination Services Ltd

General Management
Ambassador Theatre Group

Di and Viv and Rose

CMP, Greg Ripley-Duggan and Ros
Povey Productions
Celia Atkin and Rupert Gavin
present
The Hampstead Theatre production of
Di and Viv and Rose
at the Vaudeville Theatre

Running dates:
27/4/15 – 23/5/15

Cast
Tamzin Outhwaite – Di
Jenna Russell – Rose
Samantha Spiro – Viv
Emma Bown – Understudy Di / Viv
Rachel Mitchem – Understudy Rose

Creatives
Writer – Amelia Bullmore
Director – Anna Mackmin
Designer – Paul Wills
Lighting Designer – Oliver Fenwick
Sound Designer – Simon Baker
Choreographer – Scarlett Mackmin
Associate Director – Will Wrightson
Production Manager – Tariq Rifaat
Additional Casting – Amy Ball
Costume Supervisor – Jackie Orton
Dialect Coach – William Conacher

Stage Management
Company Stage Manager
 – Lizzie Chapman
Deputy Stage Manager – Maggie Tully
Assistant Stage Manager – Sarah Coates

Production
Props – Lisa Buckley
Head of Wardrobe – Denise
 Monte-Colombi
Hair and Make-up – Anna Morena
Dresser – Cáit Canavan

Elf

Michael Rose and U-Live
For Elf the Musical (UK) Limited
In association with Bord Gáis Energy
Theatre, Dublin
present
A Theatre Royal Plymouth production
of
Elf
at the Dominion Theatre

Running dates:
24/10/15 – 2/1/16

Cast

Harry Collett – Michael
Jennie Dale – Deb
Ben Forster – Buddy
Ilan Galkoff – Michael
Noah Key – Michael
Graham Lappin – Store Manager
Jessica Martin – Emily Hobbs
Joe McGann – Walter Hobbs
Mark McKerracher – Santa
   / Mr Greenway
Ewan Rutherford – Michael
Kimberley Walsh – Jovie
Katie Bradley, Charlie Bull,
   Nicola Coates, Alex Fobbester,
   Charlotte Gale, Francis Haugen,
   Paul Hutton, Mark Iles, Ceili
   O'Connor, Debbie Paul, Barnaby
   Thompson, Ed White – Ensemble
Anton Fosh, Matt Holland
   (Assistant Dance Captain),
   Tash Holway, Joanna Rennie
   (Dance Captain) – Swings
Francis Haugen – Understudy Buddy
Ceili O'Connor – Understudy Jovie
Barnaby Thompson –
   Understudy Walter Hobbs

Charlie Bull – Understudy
   Emily Hobbs
Charlotte Gale – Understudy Deb
Paul Hutton – Understudy
   Santa / Mr Greenway
Ed White – Understudy Store Manager

Creatives

Book – Thomas Meehan
Book – Bob Martin
Songs – Matthew Sklar
Songs – Chad Beguelin
Director and Choreographer
   – Morgan Young
Musical Director and Supervisor
   – Stuart Morley
Associate Choreographer
   – Helen Rymer
Production Designer – Tim Goodchild
Lighting Designer – Tim Lutkin
Video Designer – Ian
   William Galloway
Sound Designer – Clem
   Rawling for Mac Sound
Wigs and Hair Design – Richard
   Mawbey for Wig Specialities
Fight Director – Paul Benzing
Skating Consultant – Jamie Capewell
Associate / Resident Director
   – Evan Ensign
Associate Designer – Mark Friend
Associate Lighting Designer
   – Max Narula
Associate Video Designer – Ingi Bekk
Associate Sound Designer
   – Paul Delaney
Associate Musical Director
   – Jeremy Wootton
Wigs and Hair Design
   Associate – Sue Pederson
Children's Casting and
   Administration – Jo Hawes CDG
Casting – Sarah Bird CDG

Casting Associate – Mark
   Frankum CDG

Stage Management

Stage Manager – Jo Miles
Deputy Stage Manager
   – Claire Rundle
Assistant Stage Manager
   – Adam Cox
Assistant Stage Manager
   – Danyal Shafiq

Production

Production Manager –
   Richard Bullimore
Company Manager – Claire Sibley
Wardrobe Supervision – Sue
   Simmerling for Carry on Costumes
ASM Tech Swing – Jake Samuels
ASM Swing Sound – Pip Ratcliffe
Automation Operator – Nick Page
Head of Lighting and Video
   – Gary Bowman
Deputy Head of Lighting and
   Video – Peter Butler
Sound No. 1 – Graham Holder
Sound No. 2 – Katie Weatherley
Wardrobe Mistress – Rachel Morris
Deputy Wardrobe Mistress
   – Carly Turnbull
PA / Dress to Ms Walsh
   – Davina Elliott
Wig Mistress – Mel Brothwell
Deputy Wig Mistress – Julie Burnett
Head Chaperone – Pat Wallace
Chaperone – Nicky Clarke
Chaperone – Kathy Outen

Orchestra

Conductor / Keyboard – Stuart Morley
Musical Director / Keyboard
   – Jeremy Wootton
Violin – Simon Howes, Polly Wiltshire
Cello – Bryony James
Bass / Electric Bass – Harrison Wood

Oboe / Clarinet / Piccolo
   – Steve Foster
Sax / Flute / Clarinet – Chris Caldwell
Sax / Fl / Cl / Bass Cl
   – Adam Bishop
Trumpet / Flugelhorn – Nick Mead
Trumpet / Flugelhorn –
   Louis Dowdeswell
Trombone – Robbie Harvey
Trombone – Patrick Hayes
Percussion – Chris Marshall
Drum Kit – Matt Senior
Piano – Jon Ranger
Orchestral Management
   – Sylvia Addison

Everyman

at the National Theatre,
Olivier Stage

Running dates:
22/4/15 – 30/8/15

Cast

Stephen Aintree – Ensemble
Paul Bullion – Sound
Adam Burton – Goods / Passion
Michelle Butterly – Sister
Sharon D Clarke – Mother
Dermot Crowley – Death
Kate Duchêne – God / Good Deeds
Chiwetel Ejiofor – Everyman
Amy Griffiths – Goods / Vanity
Nick Holder – Strength
Nicholas Karimi – Smell /
   Understudy (Everyman)
Joshua Lacey – Goods / Sensuality
Penny Layden – Knowledge
Ira Mandela Siobhan – Sight
Philip Martin Brown – Father

Coral Messam – Conscience /
  Understudy (Mother / Sister)
Amanda Minihan – Touch /
  Understudy (God / Good Deeds)
Itxaso Moreno – Taste
Jeshaiah Murray – Everyboy
Tumo Reetsang – Everyboy
Kiruna Stamell – Discretion
Clemmie Sveaas – Goods / Insecurity
Joshua Tikare – Everyboy

Creatives

Writer – Bernard O'Donoghue
Adaptation – Carol Ann Duffy
Director – Rufus Norris
Choreographer and Movement
  Director – Javier De Frutos
Set Designer – Ian MacNeil
Costume Designer – Nicky Gillibrand
Lighting Designer – Paul Anderson
Video Designer – Tal Rosner
Music – William Lyons
Sound Designer – Paul Arditti
Music Production – Dominic Betmead
Vocal Music Director –
  Stephen Higgins
Company Voice Work – Kate Godfrey
Casting – Wendy Spon
Assistant to the Movement Director
  – Ira Mandela Siobhan

Stage Management

Stage Manager – Laura Flowers
Deputy Stage Manager – Jo Nield
Assistant Stage Manager
  – Stuart Campbell
Assistant Stage Manager
  – Tom Gilding

Production

Staff Director – Emily Lim
Production Manager – Jim Leaver
Deputy Production Manager –
  Gary Pell
Project Draughting – Paul Halter

Project Draughting – Sarah Vowles
Costume Supervisor – Claire Murphy
Costume Buyer – Sarah Holmes
Wigs, Hair and Make-up
  Supervisor – Adele Brandman
Prop Supervisor – Eleanor Smith
Prop Buyer – Jessica Sharville
Lighting Supervisor – Jeremy Turnbull
Lighting Programmer –
  Henri Charlton
Production Sound Engineer
  – Jonas Roebuck
Sound Operator – Mike Winship
Stage Supervisor – Bob Cross
Rigging Supervisor – Neil Shimmen
Video Programmer – Nick Simmons
Video Production Engineer
  – Ethan Forde
Automation – Adam Fretwell
Armourer / Special Effects
  Supervisor – Paul Wanklin
Armourer / Special Effects
  Supervisor – Steve Dart
Construction Supervisor
  – David Cotton
Scenic Painting Supervisor
  – Daina Ennis
Production Assistant – Maisy Wyer

Musicians

Music Director / Shawm /
  Recorder / Bagpipes / Rackett
  / Crumhorn / Harmonium
  / Organ – William Lyons
Shawm / Recorder / Bagpipes /
  Rackett / Crumhorn / Curtal /
  Hurdy-gurdy – Nicholas Perry
Lute / Theorbo / Gittern
  – Arngeir Hauksson
Percussion / Dulcimer –
  Louise Morgan
Percussion – Sola Akingbola

━━━━━━━━━━━━━

Farinelli and the King

Sonia Friedman Productions and
Shakespeare's Globe,
in association with Tulchin Bartner
Productions and 1001 Nights
present
the Shakespeare's Globe production
of
Farinelli and the King
by Claire van Kampen
at the Duke of York's Theatre

Running dates:
14/9/15 – 5/12/15

Cast

Sam Crane – Farinelli
Matthew Darcy – Jethro /
  Juan / Cover Farinelli
Huss Garbiya – Dr José Cervi
Melody Grove – Isabella Farnese
Colin Hurley – Metastasio
Edward Peel – De la Cuadra
Mark Rylance – Philippe V
Iestyn Davies – Singer
Rupert Enticknap – Singer
Owen Willetts – Singer
Cate Cammack – Cover
  Isabella Farnese
Andrew McDonald – Cover
  Metastasio / De la Cuadra
  / Dr José Cervi

Creatives

Writer – Claire van Kampen
Director – John Dove
Designer – Jonathan Fensom
Musical Arranger –
  Claire van Kampen
Movement Director – Siân Williams
Casting Director – Matilda James
Musical Supervisor – Bill Barclay

Voice and Dialect –
  Martin McKellan
Assistant Director – Josh Roche
Casting Associate – Karishma Balani
Assistant Musical Arranger
  – Sophie Cotton
Production Manager and Lighting
  Designer – Paul Russell

Stage Management

Company Stage Manager
  – Ben Delfont
Deputy Stage Manager –
  Becca Ridley
Assistant Stage Manager
  – Olly Clarke-Bibb
Candle Technician –
  Katherine Tippins

Production

Hair and Wigs – Campbell
  Young Associates
Costume Supervisor – Lorraine Ebdon
Wardrobe Manager –
  Heather Jane Bull
Wardrobe Deputy – Jessica Houghton
Dresser – Anna Winkler
Wigs Manager – Kathy Adams
Wigs Assistant – Nicky Ives

Musicians

Musical Director / Harpsichord
  – Robert Howarth
Violin 1 – Naomi Burrell
Violin 1 – Pavlo Beznosiuk
Violin 1 – John Crockatt
Violin 2 – James Toll
Theorbo / Baroque Guitar /
  Recorder – Arngeir Hauksson
Cello – Jonathan Byers
Bass – Pippa Macmillan
Cover Musicians – James
  Johnstone, Chad Kelly, Elin
  White, Lynda Sayce, Joanna
  Levine, Peter McCarthy

General Management
Lil Lambley and Fiona Stewart for
    Sonia Friedman Productions
Press
The Corner Shop PR
Marketing
AKA

Guys and Dolls

Runaway Entertainment, Bos
Productions, and Richard Darbourne Ltd
in association with Tulchin/Bartner
Productions present
the Chichester Festival Theatre
production of
Guys and Dolls
at the Savoy Theatre

Running dates:
6/1/16 – 12/3/16

Cast
Lucy Jane Adcock – Mimi
Cornelius Clarke – Harry the Horse
Lorna Gayle – General
    Matilda B Cartwright
Nic Greenshields – Big Jule
David Haig – Nathan Detroit
Selina Hamilton – Havana Diva
Siubhan Harrison – Sarah Brown
Ian Hughes – Benny Southstreet
Frankie Jenna – Agatha
Neil McCaul – Arvide Abernathy
William Oxborrow – Lieutenant
    Brannigan / Joey Biltmore
Jamie Parker – Sky Masterson
Carl Patrick – Rusty Charlie
Giovanni Spanó – Angie the Ox
Gavin Spokes – Nicely-Nicely Johnson
Jonathan Stewart – Calvin

Sophie Thompson – Miss Adelaide
Abigail Brodie, Momar Diagne,
    Lavinia Fitzpatrick, Jacob
    Maynard, Genevieve Nicole, Max
    Parker, James Revell, Lucie-Mae
    Sumner, Liam Wrate – Ensemble
Understudies
Carl Patrick, Cornelius Clarke
    – Nathan Detroit
Lucy Jane Adcock, Genevieve
    Nicole – Miss Adelaide
Jonathan Stewart, Max
    Parker – Sky Masterson
Frankie Jenna, Lucie-Mae
    Sumner – Sarah Brown
Giovanni Spanó, Carl Patrick
    – Nicely-Nicely Johnson
Cornelius Clarke, William Oxborrow,
    Carl Patrick – Arvide Abernathy
Jonathan Stewart, Liam Wrate
    – Lieutenant Brannigan
    / Joey Biltmore
Carl Patrick, Giovanni Spanó
    – Benny Southstreet
Genevieve Nicole, Lucy Jane Adcock
    – General Matilda B Cartwright
Giovanni Spanó, Liam Wrate
    – Harry the Horse
Max Parker, Momar Diagne – Big Jule
Max Parker, Liam Wrate – Rusty Charlie
Creatives
Music and Lyrics – Frank Loesser
Book – Abe Burrows
Director – Gordon Greenberg
Set and Costume Designer
    – Peter McKintosh
Choreographer – Carlos Acosta
Choreographer – Andrew Wright
Musical Supervisor / Musical
    Director / Dance Arrangements
    – Gareth Valentine
Orchestrations – Larry Blank

Lighting Designer – Tim Mitchell
Sound Designer – Paul Groothuis
Hair, Wig and Make-up Design –
    Campbell Young Associates
Casting Director – Pippa Ailion CDG
Casting Director – Jim Arnold CDG
Associate Director – Samuel Wood
Associate Choreographer
    – Matthew Cole
Associate Choreographer
    – Lucy Banfield
Stage Management
Stage Manager – Stew Stealey
Deputy Stage Manager – David Neill
Assistant Stage Manager
    – Fiona Samways
Assistant Stage Manager – Joe Pocket
Production
Company Manager – Mike Mansfield
Production Manager –
    Simon Godding
Chief Electrician – John Maddox
Sound No. 1 – Michael Ryles
Sound No. 2 – Andy Yiannaki
Technical Swing – Nick Hughes
Head of Wardrobe – Iwan Harries
Wardrobe Deputy – Rachael Nevill
Wardrobe Assistant – Naomi Ford
Head of Wigs – Joanna Smedley
Wigs Deputy – Jessica Plews
Wigs Assistant – Rochelle Porter
Orchestra
Musical Director –
    Gareth Valentine
Keyboard / Assistant Musical
    Director – Andy Massey
Drums – Allan Cox
Double Bass – Don Richardson
Percussion – James Turner
Trumpet – Alex Maynard
Trumpet – Stuart Brooks
Trumpet – Richard Freeman

Trombone – Tom Dunnett
Trombone – Chris Traves
French Horn – Jon Eddie
Reeds – Rupert Widdows
Reeds – Duncan Lamont
Reeds – Steve Pierce
Reeds – Jay Craig
Orchestral Management – Musical
    Coordination Services Ltd
Assistant – Peter Harrison
Producers
Chichester Festival Theatre –
    Originating Producer
Runaway Entertainment
Bos Productions
Richard Darbourne Ltd
Tulchin/Bartner Productions
General Management
Runaway Entertainment
Press
Jo Allan PR
Marketing
Dewynters

Gypsy

Michael Harrison and David Ian
with Neil Laidlaw, Lee Dean, Tulchin/
Bartner Productions, Michael Watt,
Charles Diamond / Damian Arnold,
Patrick Catullo / Aaron Glick, Ramin
Sabi / Seaview Productions and
Ambassador Theatre Group
present
the Chichester Festival Theatre
production of
Gypsy
at the Savoy Theatre

Running dates:
28/3/15 – 28/11/15

Cast (and post cast change)

Lucy Billington – Balloon Girl
Dan Burton – Tulsa
Jack Chissick – Mr Goldstone
    / Rich Man
Anita Louise Combe – Tessie Tura
Peter Davison – Herbie
Harry Dickman – Pop
Roger Dipper – L.A
Caitlin Garcia – Flower Girl
    (Cover Baby Louise)
Molly May Gibson – Balloon Girl
Louise Gold – Mazeppa
Lauren Hall – Delores / Waitress
    / Toreadorable (then June)
Clare Halse –
    Marjorie May / Toreadorable
Billy Hartman –
    Uncle Jocko / Cigar
Lauren Henson – Baby June
Tom Hodgkins – Mr Weber
    / Boucheron
Isla Huggins-Barr – Baby June
Kieran Jae – Yonkers / Pastey
Julie Legrand – Miss Cratchitt / Electra
Katie Mann – Flower Girl
    (Cover Baby June)
Danielle Morris – Geraldine
    / Toreadorable
Ruby Oliver – Flower Girl
    (Cover Baby June)
Damien Poole – Georgie / Kansas
Lara Pulver – Louise
Patrick Romer – Pop
Scarlet Roche – Baby June
Lucinda Shaw – Mother /
    Stripper / Showgirl
Imelda Staunton – Rose
Luke Street – Little Rock
Gemma Sutton – June (then Louise)
Lauren Varnham – Delores /
    Waitress / Toreadorable

Rose Walker – Baby Louise
Lara Wass – Flower Girl
    (Cover Baby Louise)
Lara Wollington – Baby Louise
Natalie Woods – Agnes
    / Toreadorable
Liz Ewing, Lauren Ingram, Tom
    Murphy, Philip Catchpole – Swing
Joseph Adams, Henry Austin, Ethan
    Bromley, Dominic Bryant, Ewan
    Hawkins, Patrick Lee, Jonah
    Mitchell, Harvey Pearce, Owen
    Pennington, Max Robson – Boys

Understudies

Louise Gold, Liz Ewing – Rose
Lauren Hall, Lauren Ingram – Louise
Tom Hodgkins, Tom Murphy – Herbie
Clare Halse, Lauren Hall – June
Kieran Jae, Philip Catchpole – Tulsa
Liz Ewing, Lucinda Shaw – Electra
Lucinda Shaw, Liz Ewing – Tessie Tura
Liz Ewing, Lucinda Shaw – Mazeppa

Creatives

Book – Arthur Laurents
Music – Jule Styne
Lyrics – Stephen Sondheim
Director – Jonathan Kent
Designer – Anthony Ward
Choreographer – Stephen Mear
Lighting Designer –
    Mark Henderson
Sound Designer – Paul Groothuis
Video Designer – Ian
    William Galloway
Musical Director / Orchestrator
    – Nicholas Skilbeck
Associate Director – Lloyd Wood
Associate Choreographer
    – Nikki Woollaston
Resident Choreographer
    and Children's Director
    – Jane McMurtrie

Hair, Wig & Make-up Design –
    Campbell Young Associates
Voice and Dialect Coach
    – Penny Dyer
Casting Director – Pippa Ailion CDG
Children's Casting Director and
    Administrator – Jo Hawes CDG
Original Production Direction and
    Choreography – Jerome Robbins
Orchestral Manager – Andy Barnwell

Stage Management

Stage Manager – John Caswell
Deputy Stage Manager – Claire Rundle
Assistant Stage Manager
    – Kay Sinclair
Assistant Stage Manager – Josh Chalk
Assistant Stage Manager –
    Hannah Swindell

Production

Company Manager – Eamonn Byrne
Head of Automation – Adam Morley
Automation Deputy – Tom King
Tech Swing – David Evans
Sound Operator No. 1 –
    Becky Stockting
Sound Operator No. 2 –
    Katie Weatherley
Sound Operator No. 3 –
    Charlie Cronin
Wardrobe Mistress – Faye Michel Jary
Wardrobe Deputy – Hannah Gibbs
Wardrobe Assistant – Clare Jay
Dresser – Michelle Hintzen-Walrond
Dresser – Tanya Aanderaa
Dresser – Marianne Adams
Dresser – Sophie Brunskill Martin
Dresser – Keshini Ranasinghe
Wigs Mistress – Lorna Stimson
Wigs Deputy – Maddy Johnson
Wigs Assistant – Henrik Torp
Wigs Dresser – Valentina Nesti
Chaperone – Misha Rowley

Chaperone – Katy Taylor
Chaperone – Kathy Outen
Chaperone – Janet O'Connor
Chaperone – Abi Marshall
Chowsie the Dog – Nessie and Scampie
    appear courtesy of A1 Animals

Orchestra

Musical Director – Nicholas Skilbeck
Keyboard / Assistant Musical
    Director – Tom Kelly
Harp / Keyboard – Carys Hughes
Drums – Matt Skelton
Double Bass – Laurence Ungless
Trumpet – Owain Harries
Trumpet – Nick Briggs
Trumpet – Dave Hopkin
Trombone – Jon Stokes
Trombone – Chris Traves
French Horn – Ruth O'Reilly
Alto Saxophone / Flute / Piccolo
    / Clarinet – Rupert Widdows
Tenor Saxophone / Clarinet
    / Flute – Steve Pierce
Tenor Saxophone / Clarinet
    / Oboe – Mike Davis
Baritone Saxophone / Clarinet / Bass
    Clarinet / Bassoon – Jay Craig
Orchestral Management – Musical
    Coordination Services Ltd

Producers

Michael Harrison Entertainment
David Ian Productions
Neil Laidlaw
Lee Dean
Tulchin/Bartner Productions
Michael Watt
Charles Diamond / Damian Arnold
Patrick Catullo / Aaron Click
Ramin Sabi / Seaview Productions
Ambassador Theatre Group
Chichester Festival Theatre

Hamlet

by William Shakespeare
Produced by Sonia Friedman
Productions
Presented by the Barbican
at the Barbican Theatre

Running dates:
5/8/15 – 31/10/15

Cast

Barry Aird – Danish Soldier /
    Norwegian Soldier / Understudy
    (Gravedigger / Priest)
Eddie Arnold – Captain / Servant
    / Understudy (Horatio /
    Guildenstern / Barnado)
Leo Bill – Horatio
Siân Brooke – Ophelia
Nigel Carrington – Cornelius /
    Understudy (Ghost / Polonius)
Ruairi Conaghan – Player King
Benedict Cumberbatch – Hamlet
Rudi Dharmalingam – Guildenstern
Colin Haigh – Priest / Messenger
    / Understudy (Claudius /
    Player King / Cornelius)
Paul Ham – Fencing Official /
    Understudy (Laertes / Rosencrantz)
Diveen Henry – Player
    Queen / Messenger
Anastasia Hille – Gertrude
Ciarán Hinds – Claudius
Kobna Holdbrook-Smith – Laertes
Karl Johnson – Ghost / Gravedigger
Jim Norton – Polonius
Amaka Okafor – Stage Manager
    / Official / Understudy
    (Ophelia / Player Queen)
Dan Parr – Barnardo /
    Understudy (Fortinbras)

Jan Shepherd – Courtier / Understudy
    (Gertrude / Voltemand)
Morag Siller – Voltemand
Matthew Steer – Rosencrantz
    / Understudy (Marcellus)
Sergo Vares – Fortinbras
Dwane Walcott – Marcellus
    / Understudy (Hamlet)

Creatives and Production Team

Director – Lyndsey Turner
Set – Es Devlin
Costume – Katrina Lindsay
Video – Luke Halls
Lighting – Jane Cox
Music – Jon Hopkins
Sound – Christopher Shutt
Movement – Sidi Larbi Cherkaoui
Fights – Bret Yount
Casting – Julia Horan CDG
Assistant Director – Sam Caird
Voice – Alison Bomber
Dialect – Majella Hurley
Production Manager – Patrick Molony
Production Manager – Kate West
Hair and Make-up – Carole Hancock
Costume Supervisor – Sabine Lemaître
Props Supervisors – Chris
    Marcus and Jonathan Hall
    for Marcus Hall Props
Visual Special Effects – The Twins FX
Associate Set Designer –
    Max Klaentschi
Associate Set Designer –
    Chiara Stephenson
Associate Set Designer –
    Machiko Weston
Associate Video Designer
    – Laura Perrett
Associate Lighting Designer
    – Victoria Brennan
Associate Lighting Designer
    – Alex Mannix

Movement Assistant –
    Navala Chaudhari
Movement Assistant –
    Jason Kittelberger
Associate Casting Director
    – Lotte Hines CDG
Assistant Costume Supervisor
    – Heidi Bryan
Company Stage Manager
    – Richard Clayton
Stage Manager – Pandora Elrington
Deputy Stage Manager – Jenefer Tait
Assistant Stage Manager –
    Oliver Bagwell Purefoy
Assistant Stage Manager
    – Genna Hill
Head of Wardrobe – Thea Kay
Deputy Head of Wardrobe
    – Emma Sheppard
Dresser – Jordan Colls
Dresser – Ellen Rey de Castro
Dresser – Emma Rosling
Dresser – Shaun Walters
Dresser – Olivia Ward
Head of Hair and Wigs –
    Rebecca Kempton
Deputy Head of Hair and
    Wigs – Kiri Mellalieu
Sound Operator – Adam Taylor
Sound No. 2 – Dan Ford

Marketing, Sales and Advertising

AKA

Press

Premier PR

General Management

Diane Benjamin and Lucie Lovatt
    for Sonia Friedman Productions

Hangmen

at the Royal Court

Running dates:
10/9/15 – 10/10/15

Cast

Josef Davies – Hennessy
James Dryden – Clegg
Johnny Flynn – Mooney
Graeme Hawley – Bill
John Hodgkinson – Pierrepoint
Ralph Ineson – Inspector Fry
Bronwyn James – Shirley
David Morrissey – Harry
Ryan Pope – Charlie
Sally Rogers – Alice
Simon Rouse – Arthur
Reece Shearsmith – Syd

Creatives

Writer – Martin McDonagh
Director – Matthew Dunster
Designer – Anna Fleischle
Lighting Designer – Joshua Carr
Sound Designer –
    Ian Dickinson for Autograph
Assistant Director – Roy
    Alexander Weise
Casting Director – Amy Ball CDG

Stage Management

Stage Manager – Heidi Lennard
Deputy Stage Manager –
    Anastasia Dyson
Assistant Stage Manager
    – Claire Baldwin
Stage Management Placement
    – Luisa Sanchez

Production

Production Manager – Jamie Maisey
Costume Supervisor –
    Lucy Walshaw
Fight Director – Kate Waters
Dialect Coach – Zabarjad Salam
Set Build – Scott Fleary
Set Build – Cardiff Theatrical Services

Press
The Corner Shop PR

Happy Days
at the Young Vic

Running dates:
13/2/15 – 21/3/15

Cast
David Beames – Willie
Juliet Stevenson – Winnie
Creatives
Writer – Samuel Beckett
Director – Natalie Abrahami
Design – Vicki Mortimer
Light – Paule Constable
Sound – Tom Gibbons
Movement – Joseph Alford
Voice – Emma Woodvine
Casting – Julia Horan CDG
Associate Lighting Designer
    – Nicki Brown
Associate Sound Designer
    – Sean Ephgrave
Assistant Director – Anna Girvan
Stage Management
Stage Manager – Laura Draper
Deputy Stage Manager –
    Catherine Buffrey
Assistant Stage Manager – Sam Shuck
Production
Production Manager – Matt Noddings
Costume Supervisor – Lynette Mauro
Props Supervisor – Lisa Buckley
Wigs, Hair and Make-up
    Manager – Claudia Stoltz
Production Electrician – Steve Andrew
Sound Operator – Jamie McIntyre
Duty Technician – Rachel Bottomley

Dresser and Costume Maintenance
    – Lauren Penfold
Make-up By – Naomi Donne
Dress Made By – Sara Mercer
Hat Made By – Mark Wheeler

Hay Fever
Theatre Royal Bath Productions
presents
Hay Fever
at the Duke of York's Theatre

Running dates:
29/4/15 – 1/8/15

Cast
Celeste Dodwell – Jackie Coryton
Edward Franklin – Simon Bliss
Felicity Kendal – Judith Bliss
Edward Killingback – Sandy Tyrell
Alice Orr-Ewing – Sorel Bliss
Simon Shepherd – David Bliss
Michael Simkins – Richard
    Greatham
Mossie Smith – Clara
Sara Stewart – Myra Arundel
Emma Bown – Understudy Judith
    Bliss / Myra Arundel / Clara
Whitney Boyd – Understudy
    Sorel Bliss / Jackie Coryton
Andy Hawthorne – Understudy
    David Bliss / Richard Greatham
James Mack – Understudy
    Simon Bliss / Sandy Tyrell
Creatives
Writer – Noël Coward
Director – Lindsay Posner
Designer – Peter McKintosh
Lighting Designer – Paul Pyant
Sound Designer – Fergus O'Hare

Composer – Michael Bruce
Casting Director – Ginny
    Schiller CDG
Associate Director – Tom
    Attenborough
Associate Set Designer –
    Simon Anthony Wells
Stage Management
Company Stage Manager
    – Adrian Ord
Deputy Stage Manager –
    William Buckenham
Assistant Stage Manager
    – Whitney Boyd
Assistant Stage Manager
    – James Mack
Production
Production Manager – Mark
    Carey for Venture-Event Ltd
Production Electrician /
    Relight – Sonic Harrison
Costume Supervisor – Mary Charlton
Properties Supervisor – Robin Morgan
Properties Supervisor – Lindah Balfour
Fight Director – Bret Yount
Voice Coach – Budgie Salam
Wardrobe and Wig Master
    – Rod Bicknell
Wardrobe and Wig Mistress
    – Jess Bishop
Press
Arthur Leone PR
Marketing
Jason Maddocks
Nicky Palmer
Alan Henning

Henry V
The Royal Shakespeare Company's
production of

Henry V
by William Shakespeare
at the Barbican Theatre

Running dates:
7/11/15 – 24/1/16

Cast
Daniel Abbott – Duke of
    Gloucester / Monsieur Le Fer
Martin Bassindale – Boy
Antony Byrne – Pistol
Sean Chapman – Exeter
Oliver Ford Davies – Chorus
Nicholas Gerard-Martin –
    Orleans / Bishop of Ely
Robert Gilbert – Dauphin
Alex Hassell – Henry V
Jim Hooper – Canterbury
    / Erpingham
Jennifer Kirby – Katherine
Jane Lapotaire – Queen Isobel
Sam Marks – Constable of France
Dale Mathurin – Bates / Bedford
Christopher Middleton – Nym /
    Warwick / Governor of Harfleur
Evelyn Miller – Rambures
    / Lady-in-waiting
Keith Osborn – Montjoy / Scroop
Sarah Parks – Mistress Quickly
Leigh Quinn – Alice
Joshua Richards – Bardolph / Fluellen
Simon Thorp – King of France
Obioma Ugoala – Grey / Gower
Andrew Westfield – Westmorland
    / MacMorris
Simon Yadoo – Cambridge /
    Michael Williams / Jamy
Creatives
Writer – William Shakespeare
Director – Gregory Doran
Designer – Stephen Brimson Lewis

Composer – Paul Englishby
Voice Coach – Kate Godfrey
Associate Director – Owen Horsley
Movement Director – Michael Ashcroft
Fight Director – Terry King
Lighting Designer – Tim Mitchell
Music Director – Gareth Ellis
Sound Designer – Martin Slavin
Casting – Helena Palmer CDG

Stage Management
Company Manager – Ben Tyreman
Stage Manager – Patricia Davenport
Deputy Stage Manager – Klare Roger
Assistant Stage Manager
  – Angela Garrick

Production
Production Manager – Simon Ash
Costume Supervisor –
  Stephanie Arditti
Assistant Costume Supervisor
  – Sarah Holmes
Senior Sound Technician
  – Steve Atkinson
Senior Lighting Technician
  – Jack Champion
Wardrobe Mistress –
  Delfina Angiolini
Deputy Wardrobe Master
  – Rhys Tucker
Wig Mistress – Emma Taylor
Deputy Wig Mistress –
  Roxanne Gatrell
Dresser – Sophie Barnes
Dresser – Sarah Burton
Dresser – Charlotte Smith
Dresser – Matthew Warhurst

Musicians
Soprano – Helena Raeburn
Woodwind – Max Gittings
Violin – Debs White
Guitar – Dario Rossetti-Bonell
Trumpet – Andrew Stone-Fewings

Trumpet – Chris Seddon
Tuba – Ian Foster
Percussion – Zands Duggan
Keyboards – Gareth Ellis

How to Hold Your Breath
at the Royal Court

Running dates:
4/2/15 – 21/3/15

Cast
Christine Bottomley – Jasmine
Neil D'Souza – Interviewer /
  Train Inspector / Punter
Peter Forbes – Librarian
Siobhán McSweeney – Interviewer
  / Marta / Telephone Operator
Maxine Peake – Dana
Danusia Samal – Interviewer
  / Doctor / Clara
Michael Shaeffer – Jarron
Joshua Campbell, Raghad Chaar,
  Soledad Delahoz, Maris Flamino,
  Michael Jinks, Djordje Jovanovic,
  Connor Mills, Mark Ota, Aaron
  Peters, Alison Porter, Ruth
  Pugh, Javier Rasero, Jessica
  Simet, Ben Tiramani, Temi
  Wilkey – Supernumeraries

Creatives
Writer – Zinnie Harris
Director – Vicky Featherstone
Designer – Chloe Lamford
Lighting Designer – Paule Constable
Composer – Stuart Earl
Sound Designer – Gareth Fry
Movement Director – Ann Yee
Assistant Director – Debbie Hannan
Casting Director – Amy Ball CDG

Stage Management
Stage Manager – Joni Carter
Deputy Stage Manager
  – Fiona Kennedy
Assistant Stage Manager
  – Heather Cryan
Stage Management Work
  Placement – Beth McKnight

Production
Production Manager – Niall Black
Costume Supervisor – Lucy Walshaw
Set construction – MDM Props Ltd
Set construction – Weld-Fab
  Stage Engineering Ltd

Press
The Corner Shop PR

Husbands & Sons
at the National Theatre,
Dorfman Stage

Running dates:
19/10/15 – 10/2/16

Cast
Flynn Allen – Jack Holroyd
Joe Armstrong – Luther Gascoigne
Matthew Barker – Joe Gascoigne
John Biggins – Carlin
Cassie Bradley – Maggie Pearson
Louise Brealey – Minnie Gascoigne
Susan Brown – Mrs Gascoigne
Anne-Marie Duff – Lizzie Holroyd
Oliver Finnegan – Jack Holroyd
Julia Ford – Lydia Lambert
Johnny Gibbon – Ernest Lambert
Tala Gouveia – Nellie
  Lambert / Laura
Lloyd Hutchinson – Walter Lambert
Martin Marquez – Charles Holroyd

Philip McGinley – Blackmore
Katherine Pearce – Gertie Coomer
Tommy Rodger – Jack Holroyd
Josie Walker – Mrs Purdy / Clara
Sue Wallace – Grandmother

Creatives
Director – Marianne Elliott
Writer – D H Lawrence
Writer / Adaptation – Ben Power
Designer – Bunny Christie
Lighting Designer – Lucy Carter
Video Designer – Tal Rosner
Movement Director – Scott Graham
Music – Adrian Sutton
Sound Designer – Ian Dickinson
Fight Director – Kate Waters
Company Voice Work –
  Jeannette Nelson
Dialect Coach – Penny Dyer
Associate Director – Katy Rudd
Casting – Charlotte Bevan CDG

Stage Management
Stage Manager – Laura Flowers
Deputy Stage Manager –
  Janice Heyes
Assistant Stage Managers –
  Katie Barrett, Leona Nally

Production
Production Manager – Martin Barron
Deputy Production Manager
  – Sarah O'Connor
Project Draughting – Alan Bain
Project Draughting – Jo Dixon
Digital Art – Daniel Radley-Bennett
Costume Supervisor –
  Caroline Waterman
Wigs, Hair and Make-up
  Supervisor – Renata Hill
Prop Supervisor – Eleanor Smith
Lighting Supervisor – Anna Matthews
Lighting Programmer –
  Nadene Wheatley

Video Production Engineer
  – Chris Jackson
Video Programmer –
  Matthew Morgans
Video Programmer – Daniel Haggerty
Production Sound Engineer
  – Alex Caplen
Sound Operator – Matthew Ferrie
Stage Supervisor – Lee Harrington
Rigging Supervisor – Riche Tarr
Rigging Supervisor – Barry Peavot
Construction Supervisor – Dave Cotton
Scenic Art Supervisor – Daina Ennis
Producer
Producer (NT) – Pádraig Cusack
Producer (Royal Exchange
  Theatre) – Richard Morgan

King Charles III

Sonia Friedman Productions, Stuart
Thompson Productions and the
Almeida Theatre
in association with Lee Dean &
Charles Diamond and Tulchin
Bartner Productions
present the Almeida Theatre
Production of
King Charles III

Running dates:
2/9/14 – 31/1/15

Cast
Katie Brayben – Sarah /
  Ghost / TV Producer
Oliver Chris – William
Richard Goulding – Harry
Nyasha Hatendi – Spencer
  / Nick / Sir Gordon
Adam James – Mr Evans

Margot Leicester – Camilla
Tim Pigott-Smith – Charles
Miles Richardson – James Reiss
  / Understudy (Charles)
Tom Robertson – Couttsey
  / Clive / Sir Michael
Nicholas Rowe – Mr Stevens
Tafline Steen – Jess
Lydia Wilson – Kate
Pete Collis – Cover Mr Evans /
  James Reiss / Mr Stevens
Edward Elgood – Cover Harry /
  Couttsey / Clive / Sir Michael
Joe Eyre – Cover William /
  Spencer / Nick / Sir Gordon
Elinor Lawless – Cover Sarah / Ghost
  / TV Producer / Jess / Kate
Emily Swain – Cover Camilla
Musicians
Musical Director / Musician
  – Belinda Sykes
Musician – Anna-Helena McLean
Creatives
Writer – Mike Bartlett
Director – Rupert Goold
Designer – Tom Scutt
Composer – Jocelyn Pook
Lighting – Jon Clark
Sound – Paul Arditti
Casting Director – Joyce Nettles
Associate Director – Whitney Mosery
Movement Director – Anna Morrissey
Associate Lighting Designer
  – Peter Harrison
Associate Sound Designer
  – Christopher Reid
Assistant Director – Jessica Edwards
Voice and Text Coach – Alison Bomber
Production
Production Manager – Patrick Molony
Costume Supervisor – Rachel Dickson
Company Stage Manager

  – Nicholas Bromley
Deputy Stage Manager
  – Katie Barrett
Assistant Stage Manager
  – Eleanor Butcher
Wardrobe Mistress – Kate Adeney
Hair and Make-up Mistress
  – Michelle Piper
Dresser – Keshini Ranasinghe
Sound Operator – Helen Skiera
Sound Operator – Charlie Simpson
Fight Director – Ruth Cooper
  Brown of RC Annie Ltd
Fight Director – Ruth Cooper
  Brown of RC Annie Ltd
Assistant Production
  Manager – Kate West
General Management
Sonia Friedman Productions
  and Almeida Theatre
Press
The Corner Shop PR
Marketing
AKA

King John

A co-production between
Shakespeare's Globe and Royal &
Derngate, Northampton.
at Shakespeare's Globe

Running dates:
1/6/15 – 27/6/15

Cast
Laurence Belcher – Arthur / Henry
Simon Coates – King Philip
  of France / Melun
Aruhan Galieva – Blanche of
  Castile / Peter of Pomfret

Joseph Marcell – Chatillon
  / Cardinal Pandulph
Barbara Marten – Eleanor of
  Aquitaine / Lady Faulconbridge
Mark Meadows – Hubert
Tanya Moodie – Constance
Ciarán Owens – Robert
  Faulconbridge / Louis the Dauphin
Daniel Rabin – Salisbury
Jo Stone-Fewings – King John
Giles Terera – Pembroke / Austria
Alex Waldmann – The Bastard
Creatives
Writer – William Shakespeare
Director – James Dacre
Designer – Jonathan Fensom
Composer – Orlando Gough
Choreographer – Scott Ambler
Lighting Designer and Production
  Manager – Paul Russell
Director of Music – Bill Barclay
Casting Director – Matilda James
Artistic Director – Dominic Dromgoole
Executive Producer – Tom Bird
Casting, Creative and Filming
  Associate – Karishma Balani
Artistic Coordinator – Jessica Lusk
Music Coordinator – James Maloney
Staff Director – Eduard Lewis
Fight Director – Rachel Bown-Williams
Fight Director – Ruth Cooper-Brown
Globe Associate – Text – Giles Block
Globe Associate – Movement
  – Glynn MacDonald
Voice and Dialect – Martin McKellan
Voice and Dialect – Alex Bingley
Costume Supervisor – Laura Rushton
Text Assistant – Hannah
  Boland Moore
Stage Management
Stage Manager – Sally Hughes
Stage Manager – Mary O'Hanlon

Deputy Stage Manager
 – Sarah Lyndon
Assistant Stage Manager
 – Rebecca Toland
Technical Stage Manager
 – Bryan Paterson

Production

Lighting Designer and Production
 Manager – Paul Russell
Company Manager – Marion Marrs
Technical Manager – Wills
Wardrobe Manager – Megan Cassidy
Wardrobe Deputy – Emma Seychell
Wardrobe Assistant – Hanna Randall
Wardrobe Assistant – Rachel Thomas
Wigs, Hair and Make-up
 Manager – Pam Humpage
Wigs, Hair and Make-up Deputy
 – Hayley Thompson
Wigs, Hair and Make-up Assistant
 – Lee Appleton
Wigs, Hair and Make-up
 Assistant – Victoria Young
Production Assistant – Lottie Newth
Assistant Company Manager
 – Harry Niland
Assistant Production Manager
 – Fay Powell-Thomas
Costume Maker – Eve Collins
Costume Maker – Helen Dyer-Grieves
Costume Maker – Becky Graham
Costume Maker – Jane Gonin
Costume Maker – Lynn Hamilton
Costume Maker – Lil Harrison
Costume Maker – Sue James
Costume Maker – Alison Kirkpatrick
Costume Maker – Wendy Knowles
Costume Maker – Aislinn Luton
Costume Maker – Lindsay Padgett
Costume Maker – Ceri Price
Costume Maker – Elspeth Threadgold
Costume Maker – Mervyn Wallace

Shoes – Trippen
Armour – Norton Armouries
Printing – Emily Hussey
Accessories – Janet Spriggs
Foiling – Nicole Killeen
Dyeing – Schultz and Wiremu
Carpenter – John Batt
Carpenter – Kes Hayter
Carpenter – Rupert Mead
Carpenter – Simeon Tachev
Scenic Artist – Toni Bysouth
Scenic Artist – Kirsty Durman
Scenic Artist – Jen Hallas-Riddick
Scenic Artist – Sarah Kier
Scenic Artist – Thomasin Marshall
Scenic Artist – Gerard Strong
Head Sculpture and Cast – Ross White
Coronation Throne – PMB Ltd

Musicians

Musical Director / Percussion
 – Phil Hopkins
Clarinet / Bass Clarinet / Soprano
 Saxophone – Sarah Homer
Wind Instruments / Harmonium
 – Paul Johnson
Music Trainee, Supported
 by Andrew Lloyd Webber
 Foundation – Aleks Giersz

Kinky Boots

Daryl Roth, Hal Luftig
James L. Nederlander, Terry Allen
Kramer, Playful Productions, CJ E&M
Jayne Baron Sherman, Just For Laughs
Theatricals/Judith Ann Abrams,
Yasuhiro Kawana, Jane Bergére
Allan S. Gordon & Adam S. Gordon,
Ken Davenport, Hunter Arnold, Lucy
& Phil Suarez, Bryan Bantry,
Ron Fierstein & Dorsey Regal,

Independent Presenters Network, Jim
Kierstead/Gregory Rae
BB Group/Christina Papagjika,
Brian Smith/Tom and Connie Walsh,
Warren Trepp and Jujamcyn Theaters
in associations with Cameron
Mackintosh
present
Kinky Boots
at the Adelphi Theatre

1st performance:
21/8/15

Cast

Nana Agyeman-Bediako – Young Lola
Paul Ayres – Harry
Jeremy Batt – Angel
Jamie Baughan – Don
Arun Blair-Mangat – Angel
Marcus Collins – Angel
Beau Cripps – Young Charlie
Ben Dawson – Young Charlie
Killian Donnelly – Charlie Price
James Gava – Young Lola
Edward Green – Young Charlie
Robert Grose – Simon Senior
Gillian Hardie – Trish
Chlöe Hart – Pat
Matt Henry – Lola
Michael Hobbs – George
Luke Jackson – Angel
Adam Lake – Angel
Amy Lennox – Lauren
Verity Quade – Milan Stage Manager
Tumo Reetsang – Young Lola
Amy Ross – Nicola
Javier Santos – Angel
Alan Vicary – Mr. Price
Michael Vinsen – Richard Bailey
Paul Ayres, Robert Grose, Gillian
 Hardie, Chlöe Hart, Sophie

Isaacs, Sean Needham, Tim
Prottey-Jones, Verity Quade,
Alan Vicary, Michael Vinsen,
Bleu Woodward – Ensemble
Gemma Atkins, Emma Crossley,
Jordan Fox, Callum Francis, Robert
Jones (Assistant Dance Captain),
Catherine Milsom, Dominic
Tribuzio (Dance Captain) – Swings

Understudies

Callum Francis, Arun Blair-
 Mangat, Marcus Collins – Lola
Paul Ayres, Michael Vinsen – Charlie
Sophie Isaacs, Emma
 Crossley – Lauren
Tim Prottey-Jones, Sean
 Needham – Don
Gemma Atkins, Bleu
 Woodward – Nicola
Sean Needham, Tim Prottey-
 Jones – George

Creatives

Book – Harvey Fierstein
Music and Lyrics – Cyndi Lauper
Director and Choreographer
 – Jerry Mitchell
Music Supervisor, Arranger and
 Orchestrator – Stephen Oremus
Scenic Design – David Rockwell
Costume Design – Gregg Barnes
Lighting Design – Kenneth Posner
Sound Design – John Shivers
Hair Design – Josh Marquette
Make-up Design – Randy
 Houston Mercer
US Properties Coordinator –
 Kathy Fabian / Propstar
US Associate Choreographer
 – Rusty Mowery
US Associate Director – D.B. Bonds
UK Associate Director –
 Dominic Shaw

UK Associate Choreographer
– Darren Carnall
UK Musical Director – Peter White
Casting Director – Jill Green CDG
Children's Casting and Children's
Administration – Debbie O'Brien
UK Props Supervisors – Chris
Marcus and Jonathan Hall
for Marcus Hall Props
Production Manager –
Patrick Molony
UK General Managers –
Playful Productions
Worldwide Management – Aaron
Lustbader for Foresight Theatrical
Producers – Daryl Roth, Hal Luftig,
James L. Nederlander, Terry Allen
Kramer, Playful Productions, CJ
E&M, Jayne Baron Sherman, Just
For Laughs Theatricals/Judith Ann
Abrams, Yasuhiro Kawana, Jane
Bergére, Allan S. Gordon & Adam
S. Gordon, Ken Davenport, Hunter
Arnold, Lucy & Phil Suarez, Bryan
Bantry, Ron Fierstein & Dorsey
Regal, Independent Presenters
Network, Jim Kierstead, Gregory
Rae, BB Group/Christina
Papagjika, Brian Smith/Tom and
Connie Walsh, Warren Trepp and
Jujamcyn Theaters in association
with Cameron Mackintosh

Stage Management
Company Manager –
Sophie Gabszewicz
Stage Manager – Jason Golbourn
Deputy Stage Manager –
Heather Teasdale
Assistant Stage Manager
– Dave Armstrong
Assistant Stage Manager
– Duncan Parker

Assistant Stage Manager –
Annique Reynolds
Orchestra
Musical Director / Keyboard 1
– Peter White
Associate Musical Director /
Keyboard 2 – Jim Henson
Drums – Andy McGlasson
Bass Guitar – Phil Mulford
Guitar 1 – Nico Sabatini
Guitar 2 – Mark Wraith
Trumpet – Mark White
Trombone – Pat Hartley
Reeds – Paul Stevens
Violin – Jo Archard
Cello – Chris Fish
Associate Music Supervisor
and Additional Music
Arrangements – Brian Usifer
Synthesizer Programmer
– Randy Cohen
Music Copying – Emily Grishman
Music Preparation
Electronic Drum Programmer
– Sammy Merendino
Music Track Editor – Derik Lee
UK Music Technology – Phij Adams
UK Orchestral Management –
Accord Music Productions Ltd

Press
Jo Allan PR

Linda
at the Royal Court

Running dates:
26/11/15 – 9/1/16

Cast
Imogen Byron – Bridget

Karla Crome – Alice
Jaz Deol – Luke
Noma Dumezweni – Linda
Amy Beth Hayes – Amy
Dominic Mafham – Neil
Merriel Plummer – Stevie
Ian Redford – Dave
Creatives
Writer – Penelope Skinner
Director – Michael Longhurst
Set Designer – Es Devlin
Costume Designer – Alex Lowde
Video Designer – Luke Halls
Lighting Designer – Lee Curran
Composer and Sound Designer
– Richard Hammarton
Movement Director – Imogen Knight
Voice and Dialect Coach – Penny Dyer
Casting Director – Amy Ball
Associate Director – Katy Rudd
Fight Director – Bret Yount
Stage Management
Stage Manager – Michael Dennis
Deputy Stage Manager – Sarah Hellicar
Assistant Stage Manager
– Osnat Koblenz
Stage Management Placement
– Samantha Leese
Production
Production Manager – Matt Noddings
Set Build – Scott Fleary

Made in Dagenham
Stage Entertainment in association
with Glass Half Full Productions,
Just for Laughs Theatricals, Paula
Marie Black
present
Made in Dagenham The Musical
at the Adelphi Theatre

Running dates:
9/10/14 – 11/4/15

Cast
Naana Agyel-Ampadu – Cass
Thomas Aldridge – Barry
Gemma Arterton – Rita O'Grady
Isla Blair – Connie
David Cardy – Monty
Kate Coysten – Flo/ Dance Captain
Heather Craney – Clare
Julius D'Silva – Hopkins
Sophie-Louise Dann – Barbara Castle
Adrian Der Gregorian –
Eddie O'Grady
Grace Doherty – Sharon O'Grady
Kath Duggan – Tea Lady /
Assistant Dance Captain
Gemma Fray – Sharon O'Grady
Naomi Frederick – Lisa Hopkins
Steve Furst – Tooley
Scott Garnham – Buddy Cortina
Annie Guy – Sharon O'Grady
Mark Hadfield – Harold Wilson
Christopher Howell – Arthur
Sophie Isaacs – Sandra
Ian Jervis – Sid
Paul Kemble – Bill
Emma Lindars – Pauline
Harry Marcus – Graham O'Grady
Ben Mineard – Graham O'Grady
Jo Napthine – Valerie
Scott Paige – Harry
Tracey Penn – Charlotte
Ivy Pratt – Sharon O'Grady
Tommy Rodger – Graham O'Grady
Gemma Salter – Joan
Josh Shadbolt – Graham O'Grady
Gareth Snook – Macer
Rachel Spurrell – Phyllis
Emily Squibb – Rose
Sophie Stanton – Beryl

Karli Vale – Jesse
René Zagger – Stan
Understudies
Gemma Salter, Kate Coysten
  – Rita O'Grady
Thomas Aldridge, Scott
  Garnham – Eddie O'Grady
Jo Napthine, Rachel Spurrell – Connie
Ian Jervis, René Zagger – Monty
Tracey Penn, Karli Vale – Clare
Rachel Spurrell, Emma
  Lindars – Barbara Castle
René Zagger, Paul Kemble – Hopkins
Kate Coysten, Tracey Penn
  – Lisa Hopkins
Gareth Snook, Scott
  Garnham – Tooley
Paul Kemble, Christopher
  Howell – Harold Wilson
Karli Vale, Gemma Salter – Sandra
Emma Lindars, Jo Napthine – Beryl
Creatives
Book – Richard Bean
Music – David Arnold
Lyrics – Richard Thomas
Director – Rupert Goold
Choreographer – Aletta Collins
Set and Costume Designer
  – Bunny Christie
Associate Set Designer – Tim
  McQuillen-Wright
Hair, Wigs and Make-up –
  Campbell Young Associates
Costume Supervisor –
  Stephanie Arditti
Production Manager – Matt Towell
Associate Director –
  Michael Fentiman
Associate Choreographer
  – Shelby Williams
Casting Director – David
  Grindrod Associates CDG

Children's Casting Director
  – Jessica Ronane CDG
Lighting Designer – Jon Clark
Sound Designer – Richard Brooker
Video Designer – Treatment
Music Supervisor – Phil Bateman
Orchestrations – Steve Sidwell
Musical Director – Tom Deering
Stage Management
Stage Manager – Stuart Tucker
Deputy Stage Manager
  – Patrick Stanier
Assistant Stage Manager / Book
  Cover – Kerstin Muller
Assistant Stage Manager / Book
  Cover – Jemma Milne
Technical Assistant Stage
  Manager – Martyn Sands
Production
Resident Director – Vik Sivalingam
Company Manager –
  Jacqueline C Morgan
Head of Sound – Digby Shaw
Sound No. 2 – Ania Klimowicz
Sound No. 3 – Kelsham
  Buckman-Drage
Head of Automation –
  Roberto Raskovsky
Automation No. 2 – Jamie Lawrence
Head of Wardrobe – Tim Gradwell
Wardrobe Deputy –
  Rachael McIntyre
Wardrobe Assistant –
  Samantha Murphy
Dresser – Sophie Barclay
Dresser – Florence Griffiths
Dresser – Leanne Hired
Dresser – Matthew McKenna
Dresser – Ben Rahman
Dresser – Mandie Wilde
Head of Wigs – Mark Marson
Wigs Deputy – Natalie Sharp

Wigs Assistant – Alice Dawson-Whale
Wigs Assistant – Carlos Fidalgo
Wigs Dresser – Ria Knoll
Head Chaperone – Anthea Conradie
Children's Chaperone –
  Nicky Downing
Orchestra
Musical Director / Piano
  – Tom Deering
Keyboards / Assistant Musical
  Director – Will Stuart
Keyboards / 2nd Cover Musical
  Director – Alf Clewlow
Drums – Andy McGlasson
Bass Guitar / Double Bass
  – Don Richardson
Guitar – Adam Goldsmith
Guitar – Daniel Short
Percussion – James Turner
Reeds – Adrian Revell
Reeds – Mike Haughton
Trumpet – Patrick White
Orchestral Management – Musical
  Services Coordination Ltd
Keyboard Programmer – Phij Adams
Producers
Producer – Stage Entertainment
Co-Producer – Glass Half
  Full Productions
Co-Producer – Just For
  Laughs Theatricals
Co-Producer – Paula Marie Black

Matilda
The Royal Shakespeare Company's
production of
Roald Dahl's
Matilda The Musical
at the Cambridge Theatre

Running dates:
25/10/11 – present

Cast
Leo Ayres – Tommy
Charlie Barnard – Tommy
Michael Begley – Mr Wormwood
Thomas Berry – Nigel
Fifi Bloomsbury-Kheier – Amanda
Robbie Boyle – Swing
John Brannoch – Rudolpho
Oliver Brooks – Children's
  Entertainer / Sergei
Tilly Cook – Hortensia
Jonathan Cordin – Swing
Bronte Cosgrave – Alice
Ellie Dadd – Amanda
Connor Deeks – Nigel
Carla Dixon – Alice
Dayna Dixon – Hortensia
Olly Dobson – Michael Wormwood
Denzel Eboji – Bruce
Craige Els – Miss Trunchbull
Demi Goodman – Cook
Hannah Hague – Lavender
Keyaan Hameed – Bruce
Elliot Harper – The Escapologist
Will Hawksworth – Doctor
Evie Hone – Matilda
Caoimhe Judd – Amanda
Sophia Keaveney – Hortensia
Kate Kenrick – Swing
Anna-Louise Knight – Matilda
Lara McDonnell – Matilda
Rachel Moran – Swing
Lia Moxom – Alice
Tom Muggeridge – Henchman
Demi Olawoyin – Lavender
Miria Parvin – Miss Honey
Ben Perkins – Eric
Max Reader – Eric
Jason Rennie – Bruce

Charlotte Scott – The Acrobat
Matthew Serafini – Henchman
Joe Sheridan – Tommy
Jacob Smith – Nigel
Biancha Szynal – Swing
Rebecca Thornhill –
    Mrs Wormwood
Eva Trodd – Lavender
Laura Tyrer – Henchwoman
Harrison Vaughan – Bruce
Lizzie Wells – Matilda
Sharlene Whyte – Mrs Phelps
Jamie Wilding – Eric

Creatives
Book – Dennis Kelly
Music and Lyrics – Tim Minchin
Director – Matthew Warchus
Choreographer – Peter Darling
Set and Costume Design – Rob Howell
Orchestrations and Additional
    Music – Christopher Nightingale
Lighting Design – Hugh Vanstone
Sound Design – Simon Baker
Illusion – Paul Kieve
Producer – The Royal
    Shakespeare Company
Executive Producer –
    André Ptaszynski
Executive Producer – Denise Wood
Resident Director – Joseph Pitcher
Resident Choreographer
    – Fabian Aloise
Children's Musical Director
    – Laura Bangay
Voice Coach – Liz Flint
Assistant Director – Anna Fox

Stage Management
Stage Manager – Rhian Thomas
Deputy Stage Manager –
    Claire Rees-Smith
Assistant Stage Manager
    – Ceejay Davies

Assistant Stage Manager
    – Ricky Greene
Assistant Stage Manager –
    Chelsea Shorrock
Assistant Stage Manager
    – Calum Wyllie

Production
Company Manager – Roger Penhale
Deputy Company Manager
    – Lisa McLean
Head of Wardrobe – Reah Butterly
Deputy Head of Wardrobe
    – Helena Rose
Wardrobe Assistant –
    Emma Holdsworth
Wardrobe Assistant – Cara Kingsley
Wardrobe Assistant – Kyle Stewart
Dresser – Mary Nguyen
Dresser – David Tate
Head of Wigs and Make-up
    – Anita Zuberbühler
Deputy Head of Wigs and
    Make-up – Kirsty Lamb
Wigs and Make-up Assistant
    – Carlos Fidalgo
Wigs and Make-up Assistant
    – Lydia Bailey
Head of Sound – Leigh Davies
Deputy Head of Sound –
    Mark Edmondson
Sound Technician – Peter Reed
Sound Technician – Sammy Myers
Head of Automation – Adam Calver
Deputy Head of Automation –
    Christopher Ashmore-Short
Automation Technician
    – Karen Wychgel
Lead Chaperone – Sue De Souza
Deputy Lead Chaperone
    – Charlotte Green
Chaperone – Donna Blake
Chaperone – Abigail Bourne

Chaperone – Mike Marison
Chaperone – Hayley Sperring
Chaperone – Jess Steffen
House Mother – Sandra Chapman
House Mother – Maggie Colbert

Musicians
Musical Director / Keyboard
    – Laurie Perkins
Assistant Musical Director /
    Keyboard – Spencer James
Flute / Alto Saxophone /
    Clarinet – Kay Bywater
Tenor Saxophone / Clarinet /
    Bass Clarinet – Pete Whyman
Trumpet / Cornet / Piccolo
    Trumpet – Simon Lenton
Trumpet / Flugelhorn / Piccolo
    Trumpet – Toby Coles
Trombone / Bass Trombone
    – Richard Edwards
Cello – Justin Pearson
Guitars – Peter Walton
Upright Bass / Electric Bass
    – Rutledge Turnlund
Kit / Percussion – Jim Fleeman

Press
The Corner Shop PR

McQueen
at the Theatre Royal Haymarket

Running dates:
24/8/15 – 17/10/15

The Cast
Carly Bawden – Dahlia
Michael Bertenshaw – Mr Hitchcock
Amber Doyle – Dance Captain
Eloise Hymas– Twin /
    Ensemble Dancer

Amelia Jackson – Twin /
    Ensemble Dancer
Tracy-Ann Oberman – Isabella
Laura Rees – Arabella
Stephen Wight – Lee
Harry Alexander, Sophia
    Apollonia, Amber Doyle,
    George Hill, Rachel Louisa
    Maybank – Ensemble Dancers
Jessica Buckby, Andrei Teodor Iliescu
    – Onstage Swing Ensemble Dancers
Emma Bown – Understudy
    Isabella / Arabella
Abby Cassidy – Understudy
    Dahlia / Arabella
Michael Eaves – Understudy
    Mr Hitchcock
Kevin Wathen – Understudy Lee

Creatives
Writer – James Phillips
Director – John Caird
Production Designer – David Farley
Choreographer – Christopher Marney
Video Designer – Timothy Bird
Lighting Designer – David Howe
Sound Designer – John Leonard
Wig Designer – Linda McKnight
Associate Director – Emma Baggott
Casting Director – Kate Plantin CDG
Casting Director – Jayne Collins CDG
Casting Director – Adam Maskell

Stage Management
Stage Manager – Gaz Wall
Deputy Stage Manager –
    John Pemberton
Assistant Stage Manager
    – Erin Coubrough

Production
Company Manager –
    Jacqueline C Morgan
Wardrobe Mistress – Katy
    Kettleborough

Wardrobe Deputy –
William McGovern
Wardrobe Assistant – Rose Adolph
Wig, Hair and Make-up
Mistress – Sophie Bolton
Props Supervisor – Lizzie Frankl
Costume Supervisor – Katy
Kettleborough

Producers
Executive Producer – Julian
Stoneman Associates
Producer – Robert Mackintosh
Producer – Amir Ltd
Producer – Hilary A. Williams
Producer – Deborah Negri
Producer – Dead Posh Productions
General Manager – Julian
Stoneman Associates

Medea,
by Euripides,
a new version
by Rachel Cusk
at the Almeida Theatre

Running dates:
25/9/15 – 14/11/15

Company
Michele Austin – Cleaner
Amanda Boxer – Nurse
Richard Cant – Aegeus
Andy de la Tour – Creon / Tutor
Kate Fleetwood – Medea
Charlotte Randle –
Messenger / Chorus
Justin Salinger – Jason
Guillermo Bedward, Xavi Moras
Spencer, Lukas Rolfe, Louis Sayers,
Sam Smith, Joseph West – Boys

Sarah Belcher, Ruth Everett, Georgina
Lamb, Emily Mutton – Chorus

Creatives
Writer – Rachel Cusk
Director – Rupert Goold
Set Designer – Ian MacNeil
Costume Designer – Holly
Waddington
Composition and Sound
– Adam Cork
Lighting Designer – Neil Austin
Choreography – Scott Ambler
Casting – Julia Horan CDG
Assistant Direction – Sara Joyce
Costume Supervision –
Deborah Andrews
Design Assistant – Jim Gaffney
Trainee Director – David Loumgair

Stage Management
Company Stage Manager
– Graham Michael
Deputy Stage Manager –
Lorna Seymour
Assistant Stage Manager – Chris Carr

Production
Production Manager – Aggi Agostino
Wardrobe Manager – Eleanor Dolan
Deputy Wardrobe Manager
– Rachael Higham
Hair and Wigs Manager – Anna Pileci
Dresser – Johanne Bertaux-Strenna
Chief Technician – Jason Wescombe
Lighting Technician – Robin Fisher
Sound Technician – Andrew Josephs
Production Carpenter – Gruff Carro
Medea's Costume – Marlin Anderson
Medea's Costume – Deborah Andrews
Chorus Costume Maker
– Rosa Prados
Tailor – Maureen Cordwell
Hair, Wigs and Make-up / Chorus
Masks – Susanna Peretz

Wardrobe Student Placement
– Josephine Fauchier
Set Build – Miraculous Engineering
Set Painter – Kerry Jarrett

Press
The Corner Shop PR

Memphis the Musical
at the Shaftesbury Theatre

Running dates:
9/10/14 – 31/10/15

Cast
Rolan Bell – Delray
Matt Cardle – Huey
Tyrone Huntley – Gator
Rachel John – Alternate Felicia
Beverley Knight – Felicia
Claire Machin – Gladys
Jason Pennycooke – Bobby
Jon Robyns – Alternate Huey
Mark Rope – Mr Simmons
Keisha Atwell, Arielle Campbell,
Mark Carroll, Joseph Davenport,
Momar Diagne, Carly Mercedes
Dyer, Kimmy Edwards, Laura
Ellis, Hillary Elk (Assistant Dance
Captain), Charlotte Gorton, Yasmin
Harrison, Benjamin Harrold,
Waylon Jacobs, Dean Maynard,
Devon McKenzie-Smith, Tim
Newman, Simon Ray-Harvey,
Ashley Rumble, Kyle Seeley (Dance
Captain), Helen Siveter, Dawnita
Smith, Alex Thomas – Ensemble

Understudies
Keisha Atwell, Kimmy
Edwards – Felicia
Tim Newman – Huey

Simon Ray-Harvey, Waylon
Jacobs – Delray
Waylon Jacobs, Momar Diagne – Gator
Simon Ray-Harvey, Waylon
Jacobs – Bobby
Charlotte Gorton, Helen
Siveter – Gladys
Mark Carroll, Dean Maynard
– Mr Simmons

Creative Team
Book and Lyrics – Joe DiPietro
Music and Lyrics – David Bryan
Concept – George W George
Director – Christopher Ashley
Choreographer – Sergio Trujillo
Music Producer / UK Music
Supervisor – Christopher Jahnke
Designer – David Gallo
Costume Designer – Paul Tazewell
Lighting Designer – Howell Binkley
Sound Designer – Gareth Owen
Projection Design – David Gallo
Projection Design – Shawn Sagady
Hair and Wig Design –
Charles G LaPointe
Fight Director – Steve Rankin
Fight Director – Tristan Adams
Hair and Wig Design –
Pippa Ailion CDG
Orchestrations – Daryl Waters
Orchestrations – David Bryan
UK Musical Supervisor – Nick Finlow
Musical Director – Tim Sutton
UK Associate Director – Tara Wilkinson
Associate Choreographer –
Edgar Godineaux
Dance Arrangements –
August Eriksmoen
Dance Assistant – Leonora Stapleton
Set Designer – Andrew D Edwards
Assistant Costume Designer
– Rory Powers

Associate Sound Designer
  – Russell Godwin
UK Associate Lighting
  Designer – John Harris
Dramaturgist – Gabriel Greene
Dialect Coach – Michaela Kennen

Stage Management

Stage Manager – Natalie Wood
Deputy Stage Manager –
  Rosalie Fenelon
Assistant Stage Manager – Beverley Else
Assistant Stage Manager –
  Robert Le Maistre
Technical Swing / Assistant Stage
  Manager – Lee Fowler

Production

Production Manager – Rich Blacksell
Company Manager – Stephen Burnett
Costume Supervisor – Hannah Bell
Assistant Costume Supervisor
  – Lisa Makin
Wigs Supervisor – Linda McKnight
Props Buyer – Marcus Hall
Head of Lighting – Gary Bowman
Deputy Head of Lighting – Pete Butler
Head of Sound – Dave Palmer
Sound No. 2 – Andy Yiannaki
Sound No. 3 – Zoe Blackford
Head of Automation – Tom Hawes
Automation No. 2 – Nick Szewciw
Head of Wardrobe – Alex Surridge
Wardrobe Deputy – Corrine Tookey
Wardrobe Assistant – Carly Turnbull
Wardrobe Assistant –
  Charlotte H Smith
Head of Wigs – Katie Marson
Wigs Deputy – Cheryl Garvey
Wigs Assistant – Holly
  Packham O'Brien
Wigs Assistant – Dominique Torres
Wigs Dresser – Rhona Phipps-Tyndall
Dresser – Ursula Crocker

Dresser – Jenni Carvell
Dresser – Tim Chketiani
Dresser – Emma Clarke
Dresser – Alison Littlewood
Dresser – Emma Shortland
Dresser – Cheryl Sime
Dresser – Anna Witcombe

Musicians

Musical Director / Piano
  – Tim Sutton
Assistant Musical Director /
  Keyboard – Benjamin Burrell
Drums – Justin Shaw
Bass – John McKenzie
Guitar – James Pusey
Reeds – Paul Jones
Reeds – Paul Nathaniel
Trumpet – Mark White
Trombone – Pat Hartley
Orchestral Management – Musical
  Coordination Services Ltd
Keyboard Programmer – Phij Adams

Producers

Executive Producers – Smith
  & Brant Theatricals

General Management

Stage Entertainment

Press

The Corner Shop PR

Mr Foote's Other Leg
at the Hampstead Theatre

Running dates:
14/9/15 – 17/10/15

Cast

Micah Balfour – Frank Barber
Sophie Bleasdale – Miss Chudleigh
Joshua Elliott – Mr Hallam

Jenny Galloway – Mrs Garner
Ian Kelly – Prince George
Dervla Kirwan – Peg Woffington
Forbes Masson – John Hunter
Joseph Millson – David Garrick
Simon Russell Beale – Samuel Foote
Colin Stinton – Charles Macklin
  / Benjamin Franklin
Canavan Connolly – Supernumerary
Julian Pichelski – Supernumerary

Creatives

Writer – Ian Kelly
Director – Richard Eyre
Set and Costume Designer
  – Tim Hatley
Assistant Designer – Ross Edwards
Lighting Designer – Peter Mumford
Sound Designer – John Leonard
Composer – Richard Hartley
Casting Director – Cara Beckinsale
Assistant Director – Nick Bromley

Stage Management

Company Stage Manager
  – Robyn Hardy
Deputy Stage Manager – Helen Smith
Assistant Stage Manager
  – Kezia Beament

Production

Production Manager – Matt Towell
Costume Supervisor –
  Sabrina Cuniberto
Wardrobe Mistress – Rosy Emmerich
Wigs Supervisor – Betty Marini
Wigs Mistress – Emily Grove
Dresser – Sim Camps
Props Supervisor – Lizzie Frankl
Props Assistant – Claire Turner
Lighting Assistant – Charlotte Burton
Scenic Construction and
  Paint – Souvenir

Press

The Corner Shop PR

My Night with Reg
at the Apollo Theatre
transfer from the Donmar Warehouse

Running dates:
17/1/15 – 11/4/15

Cast

Matt Bardock – Benny
Jonathan Broadbent – Guy
Richard Cant – Bernie
Julian Ovenden – John
Lewis Reeves – Eric
Geoffrey Streatfeild – Daniel
Paul Giddings – Understudy
  Guy / Bernie
Richard Hurst – Understudy John
Matthew Pattimore –
  Understudy Eric
Daniel Robinson – Understudy
  Daniel / Benny

Creative Team

Writer – Kevin Elyot
Director – Robert Hastie
Designer – Peter McKintosh
Lighting Designer – Paul Pyant
Sound Designer – Gregory Clarke
Casting Director – Alastair
  Coomer CDG
Associate Director – Josh Seymour

Stage Management

Company Stage Manager
  – Pandora Erlington
Deputy Stage Manager – Mary Hely
Assistant Stage Manager –
  Matthew Pattimore

Production

Production Manager –
  Matt Noddings
Voice and Dialect Coach
  – Zabarjad Salam

Movement Director – Ben Wright
Costume Supervisor – Angie Burns
Wardrobe Master –
    Christopher Cope
Promotions – Bright
    Green Promotions

General Management

Producer – Eleanor Lloyd
    Productions

Press

Jo Allan PR

Marketing

AKA

Oresteia

at Trafalgar Studios 1
Transfer from Almeida Theatre

Running dates:
22/8/15 – 7/11/15

Cast

Lorna Brown
Jessica Brown Findlay
Cleopatra Dickens
Dixie Egerickx
Annie Firbank
Matt Goldberg
Joshua Higgott
Joshua Lester
Jonathan McGuinness
Oliver Ryan
Ophelia Standen
Jacob Swann
Luke Thompson
Lia Williams
Angus Wright
Hara Yannas

Understudies

Robyn Moore

Saskia Roddick
Neil Stewart

Creatives

Adaptation / Direction – Robert Icke
Design – Hildegard Bechtler
Lighting – Natasha Chivers
Sound – Tom Gibbons
Video – Tim Reid
Casting – Julia Horan CDG
Associate Direction –
    Anthony Almeida
Consultant Academic –
    Simon Goldhill
Dramaturg – Duška Radosavljevic
Casting Associate – Lotte Hines
Assistant Lighting Design
    – Peter Harrison
Sound Associate – Sean Ephgrave
Sound Associate – Pete Malkin

Stage Management

Company Stage Manager
    – Penny Foxley
Deputy Stage Manager – Nicki Barry
Assistant Stage Manager / Book
    Cover – Ellen Hulme
Technical Assistant Stage Manager
    – Matthew Richard Smith

Production

Production Manager (West End
    Transfer) – Gary Beestone
Production Manager (Original
    Almeida) – James Crout
Deputy Production Manager (Original
    Almeida) – Aggi Agostino
Wardrobe Master – Chris Cope
Wardrobe Deputy – Emily Moore
Wardrobe Assistant – Sarah Burton
Costume Supervision – Laura Hunt
Lighting Operator – Gareth Jones
Sound Operator – Daniel Balfour
Chaperone – Kay Elliott
Chaperone – Theresa Taylor

Press

The Corner Shop PR

General Management

Ambassador Theatre Group

Seven Brides for Seven Brothers

Regent's Park Theatre, Ltd presents
Seven Brides for Seven Brothers
at Regent's Park Open Air Theatre

Running dates:
16/7/15 – 29/8/15

Cast

Rosanna Bates – Liza
David Burrows – Mr Hoallum
Leon Cooke – Daniel
Eamonn Cox – Matt
Jacob Fisher – Jeb /
    Understudy (Gideon)
Charlene Ford – Dorcas
Steve Fortune – Mr Sander
Alex Gaumond – Adam
Bob Harms – Ephraim
Bethany Huckle – Alice
Frankie Jenna – Sarah
James Leece – Benjamin
Angela M. Caesar – Mrs Sander
Philip Marriott – Zeke
Dylan Mason – Joel
Trevor Michael Georges – Preacher
Natasha Mould – Martha
Peter Nash – Nathan
Sam O'Rourke – Gideon
Ryan Pidgen – Luke
Laura Pitt-Pulford – Milly
Adam Rhys-Charles – Frank
    / Understudy (Adam)
Karli Vale – Ruth / Understudy (Milly)

Annie Wensak – Mrs Hoallum
Matthew Whennell-Clark – Swing
    / Deputy Dance Captain
Ed White – Caleb
Emma Woods – Swing /
    Dance Captain

Creative Team

Book – Lawrence Kasha
Book – David S Landay
Music – Gene de Paul
Lyrics – Johnny Mercer
New Songs – Al Kasha
New Songs – Joel Hirschhorn
Director – Rachel Kavanaugh
Set and Costume Designer
    – Peter McKintosh
Choreographer – Alistair David
Musical Supervisor / Dance
    Arrangements – Gareth Valentine
Musical Director – Stephen Ridley
Lighting Designer – Tim Mitchell
Orchestrations – Larry Blank
Orchestrations – Mark Cumberland
Sound Designer – Nick
    Lidster for Autograph
Casting Director – James Orange CDG
Fight Director – Kate Waters
Voice and Text Coach –
    Barbara Houseman
Dialect Coach – Charmian Hoare
Associate Director – Tom
    Attenborough
Assistant Musical Director
    – Peter McCarthy
Assistant Choreographer
    – Emma Woods
Associate Fight Director
    – Jonathan Holby
Associate Fight Director
    – Owain Gwynn
Assistant to the Designer
    – Simon Wells

Stage Management

Company Stage Manager
– Maria Baker
Deputy Stage Manager
– Helen Bowen
Assistant Stage Manager
– Freddie Harris
Assistant Stage Manager
– Sarah Phillips
Stage Management Placement
– Christina Leach

Production

Production Manager – Rich Blacksell
Season Production Manager
– Andy Beardmore
Costume Supervisor – Angie Burns
Assistant Costume Supervisor
– Morag Pirrie
Props Supervisor – Lizzie Frank
Props Assistant – Claire Turner

Orchestra

Musical Director / Keyboards
– Stephen Ridley
Assistant Musical Director /
Keyboards – Peter McCarthy
Drums / Percussion – Dominic Sales
Double Bass – Joe Pettitt
Violin – Shelley Tucker
Trumpet / Flugel – Jean-Paul Gervasoni
Trombone / Euphonium
– Tom Dunnett
French Horn – Dan Beer
Alto Saxophone / Flute / Piccolo /
Clarinet / Baritone Saxophone
/ Clarinet – Adrian Revell
Bass Clarinet / Flute – Emma Fowler
Orchestral Management – Musical
Coordination Services Ltd
Keyboard Programming
– Stuart Andrews

Press

The Corner Shop PR

Sinatra:
The Man and His Music

Karl Sydow in association with
Frank Sinatra Enterprises presents
Sinatra: The Man and His Music
at the London Palladium

Running dates:
10/7/15 – 10/10/15

Cast

Lucy Banfield
Faye Best
Christopher Black
Nicola Coates
Rachel Ensor
Jamie Firth
Francis Haugen
Matt Holland
Amy Hollins
Aaron James
Anabel Kutay
Aston Newman Hannington
Ashley Nottingham
Charis O'Connor
Liam Paul Jennings
Alastair Postlethwaite
Jamie Revell
Niall Swords
Gemma Whitelam
Bryony Whitfield

Creatives

Director – David Gilmore
Choreographer – GJD Choreography
Set Designer – Stufish
Entertainment Architects
Video Designer – 59 Productions
Lighting Designer –
Patrick Woodroffe
Lighting Designer – Adam Bassett

Musical Supervisor and New Musical
Arrangements – Gareth Valentine
Orchestrations – Don Sebeskey
Orchestrations – David Pierce
Sound Designer – Dan Samson
Costume Designer – Laura Hopkins
Casting Director – Debbie O'Brien
Associate Lighting Designer and
Programmer – Tim Oliver
Associate Lighting Designer
– Adam Bassett
Lighting Design Associate
– Miriam Bull
Associate Sound Designer
– Gary Hickeson
Associate Costume Designer
– Helen Johnson

Stage Management

Deputy Stage Manager – Chris Fossey
Assistant Stage Manager
– Becky Hartnett
Technical Assistant Stage
Manager – Sky Palin

Production

General / Production Manager
– David Stothard
Company Manager – Terri Baker

Orchestra

Musical Director / Conductor
– Richard John
Keyboards / Assistant Musical
Director – Will Stuart
Piano – Rob Barron
Drums – Ed Richardson
Double Bass – Don Richardson
Percussion – James Turner
Trumpet – Mike Lovatt
Trumpet – Andy Gathercole
Trumpet – Alan Berlyn
Trombone – Ashley Horton
Trombone – Richard Wigley
Bass Trombone – Dave Stewart

French Horn – Richard Bayliss
Alto Saxophone / Flute /
Clarinet – Graeme Blevins
Alto Saxophone / Flute /
Clarinet – Sam Maine
Tenor Saxophone / Flute /
Clarinet – Rob Fowler
Tenor and Soprano Saxophones
/ Clarinet – Simon Allen
Baritone Saxophone / Bass Clarinet
/ Clarinet – Claire McInerney
Violin (Leader) – Marianne Haynes
Violin – Ros Stephen
Violin – Ciaran McCabe
Violin – Tina Jacobs-Lim
Violin – Naomi Rump
Violin – Ali Gordon
Cello – Vicky Matthews
Orchestral Management – Musical
Coordination Services Ltd

Producers

Producer – Karl Sydow
Executive Producer – Ivan MacTaggart
Producer for FSE – Charlie Pignone
Associate Producers – NGM

Splendour
at the Donmar Warehouse

Running dates:
30/7/15 – 26/9/15

Cast

Zawe Ashton – Gilma
Sinéad Cusack – Micheleine
Michelle Fairley – Genevieve
Genevieve O'Reilly – Kathryn

Creatives

Writer – Abi Morgan
Director – Robert Hastie

Designer – Peter McKintosh
Lighting Designer – Lee Curran
Sound Designer – Adrienne Quartly
Movement Director – Jack Murphy
Casting Director – Alastair
  Coomer CDG
Resident Assistant Director – Zoé Ford
Fight Director – Bret Yount
Voice and Dialect Coach
  – Zabarjad Salam
Design Assistant – Ben Davies
Design Assistant – Grace Smart

Stage Management
Company Stage Manager
  – Clare Whitfield
Deputy Stage Manager
  – Caroline Meer
Assistant Stage Manager – Cheryl Firth
Stage Management Intern
  – Rebecca Gee

Production
Production Manager –
  Jasmine Sandalli
Costume Supervisor – Angie Burns
Production Sound Engineer
  – Sarah Weltman
Scenery Construction and Paint
  – All Scene All Props
Lighting Equipment – PRG
Sound Equipment – Autograph
Make-up Provider – MAC

Temple
at the Donmar Warehouse

Running dates:
21/5/15 – 25/7/15

Cast
Anna Calder-Marshall – The Virger

Richard Griffiths – Chorister
Paul Higgins – The Canon Chancellor
Rebecca Humphries – The PA
Luca Latchman – Chorister
Shereen Martin – The City Lawyer
Eigo Matsumoto – Chorister
James Murray – Chorister
Eskandar Rashidian – Chorister
Simon Russell Beale – The Dean
Malcolm Sinclair – The
  Bishop of London
Lucas Watson – Chorister

Creatives
Writer – Steve Waters
Director – Howard Davies
Designer – Tim Hatley
Lighting Designer – Mark Henderson
Sound Designer – Mike Walker
Composer – Stephen Warbeck
Casting Director – Alastair
  Coomer CDG
Assistant Director – Jez Pike
Children's Casting – Vicky Richardson
Assistant Designer – Ross Edwards

Stage Management
Company Stage Manager
  – Linsey Hall
Deputy Stage Manager – Mary Hely
Assistant Stage Manager
  – Katie Barrett
Stage Management Intern
  – Hannah Gregory

Production
Production Manager – Igor
Costume Supervisor – Jack Galloway
Voice Coach – Barbara Houseman
Choir Master – Matthew Scott
Digital Art – Graeme Crowley
Digital Printing – Service Graphics
Set built and painted by – Bower
  Wood Production Services
Lighting equipment provided by – PRG

Sound Equipment provided by
  – Autograph
Education Practitioners – Simon
  Evans and Sophie Watkiss
Chaperone – Claire Russell
Chaperone – David Russell
Chaperone – Linda Russell
Chaperone – Rachael Walker

The 39 Steps
Edward Snape for Fiery Angel Ltd
and Tricycle London Productions Ltd
present
in Association with West Yorkshire
Playhouse
The 39 Steps
at the Criterion Theatre

Running dates:
14/9/06 – 5/9/15

Cast
Alix Dunmore – Pamela /
  Annabella / Margaret
Tim Frances – Man 2
Richard Galazka – Richard Hannay
Daniel Tuite – Man 1
Matthew Bancroft –
  Understudy Hannay
Paul Critoph – Understudy Man
Hazel Gardner – Understudy
  Annabella / Margaret / Pamela

Creatives
Adaptation – Patrick Barlow
Original Concept – Simon
  Corble and Nobby Dimon
Director – Maria Aitken
Designer – Peter McKintosh
Lighting Designer – Ian Scott
Sound Designer – Mic Pool

Movement Director – Toby Sedgwick
Associate Producer – Marilyn Eardley
Associate Director – James Farrell
Associate Movement Director
  – Emily Mytton

Stage Management
Company and Stage
  Manager – Jasper Fox
Deputy Stage Manager
  – Andrew Sloane
Assistant Stage Manager
  – Bex Harding
Assistant Stage Manager
  – Elizabeth Patrick

Production
Costume Supervisor – Mary Charlton
Wardrobe Mistress – Alexa Day
Dresser – Carys Reynolds

Press
Fiery Angel

Marketing
AKA

The Audience
Matthew Byam Shaw,
Robert Fox and Andy Harries
present
The Audience
by Peter Morgan
at the Apollo Theatre

Running dates:
21/4/15 – 25/7/15

Cast
Marnie Brighton – Young Elizabeth
David Calder – Winston Churchill
Jonathan Coote – Archbishop / Cecil
  Beaton / Detective / Understudy
  (Gordon Brown / Anthony Eden)

Mark Dexter – David
 Cameron / Tony Blair
Harry Feltham – Footman
 / Horse Guard
Michael Gould – John Major
Madeleine Jackson Smith
 – Young Elizabeth
Gordon Kennedy – Bishop
 / Gordon Brown
Sylvestra Le Touzel –
 Margaret Thatcher
Izzy Meikle-Small – Young
 Elizabeth / Understudy (Bobo
 McDonald / Private Secretary)
Charlotte Moore – Bobo MacDonald
 / Private Secretary / Understudy
 (The Queen / Margaret Thatcher)
David Peart – Equerry /
 Understudy (Harold Wilson
 / Winston Churchill)
Matt Plumb – Footman / Horse Guard
David Robb – Anthony Eden
Kristin Scott Thomas – The Queen
Sarah Spears – The Queen's Dresser
Philip Stewart – Bishop / Detective
 / Policeman / Understudy
 (Equerry / John Major / David
 Cameron / Tony Blair)
Olivia Ward – The Queen's Dresser
Nicholas Woodeson – Harold Wilson

Creative Team

Writer – Peter Morgan
Director – Stephen Daldry
Designer – Bob Crowley
Lighting Designer – Rick Fisher
Sound Designer – Paul Arditti
Composer – Paul Englishby
Hair and Make-up Designer
 – Ivana Primorac
Casting Director – Robert Sterne CDG
Children's Casting – Jessica
 Ronane CDG

Associate Director – Justin Martin

Stage Management

Company Stage Manager
 – Howard Jepson
Deputy Stage Manager – Georgia Bird
Assistant Stage Manager
 – James Minihane

Production

Production Manager – Matt Noddings
Props Supervisor – Chris Lake
Dialect Coach – William Conacher
Associate Designer – Rosalind Coombes
Associate Lighting Designer
 – Rob Casey
Associate Sound Designer – Chris Reid
Associate Costume Designer
 – Irene Bohan
Resident Director – Oonagh Murphy
Wardrobe Manager – Charlie Stidwill
Wigs Manager – Sarah Spears
Wigs Deputy – Kathy Adams
Dresser to Kristin Scott Thomas
 – Olivia Ward
Dresser – Amanda Wilde
Sound Operator – Alexander Broad
Children's Chaperone –
 Jacqueline Moore
Children's Chaperone –
 Catherine Dunne

Producers

Playful Productions
Robert Fox
Andy Harris

The Beaux' Stratagem
at the National Theatre,
Olivier Stage

Running dates:
19/5/15 – 20/9/15

Cast

Esh Alladi – Bagshot /
 Understudy (Aimwell)
Samuel Barnett – Aimwell
Jamie Beamish – Foigard
Pippa Bennett-Warner – Dorinda
Jane Booker – Lady Bountiful
Cornelius Clarke – Tapster
 / Understudy (Foigard /
 Scrub / Hounslow)
Susannah Fielding – Mrs Sullen
Molly Gromadzki – Gipsy /
 Understudy (Dorinda / Cherry)
John Hastings – Chamberlain /
 Understudy (Archer / Bagshot)
Richard Henders – Mr Sullen
Lloyd Hutchinson – Boniface
Chris Kelham – Footman
 / Understudy (Sullen /
 Bellair / Sir Charles)
Nicholas Khan – Sir
 Charles Freeman
Barbara Kirby – Countrywoman
 / Understudy (Lady Bountiful)
Ana-Maria Maskell – Maid /
 Understudy (Mrs Sullen /
 Gipsy / Countrywoman)
Amy Morgan – Cherry
Pearce Quigley – Scrub
Mark Rose – Hounslow / Understudy
 (Boniface / Gibbet / Tapster)
Chook Sibtain – Gibbet
Geoffrey Streatfeild – Archer
Timothy Watson – Count Bellair

Creatives

Writer – George Farquhar
Director – Simon Godwin
Designer – Lizzie Clachan
Lighting Designer – Jon Clark
Movement Director –
 Jonathan Goddard
Music – Michael Bruce

Sound Designer – Christopher Shutt
Fight Director – Kev McCurdy
Company Voice Work –
 Jeannette Nelson
Dialect Coach – Michaela Kennen
Staff Director – Lily McLeish
Dramaturgy – Simon Godwin
Dramaturgy – Patrick Marber
Casting – Wendy Spon

Stage Management

Stage Manager – Alison Rankin
Deputy Stage Manager
 – Nik Haffenden
Assistant Stage Manager
 – Susan Ellicott
Assistant Stage Manager
 – Abbie Procter

Production

Production Manager – Jim Leaver
Deputy Production Manager
 – Sarah O'Connor
Project Draughting – Alan Bain
Digital Art – Emma Pile
Costume Supervisor – Johanna Coe
Costume Buyer – Charlotte McGarrie
Wigs, Hair and Make-up Supervisor
 – Sara Lou Packham
Prop Supervisor – Rebecca Johnston
Prop Buyer – Sian Willis
Lighting Supervisor – Jeremy Turnbull
Lighting Programmer –
 Daniel Haggerty
Production Sound Engineer
 – Jonas Roebuck
Sound Operator – Clive Bryan
Stage Supervisor – Gary Tollhurst
Rigging Supervisor –
 Neill Shimmens
Automation Supervisor – Jay Bruce
Armourer – Paul Wanklin
Construction Supervisor
 – Paul Sheppard

Scenic Painting Supervisor
    – Cass Kirchner
Production Assistant – Maisy Wyer
Musicians
Music Director / Bassist
    – Richard Hart
Violin – Sarah Crisp
Acoustic Guitar / Banjo –
    Oliver Seymour-Marsh
Percussion – Billy Stookes
Accordion – Ian Watson

The Father
Theatre Royal Bath Productions
and Tricycle Theatre present
The Father
at the Wyndham's Theatre

Running dates:
30/9/15 – 21/11/15

Cast
Rebecca Charles – Woman
Kenneth Cranham – André
Nicholas Gleaves – Pierre
Kirsty Oswald – Laura
Claire Skinner – Anne
Jim Sturgeon – Man
Tom Michael Blyth –
    Understudy Pierre / Man
Ellis Jones – Understudy André
Emily Stride – Understudy
    Anne / Laura / Woman
Creatives
Writer – Florian Zeller
Translation – Christopher Hampton
Director – James Mcdonald
Associate Director – Stella Powell-Jones
Designer – Miriam Buether
Lighting Designer – Guy Hoare

Sound Designer – Christopher Shutt
Casting Director – Ginny
    Schiller CDG
Stage Management
Company Stage Manager (On
    the Book) – Xenia Lewis
Assistant Stage Manager / Book
    Cover – Georgia Pavelková
Production
Production Manager (Cambridge
    and West End) – Mark Carey
Production Manager (Ustonov Studios
    and Tour) – Kate Edwards
Costume Supervisor – Jackie Orton
Associate Designer – Natasha Piper
Associate Lighting Design and
    Programmer – Rebecca Stoddart
Production Electrician /
    Relight – Barry Abbotts
Production Carpenter –
    Andy Stubbs
Production Sound – Jon Everett
Casting Assistant – Emily Jones
Casting Assistant – Liz Bichard
Wardrobe Manager –
    Emma Northcott
Producers
Theatre Royal Bath Productions
Tricycle Theatre
Simon Friend
Press
Arthur Leone PR

The Homecoming
The Jamie Lloyd Company presents
The Homecoming
at Trafalgar Studios 1

Running dates:
14/11/15 – 13/2/16

Cast
Keith Allen – Sam
Gemma Chan – Ruth
Ron Cook – Max
Gary Kemp – Teddy
John Macmillan – Joey
John Simm – Lenny
John Hastings – Understudy
    Teddy / Lenny / Joey
Millie Reeves – Understudy Ruth
Geoffrey Towers – Understudy
    Max / Sam
Creatives
Writer – Harold Pinter
Director – Jamie Lloyd
Designer – Soutra Gilmour
Lighting Designer – Richard Howell
Sound Designer – George Dennis
Associate Director – Luke Kernaghan
Fight Director – Owain Gwynn
Stage Management
Company Stage Manager
    – Martin Hope
Deputy Stage Manager – Kirsty Nixon
Assistant Stage Manager
    – Laura Cunnick
Production
Production Manager –
    Dominic Fraser
Costume Supervisor –
    Binnie Bowerman
Props Supervisor – Fahmida Bakht
Wardrobe Master –
    William Portch-Burgess
LX Board Operator / Technician
    – Michael Corcoran
General Management
Ambassador Theatre Group
Press
The Corner Shop PR
Marketing
Maidwell Marketing

The Importance of Being Earnest
First performance of this production
of The Importance of Being Earnest
was at the Vaudeville Theatre on 24
June 2015, produced by Kim Poster
and Nica Burns.
at the Vaudeville Theatre

Running dates:
24/6/15 – 7/11/15

Cast
Emily Barber –
    Hon Gwendolen Fairfax
Michael Benz – John Worthing / J P
Philip Cumbus –
    Algernon Moncrieff
Imogen Doel – Cecily Cardew
Michele Dotrice – Miss
    Prism / Governess
Mark Hammersley – Footman /
    Understudy (John Worthing /
    J P / Algernon Moncrieff)
Brendan Hooper – Merriman /
    Butler / Understudy (Rev Canon
    Chasuble / D D / Lane)
David Killick – Lane / Manservant
Richard O'Callaghan – Rev
    Canon Chasuble / D D
David Suchet – Lady Bracknell
Charlotte Blackledge –
    Understudy Hon Gwendolen
    Fairfax / Cecily Cardew
Pamela Harman – Understudy
    Lady Bracknell / Miss Prism
Creatives
Writer – Oscar Wilde
Director – Adrian Noble
Set and Costume Designer
    – Peter McKintosh

Associate Set Designer –
  Simon Anthony Wells
Lighting Designer –
  Howard Harrison
Music – Larry Blank
Sound Designer – Gareth Owen
Associate Sound Designer
  – Mike Thacker
Casting Director – Gabrielle Dawes
Movement – Jack Murphy
Vocal Coach – Charmian Hoare

Stage Management

Company Stage Manager
  – Elaine De Saulles
Deputy Stage Manager –
  Ruthie Philip-Smith
Assistant Stage Manager
  – Penelope Ayles
Tech Assistant Stage Manager
  – Aaron Carrington

Production

Production Consultant – John Dalston
Production Consultant –
  Digby Robinson
Costume Supervisor – Yvonne Milnes
Property Supervisor – Simon Wilcock
Wardrobe Master –
  Christopher Cope
Assistant Wardrobe Mistress
  – Sinéad Francis
Wigs Mistress – Lucy Horton
Theatre Apprentice – Allegra
  Campbell Boreham
Promotions – Rebekah Macleary

General Management

Stanhope Productions

Press

Jo Allan PR

Marketing

AKA

The Merchant of Venice
at Shakespeare's Globe

Running dates:
23/4/15 – 7/6/15

Cast

Stefan Adegbola – Launcelot Gobbo
Michael Bertenshaw – Duke
  of Venice / Tubal
Philip Cox – Balthasar / Chus
Scott Karim – Prince of Morocco
Ben Lamb – Lorenzo
Daniel Lapaine – Bassanio
Christopher Logan –
  Prince of Arragon
Dominic Mafham – Antonio
Brian Martin – Salarino
Dorothea Myer-Bennett – Nerissa
Regé-Jean Page – Solanio
Rachel Pickup – Portia
Jonathan Pryce – Shylock
Phoebe Pryce – Jessica
David Sturzaker – Gratiano
Sydney Aldridge, Jack Joseph,
  Jimmy Roye-Dunne – Ensemble

Creatives

Writer – William Shakespeare
Director – Jonathan Munby
Designer – Mike Britton
Composer – Jules Maxwell
Choreographer – Lucy Hind
Fight Director – Kate Waters
Globe Associate – Text – Giles Block
Globe Associate – Movement
  – Glynn Macdonald
Casting Director – Matilda James
Voice and Dialect – Martin McKellan
Assistant Director – Kevin Bennett

Stage Management

Stage Manager – Ian Farmery

Deputy Stage Manager
  – Danni Bastian
Assistant Stage Manager –
  Anastasia Kaimakamis
Technical Stage Manager
  – Bryan Paterson

Production

Production Manager – Wills
Production Manager – Paul Russell
Company Manager – Marion Marrs
Costume Supervisor – Sydney Florence
Text Assistant – Hannah
  Boland Moore
Wardrobe Manager – Megan Cassidy
Wardrobe Deputy – Emma Seychell
Wardrobe Assistant – Heather Bull
Wardrobe Assistant – Paula Eastman
Wardrobe Assistant – Sally Fernandes
Wardrobe Assistant –
  Samantha Murphy
Wardrobe Assistant – Hanna Randall
Wardrobe Assistant – Rachel Thomas
Wigs, Hair and Make-up
  Manager – Pam Humpage
Wigs, Hair and Make-up Deputy
  – Hayley Thompson
Wigs, Hair and Make-up
  Assistant – Lee Appleton
Wigs, Hair and Make-up
  Assistant – Victoria Young
Carpenter – Jon Batt
Carpenter – Kes Hayter
Carpenter – Rupert Mead
Carpenter – Simeon Tachev
Assistant Company Manager
  – Harry Niland
Assistant Production Manager
  – Fay Powell-Thomas
Costume Assistant – Ruitin Gan
Costume Assistant –
  Kristina Gumpinger
Costume Assistant – Rebecca Lesley

Costume Assistant – Aislinn Luton
Costume Maker – Carole Coates
Costume Maker – Jane Colquhoun
Costume Maker – Vanessa Coupe
Costume Maker – Sil Devilly
Costume Maker – Lois Edmunds
Costume Maker – Jane Gonin
Costume Maker – Glenn Hills
Costume Maker – Dawn Korner
Costume Maker – Kirsti Spence
Costume Maker – Jeffrey Portman
Costume Maker – Karen Sharp
Costume Maker – Kirsti Spence
Costume Maker – Sheila White
Prop Maker – Charlotte Austen
Prop Maker – Alice Firebrace
Prop Maker – Emma Hughes
Prop Maker – Hannah Williams
Scenic Artist – Sarah Kier
Scenic Artist – Thomasin Marshall
Scenic Artist – Fiona Stewart
Scenic Artist – Lizzie Wilkinson

Musicians

Musical Director / Singer
  – Jeremy Avis
Singer – Michael Henry
Clarinets – Dai Pritchard
Cello – Catherine Rimer
Singer – Nuno Silva

The Ruling Class
at Trafalgar Studios 1

Running dates:
16/1/15 – 11/4/15

Cast

Rosy Benjamin – Ensemble /
  Understudy (Grace Shelley
  / Lady Claire Gurney)

Andrew Bloomer – Ensemble / Understudy (Dinsdale Gurney / Dr Herder) / Multi-roles
Ron Cook – Sir Charles Gurney
Michael Cronin – Bishop Bertie Lampton
Kathryn Drysdale – Grace Shelley
Serena Evans – Lady Claire Gurney
Oliver Lavery – Ensemble / Understudy (Jack, 14th Earl of Gurney)
Paul Leonard – 13th Earl of Gurney / Mrs Piggot-Jones / McKyle's Assistant / Detective Inspector Brockett / 2nd Lord
Elliot Levey – Dr Herder
Forbes Masson – Toastmaster / Matthew Peake / Mrs Treadwell / McKyle / Kelso Truscott / Q.C. / Detective Sergeant Fraser / 1st Lord
James McAvoy – Jack, 14th Earl of Gurney
Joshua McGuire – Dinsdale Gurney
Anthony O'Donnell – Daniel Tucker
Geoffrey Towers – Ensemble / Understudy (Charles Gurney / Tucker / Bishop Bertie Lampton / 13th Earl of Gurney)

Creatives
Writer – Peter Barnes
Director – Jamie Lloyd
Designer – Soutra Gilmour
Lighting – Jon Clark
Sound and Music – Ben Ringham
Sound and Music – Max Ringham
Choreographer – Darren Carnall
Musical Director – Huw Evans
Wigs and Hair – Richard Mawbey
Fight Director – Kate Waters
Voice and Dialect Coach – Penny Dyer

Associate Director – Richard Fitch
Associate Designer – Rachel Wingate
Associate Costume Designer / Costume Supervisor – Christopher Cahill
Creature Design – Max Humphries

Stage Management
Company Stage Manager – Emma Banwell-Knight
Deputy Stage Manager – Vicky Eames
Assistant Stage Manager – Annie Kalinauckas
Technical Assistant Stage Managers – Laura Curd
Technical Assistant Stage Managers – Pete Hayes

Production
Production Manager – Dominic Fraser
Props Supervisor – Lizzie Frankl
Wardrobe Mistress – Nina Kendall Wardrobe Mistress
Wardrobe Deputy – Rachel Wood
Wigs Mistress – Julie Burnett
LX Board Operator / Technician – Jude Malcomson

General Management
Ambassador Theatre Group

The Trial
at the Young Vic
By Franz Kafka, Adapted by Nick Gill

Running dates:
19/6/15 – 22/8/15

Cast
Marc Antolin – Law Student / Flogger

Steven Beard – Uncle Albert / Magistrate
Richard Cant – Male Guard / Assistant / Tudor
Sarah Crowden – Mrs Barrow / Information Officer
Charlie Folorunsho – Bank Clerk / Defendant in Tattooist
Neil Haigh – Bank Clerk / Defendant in Information Office
Suzy King – Bank Clerk / Faye
Rory Kinnear – Josef K
Kate O'Flynn – Tiffany / Female Guard / Rosa / Chastity / Cherry / Girl
Weruche Opia – Comptroller / Bank Clerk / Defendant / Prostitute
Hugh Skinner – Kyle / Block
Sian Thomas – Mrs Grace / Doctor

Creatives
Writer – Franz Kafka
Adaptation – Nick Gill
Director – Richard Jones
Design – Miriam Buether
Costumes – Nicky Gillibrand
Light – Mimi Jordan Sherin
Music – David Sawer
Sound – David Sawer and Alex Twiselton
Movement – Sarah Fahie
Casting – Julia Horan CDG
Hair, Wigs and Make-up Design – Campbell Young Associates
Fights – Bret Yount
Jerwood Assistant Director – Nel Crouch
Boris Karloff Trainee / Assistant Director – Robert Awosusi

Stage Management
Stage Manager – Daniel Gammon
Deputy Stage Manager – Charlotte Hall

Assistant Stage Manager – Sally Inch
Assistant Stage Manager – Greg Sharman

Production
Production Manager – Bernd Fauler
Costumer Supervisor – Claire Murphy
Props Supervisor – Jo Maund
Lighting Operator – Sebastian Barresi / Jess Glaisher
Sound Operator – Amy Bramma / Jamie McIntyre
Automation Operator – Nell Allen
Automation Operator – Zoë Cotton
Stage Crew – Adam Bouras
Stage Crew – Nicola Donithorn
Stage Crew – Matt Fletcher
Stage Crew – Deborah Machin
Wardrobe Manager – Heather Bull
Wardrobe Assistant and Dresser – Claire Wardroper
Hair, Wigs and Make-up – Jenny Glynn
Costume Assistant – Rosey Morling
Costume Maker – Mark Costello
Costume Maker – Phil Reynolds

The Twits
at the Royal Court

Running dates:
7/4/15 – 31/5/15

Cast
Sam Cox – Yorkshire Terrier Man
Cait Davis – Monkey Mum
Monica Dolan – Mrs Twit
Aimée-Ffion Edwards – Monkey Daughter
Christine Entwisle – Tattooed Fortune Teller Lady

Oliver Llewellyn-Jenkins
– Monkey Son
Glyn Pritchard – Monkey Father
Dwane Walcott – Handsome
Waltzer Boy
Jason Watkins – Mr Twit
Creatives
Writer – Roald Dahl
Adaptation – Enda Walsh
Director – John Tiffany
Associate Director / Movement
– Steven Hoggett
Composer and Musical
Supervisor – Martin Lowe
Designer – Chloe Lamford
Lighting Designer – Philip Gladwell
Sound Designer – Gregory Clarke
Music Production – Phij Adams
Associate Director – Katy Rudd
Associate Movement Director
– Vicki Manderson
Associate Designer – Fly Davis
Casting Director – Amy Ball
Stage Management
Stage Manager – Rebecca Maltby
Deputy Stage Manager
– Sarah Hellicar
Assistant Stage Manager
– Greg Sharman
Stage Management Work
Placement – Libbie Khabaza
Production
Production Manager – Niall Black
Costume Supervisor – Lucy Walshaw
Company Manager – Heidi Lennard
Set Construction – Miraculous
Engineering
Set Painter – Lisa Dickson
Set Painter – Sarah Hrida
Set Painter – Kerry Jarrett

Three Days in the Country
at the National Theatre,
Lyttelton Stage

Running dates:
28/7/15 – 21/10/15

Cast
Nigel Betts – Bolshintsov
Nicholas Bishop – Matvey
Tom Burgering – Kolya
Paige Carter – Ensemble /
Understudy (Vera / Katya)
Amanda Drew – Natalya
Mark Extance – Ensemble
/ Understudy (Schaaf /
Shpigelsky / Bolshintsov)
Lynn Farleigh – Anna
Mark Gatiss – Shpigelsky
Debra Gillett – Lizaveta
Gawn Grainger – Schaaf
Joel Thomas – Kolya
Joshua Gringas – Kolya
John Light – Arkady
Matthew Lloyd Davies – Ensemble
/ Understudy (Arkady / Rakitin)
Mateo Oxley – Ensemble /
Understudy (Belyaev / Matvey)
Royce Pierreson – Belyaev
Cassie Raine – Ensemble /
Understudy (Natalya / Lizaveta)
Lily Sacofsky – Vera
John Simm – Rakitin
Cherrelle Skeete – Katya
Lisa Tramontin – Ensemble
/ Understudy (Anna)
Paige Carter, Mark Extance,
Matthew Lloyd Davies, Mateo
Oxley, Cassie Raine, Lisa
Tramontin – Ensemble
Creatives

Writer – Patrick Marber
Director – Patrick Marber
Designer – Mark Thompson
Lighting Designer – Neil Austin
Music and Sound – Adam Cork
Movement – Polly Bennett
Music Director – Sam Cable
Company Voice Work – Kate Godfrey
Company Voice Work –
Jeanette Nelson
Staff Director – Daniel Raggett
Literal Translation – Patrick Miles
Stage Management
Stage Manager – David Marsland
Deputy Stage Manager
– Fiona Bardsley
Assistant Stage Manager – Polly Rowe
Production
Production Manager – Matt Noddings
Casting – Wendy Spon
Deputy Production Manager
– Richard Eustace
Project Draughting – Paul Halter
Costume Supervisor – Irene Bohan
Costume Buyer – Charlotte McGarrie
Wigs, Hair and Make-up
Supervisor – Adele Brandman
Prop Supervisor – Richard Watson
Prop Buyer – Jessica Sharville
Lighting Supervisor – Laurie Clayton
Lighting Programmer – Jane Dutton
Production Sound Engineer
– Joel Price
Sound Operator – Ben Vernon
Stage Supervisor – Ken Pedersen
Rigging Supervisor – Barry Peavot
Armourer – Paul Wanklin
Construction Supervisor
– Paul Sheppard
Scenic Painting Supervisor
– Jennifer Espley
Assistant to the Designer – Ben Davies

Musicians
Piano – Sam Cable
Producers
Produced in association with
Sonia Friedman Productions

To Kill a Mockingbird
presented at the Barbican Theatre

Running dates:
24/6/15 – 25/7/15
Cast
Christopher Akrill – Boo Radley
Geoff Aymer – Reverend Sykes
Jemima Bennett – Scout
Harry Bennett – Jem
Victoria Bewick – Mayella Ewell
Rosie Boore – Scout
Connor Brundish – Dill
David Carlyle – Nathan
Radley / Mr Gilmer
Natalie Grady – Maudie Atkinson
Leo Heller – Dill
Jamie Kenna – Heck Tate
Phil King – Link Deas / Musician
Susan Lawson-Reynolds – Calpurnia
Zackary Momoh – Tom Robinson
Milo Panni – Dill
Ryan Pope – Bob Ewell
Ava Potter – Scout
Billy Price – Jem
Tommy Rodger – Jem
Christopher Saul – Walter
Cunningham / Judge Taylor
Robert Sean Leonard – Atticus Finch
Connie Walker – Stephanie
Crawford / Mrs Dubose
Matt Brewer – Understudy Bob
Ewell / Boo Radley / Heck Tate
/ Nathan Radley / Mr Gilmer /

Walter Cunningham / Judge Taylor

Eke Chuckwu – Understudy
Reverend Sykes / Tom Robinson

Kate England – Understudy Maudie
Atkinson / Mayella Ewell /
Stephanie Crawford / Mrs Dubose

Natasha Magigi – Understudy
Calpurnia

Creatives

Writer / Adaptation –
Christopher Sergel

Author of the Novel *To Kill a
Mockingbird* – Harper Lee

Director – Timothy Sheader

Designer – Jon Bausor

Composer – Phil King

Original Movement – Naomi Said

Movement Director – Polly Bennett

Lighting Designer – Oliver Fenwick

Sound Designer –
Ian Dickinson for Autograph

Casting Director – Lucy Jenkins
CDG and Sooki McShane CDG

Casting Director (Children)
– Jessica Ronane CDG

Associate Director –
Barbara Houseman

Associate Sound Designer – Nick
Lidster for Autograph

Dialect Coach – Majella Hurley

Resident Director (Regent's Park
and UK Tour) – Fiona Dunn

Resident Director (UK Tour and
Barbican) – Paul Foster

Assistant Designer – Rebecca Brower

Stage Management

Company Stage Manager
– Davin Patrick

Deputy Stage Manager
– Robyn Clogg

Assistant Stage Manager – Rick Barlow

Assistant Stage Manager – Jason Mills

Production

Production Manager –
Matt Noddings

Deputy Production Manager
– Andy Beardmore

Production Coordinator –
Hugh de la Bédoyère

Costume Supervisor – Holly White

Deputy Costume Supervisor
– Molly Syrett

Production Assistant – Nick Morrison

Production Assistant – Rachel Francis

Production Electrician – Liam Cleary

Production Sound Engineer
– Mark Cunningham

Sound No. 1 – Matt Russell

Sound No. 2 – Rick Barlow

Wardrobe Mistress –
Rachel Schofield

Chaperone – Kate Brayn

Chaperone – Sophie Cathersides

Chaperone – Elaine Morris

Chaperone – Keith de Souza

Chaperone – Phil Thomas

Children's Casting Assistant
– Verity Naughton

Costume Maker – Wendy Knowles

Costume Maker – Sarah Ninot

Tailoring – Rachel Pashley

Costume Dyeing and Distressing
– Gabrielle Firth

Costume Hires – Academy Costume

Set Construction – Belgrade
Production Services

Tree Supplier – Souvenir

Lighting Equipment – White Light Ltd

Sound Equipment – Autograph

Producers

Regent's Park Theatre Ltd

Fiery Angel

Adam Spiegel Productions

William Village

General Management

Fiery Angel Ltd

Press

The Corner Shop PR

Marketing

Dressing Room 5

Urinetown
at the Apollo Theatre

Running dates:
8/10/14 – 3/1/15

Cast

Nathan Amzi – Officer Barrel

Katie Bernstein – Little Becky
Two Shoes / Mrs Millennium

Marc Elliott – Mr McQueen

Cory English – Old Man Strong
/ Hot Blades Harry

Madeleine Harland – Soupy Sue

Rosanna Hyland – Hope Cladwell

Karis Jack – Little Sally

Julie Jupp – Old Woman
/ Josephine Strong

Aaron Lee Lambert – Billy Boy
Bill / UGC Executive

Mark Meadows – Senator Fipp

Jeff Nicholson – Tiny Tom / Dr Billeaux

Kane Oliver Parry – Robbie the
Stockfish / UGC Executive

Simon Paisley Day –
Caldwell B Cladwell

Jenna Russell – Penelope Pennywise

Matthew Seadon-Young
– Bobby Strong

Jonathan Slinger – Officer Lockstock

Chris Bennett – Swing /
Dance Captain

Joel Montague – Swing / Fight
Captain / Assistant Dance Captain

Alasdair Buchan, Vicki Lee Taylor,
Christina Modestou – Swings

Understudies

Alasdair Buchan, Jeff Nicholson
– Officer Lockstock

Katie Bernstein, Christina
Modestou – Little Sally

Joel Montague, Aaron Lee
Lambert – Bobby Strong

Julie Jupp, Vicki Lee Taylor
– Penelope Pennywise

Joel Montague, Christ Bennett
– Robbie the Stockfish
/ UCG Executive

Vicki Lee Taylor, Christina Modestou
– Old Woman / Josephine Strong

Vicki Lee Taylor, Christina
Modestou – Soupy Sue

Joel Montague, Chris Bennett
– Tiny Tom / Dr Billeaux

Christina Modestou, Vicki Lee
Taylor – Little Becky Two
Shoes / Mrs Millennium

Joel Montague, Christ Bennett –
Billy Boy Bill / UGC Executive

Chris Bennett, Joel Montague – Old
Man Strong / Hot Blades Harry

Madeleine Harland, Christina
Modestou – Hope Cladwell

Chris Bennett, Alasdair
Buchan – Officer Barrel

Aaron Lee Lambert, Alasdair
Buchan – Mr McQueen

Alasdair Buchan, Joel
Montague – Senator Fipp

Jeff Nicholson, Nathan Amzi
– Caldwell B Cladwell

Creatives

Music and Lyrics – Mark Hollmann

Book and Lyrics – Greg Kotis

Director – Jamie Lloyd

Production Designer – Soutra Gilmour

403

Choreographer – Ann Yee
Musical Supervisor and
    Director – Alan Williams
Lighting Designer – Adam Silverman
Sound Designer – Terry Jardine
Sound Designer – Nick Lidster
Casting Director –
    David Grindrod Associates
Hair and Wig Designer –
    Richard Mawbey
Fight Director – Kate Waters
Orchestrations – Bruce Coughlin
Associate Lighting Designer
    – Chris Mercer
Projection Designer –
    Duncan McLean
Associate Director – Richard Fitch
Associate Choreographer
    – Richard Roe
Associate Musical Director
    – Mark Etherington

Stage Management

Company Stage Manager
    – John Power
Senior Stage Manager –
    Graham Hookham
Deputy Stage Manager
    – Briony Allen
Technical Assistant / Stage
    Manager – Will Herman
Assistant Stage Manager – Laura Sully

Production

Sound No. 1 – Gareth Tucker
Sound No. 2 – Daniel Higgott
Wardrobe Master – Chris Cope
Wardrobe Deputy – Caroline Andrew
Wardrobe Assistant – Anna Robson
Head of Wigs and Make-up
    – Sally-Kate Duboux
Deputy Head of Wigs and
    Make-up – Elaine Amielle
Props Supervisor – Lizzie Frankl

Costume Supervisor – Chris Cahill

Orchestra

Musical Director / Piano
    – Alan Williams
Drums / Percussion – Tom Clare
Trumpet – Jean-Paul Gervasoni
Bass Trombone / Euphonium
    – Steve Haynes
Double Bass – Jo Nichols
Reeds – Paul Stevens
Orchestral Management – Musical
    Coordination Services Ltd

Producers

Julian Stoneman Associates
The Araca Group
Jennifer Evans
Tulchin/Bartner Productions
Greenleaf Productions
Flora Suk-Hwa Yoon
Los Foleys
Olympus Theatricals
Deborah Negri
Richard Winkler
Manal Morrar

Women on the Verge of a Nervous Breakdown
at the Playhouse Theatre

Running dates:
17/12/14 – 23/5/15

Cast

Ricardo Afonso – Taxi Driver
Marianne Benedict – Rosalia
    / Hair Stylist / Understudy
    (Pepa / Candela / Marisa)
Tamsin Greig – Pepa
Haydn Gwynne – Lucia
Seline Hizli – Marisa

Holly James – Matador / Dance
    Captain / Understudy (Candela
    / Paulina / Marisa)
Perry Lambert – Swing
Michael Matus – Hector /
    Magistrate / Understudy (Ivan)
Rebecca McKinnis – Christina /
    Understudy (Pepa / Lucia / Paulina)
Sarah Moyle – Concierge /
    Understudy (Lucia)
Alastair Natkiel – Telephone
    Repairman / Ambite /
    Understudy (Ivan / Taxi Driver
    / Carlos / Doctor / Hector)
Haydn Oakley – Carlos
Jérôme Pradon – Ivan
Nuno Queimado – Malik /
    Understudy (Taxi Driver /
    Carlos / Doctor / Hector)
Dale Rapley – Doctor /
    Chief Inspector
Anna Skellern – Candela
Willemijn Verkaik – Paulina

Creatives

Book – Jeffrey Lane
Music and Lyrics – David Yazbek
Based on the Film by –
    Pedro Almodóvar
Director – Bartlett Sher
Musical Supervisor – Matthew Brind
Choreography – Ellen Kane
Set Design – Anthony Ward
Costume Design – Caitlin Ward
Lighting Design – Peter Mumford
Sound Design – Paul Groothuis
Sound Design – Tom Marshall
Orchestrations – Simon Hale
Musical Director – Greg Arrowsmith
Associate Director – Tyne Rafaeli
Resident Director – Jason Lawson
Resident Choreographer
    – Holly James

Stage Management

Company Stage Manager
    – Wyn Williams
Deputy Stage Manager –
    Woody Woodcock
Assistant Stage Manager /
    Book Cover – John Hicks
Technical Assistant Stage
    Manager – Chris Deasey

Production

Production Manager –
    Richard Bullimore
Props Supervisor – Lisa Buckley
Props Supervisor – Mary Halliday
Costume Supervisor –
    Deborah Andrews
Wigs, Hair and Make-up
    – Carole Hancock
Wardrobe Mistress –
    Sharon Williams
Deputy Wardrobe Mistress
    – Laura Crosbie
Wigs Mistress – Anna Pileci
Sound No. 1 – Paul Allen
Sound No. 2 – Daniel Higgott
Lighting Board Operator
    – Cormac O'Brien

Musicians

Musical Director / Piano
    – Greg Arrowsmith
Keyboard / Accordion / Deputy
    Musical Director – Irvin Duguid
Drums – Joe Evans
Percussion – Hugh Wilkinson
Double Bass / Bass Guitar
    – Jo Nichols
Guitar – Andy Jones
Orchestral Management – Musical
    Coordination Services Ltd

Producers

Howard Panter for The
    Ambassador Theatre Group

General Management

Ambassador Theatre Group

---

wonder.land

at the National Theatre,
Olivier Stage

Running dates:
27/11/15 – 30/4/16

Cast

Simon Anthony – Swing /
   Ensemble / Understudy (Mr
   King / Dum / Dee / Dodo)
Sam Archer – Dum / Dance Captain
Carly Bawden – Alice
Lois Chimimba – Aly
Leon Cooke – Dee
Nadine Cox – WPC Rook
Ivan de Freitas – Dodo
Hal Fowler – MC (Cheshire
   Cat / Caterpillar)
Anna Francolini – Mrs Manxome
Adrian Grove – Mr King /
   Understudy (MC / Matt / PC Rock)
Paul Hilton – Matt
Joshua Lacey – White Rabbit
Dylan Mason – Swing / Ensemble
   / Understudy (White Rabbit
   / Luke / Mouse / Kieran)
Daisy Maywood – Humpty
Enyi Okoronkwo – Luke Laprel
Lisa Ritchie – Swing / Ensemble
   / Understudy (Dinah / Kitty
   / Mary Ann / Mock Turtle)
Stephanie Rojas – Mary Ann
   / Understudy (Humpty)
Abigail Rose – Kitty /
   Understudy (Alice)
Golda Rosheuvel – Bianca

Cydney Uffindell-Phillips
   – Mock Turtle
Ed Wade – Mouse / Kieran
Witney White – Dinah /
   Understudy (Aly)

Creatives

Author of *Alice's Adventures in
   Wonderland* – Lewis Carroll
Co-Creator / Music –
   Damon Albarn
Co-Creator / Book and
   Lyrics – Moira Buffini
Co-Creator / Director –
   Rufus Norris
Set Designer – Rae Smith
Projections – 59 Productions
Costume Designer – Katrina Lindsay
Lighting Designer – Paule Constable
Music Supervisor / Music
   Director – Tom Deering
Music Associate – Malcolm
   Forbes-Peckham
Sound Designer – Paul Arditti
Choreographer – Javier de Frutos
Associate Director – James Bonas
Associate Set Designer – Tom Paris
Associate Choreographer –
   Cydney Uffindell-Phillips
Staff Director – Tinuke Craig
Puppet Design 'Charlie' – Toby Olié
Company Voice Work –
   Jeanette Nelson

Stage Management

Stage Manager – Shane Thom
Deputy Stage Manager – Ruth Taylor
Assistant Stage Manager
   – Ian Connop
Assistant Stage Manager
   – Bryony Peach

Production

Deputy Production Manager
   – Emily Seekings

Project Draughting – Oliver Cooper
Digital Art – Daniel Radley-Bennett
Orchestrations – Damon Albarn
Additional Vocal Arrangements and
   Orchestrations – Tom Deering
Additional Vocal Arrangements and
   Orchestrations – David Shrubsole
Keyboard Programming
   – Jon Gingell
Music Preparation – Mark Dickman
Music Preparation – Tom Kelly
Music Consultant – David Shrubsole
Recording Engineer – Stephen
   Sedgwick, Studio 13
Costume Supervisor –
   Sabine Lamaître
Costume Prop Supervisor
   – Catherine Ladd
Assistant Costume Supervisor
   – Bryony Fayers
Assistant Costume Supervisor
   – Ashley Holtom
Wigs, Hair and Make-up
   Supervisor – Carole Hancock
Wigs, Hair and Make-up
   Supervisor – Suzanne Scotcher
Prop Supervisor – Eleanor Smith
Prop Buyer – Sian Willis
Lighting Supervisor –
   Brendan Arsdell
Lighting Programmer –
   Daniel Haggerty
Production Sound Engineer
   – Ed Ferguson
Sound Operator – Jonas Roebuck
Sound Associate – Giles Thomas
Stage Supervisor – Richard Gosling
Rigging Supervisor – Neill Shimmen
Video Programmer – Katie Pitt
Video Production Engineer
   – Matthew Morgans
Automation Supervisor – Simon Nott

Armourer / Special Effects
   Supervisor – Paul Wanklin
Armourer / Special Effects
   Supervisor – Steve Dart
Construction Supervisor
   – David Cotton
Scenic Art Supervisor –
   Lindsay Tufnell

Musicians

Music Director / Piano /
   Keyboard 1 – Tom Deering
Piano / Keyboard 2 – Ian Watson
Violin / Acoustic Guitar / Ukelele
   and Banjo – Sarah Freestone
Percussion / Kit – Tony McVey
Electric Bass – Tim Harries
Electric Guitar – Simon Tong
Flute / Piccolo / Alto Saxophone
   / Bass Flute – Andy Findon
Clarinet / Bass Clarinet / Soprano,
   Baritone and Tenor Saxophones
   – Christian Forshaw
Orchestral Management
   – Terry Eldridge
Orchestral Management
   – Rocky Shahan

Acknowledgements

Matt:

Firstly, I would simply not have been able to take on this daunting and rewarding project without the support and patience of my amazing wife Lou – to whom I dedicate this book. Huge respect in his 40th year also goes to my brother, Tom, who gave me my first job in theatre; Mum and Dad who have always supported me and encouraged me to follow my dreams; Anandh for his generous support and friendship; David Suchet for his interest, patience and support of the project; and to all our friends and family for their support – Thank You.

John:

Without the enduring love, patience and support of my family, not just Tat, Jack and Sammy, but my extended family both in the UK and the USA, I wouldn't be where I am today, and you wouldn't be holding this – the very first Curtain Call Annual. Dad, Mom, Liz, Kathy and T.J. - I love you and miss you. This book is dedicated to all of you. And to my friends, many of whose names appear within these pages, the same goes to you. See you on the boards! Ed Stoppard (who, I know, will hate this), is deserving of a special thanks.

Curtain Call would like to thank:

Caro Newling – for her support of and enthusiasm for the project from the outset; Emma De Souza – surely the hardest working person in London theatre – for her enduring support, patience, thought and encouragement throughout; Catherine Bowell for the countless emails and hustling on our behalf; Anthony McNeil – for the myriad opportunities and diligent work behind the scenes; Harriet Usher for guiding us through our first exhibition; and, last but not least, Julian Bird whose vision and positivity heads up the entire hard-working team at the Society of London Theatre.

Fred and Karim – for all the breakfasts, lunches, after hours talks, tough love, conference calls, crisis talks, direction, redirection, misdirection, advice, encouragement and, ultimately, your support and belief in establishing Curtain Call – Thank You.

Peter Aspbury, Edward Bearcroft, Gerard Boujo, David Brown, Haydn Cole, Robert Hanna, Annette Harris, Jennifer Horsman, Christopher Huddlestone, Des Humphrey, Nicholas Lyster, Carolyn Madley, Tim Norman, Rosemary Pearson, Jonathan Perkins, Serena Perkins, David Pilgrim, Ian Poulter, John Richardson, Martin Scorer, Margaret Sparks, Geoff Stanley, Andrew Strong, Carol Tsivanidis, Robert Winter, Liz Winter, Charlotte Winter, Ellie Winter and Georgie Winter.

A huge thank you to all the theatres, producers, stage management teams, crew members, stage door keeper's, front of house staff, theatre managers, publicists, marketing departments, agents and all other unsung heroes who have assisted us along the way including (and in no particular order): Jamie Lloyd – for his early belief and support of the project; Tim Pigott-Smith – for his belief and support of the project from the outset; Fiona Stewart, Lucie Lovatt, Lil Lambley and Sonia at Sonia Friedman Productions; Stacy Coyne, Charlotte Bayley, Priya Roy, Daisy Heath, Lucy Woollatt and David Lan at Young Vic; Vicky Featherstone, Anoushka Hay, Ryan Govin, Joni Carter, Lucy Davies, Becky Wootton and all of the team at the Royal Court; Marion Marrs, Claudia Conway, Harry Niland and all the team at Shakespeare's Globe; Holly Aston, Tom Robertson, Lydia Cotton, David Griffiths, Josie Rourke and Kate Pakenham at Donmar Warehouse; Rufus Norris, Lucinda Morrison, Mary Parker, Martin Shippen and Susie Newbery at the National Theatre; Nicky Palmer and all at Theatre Royal Bath; The Jamie Lloyd Company; Susie McKenna and all the team at the Hackney Empire; Colin Sumsion and all the teams at Big Buoy and Big Chop; Nicole Kidman; Kate Morley; Gemma Sutton; Sophie Thompson; Ros Povey; Jane Semark; Mark Rylance; Claire van Kampen; James McAvoy and Anne-Marie Duff; Kate Fleetwood; Emma Higginbottom; Maria Friedman; Jessica

Ronane CDG; George MacKay; Mark Strong; Nicola Walker; Barnaby Kay; Simon Russell Beale; Richard Eyre; Ivo van Hove and Jan Versweyveld; Jenna Russell; Yasheen Rajan; Tom Stoppard; Alan Scales; Andy Locke, Morag Shackerly–Bennett and all the team at Regent's Park Open Air Theatre; Edward Snape, Marilyn Eardley, Jon Bath, Hugh de la Bodeyere, Bonnie Royal and all the team at Fiery Angel; Susan Butterly, David Massey, Sara Lee, James-Paul Hayden and everyone at Working Title, Billy London Ltd, and Billy Elliot the Musical for helping to make the Billy shoot happen; Sally Greene and Sara White – for their early support of and belief in the project; Peter Clayton; Chichester Festival Theatre; Nicky Wingfield, Michael Rose and the team at London Management; Rosamund Cranmer, Sarah Brown and the team at David Ian Productions; Robyn Keynes and all the team at Smith & Brant; Tim Leist, Victoria Butler and all the team at Stage Entertainment; Rupert Goold, Simone Finney, Emma Pritchard, Jane Macpherson and all the team at the Almeida; Nica Burns, Max Weitzenhoffer and all the team at Nimax; Runaway Entertainment and Rock the Boat Ltd; Stephen McGill, David Hutchison, Phillip Rowntree and all the team at Sell A Door Theatre Company; Warner Bros. Theatre Ventures; Langley Park Productions; Neal Street Productions; Tom Siracusa and all the team at the Menier Chocolate Factory Productions; Jerry Mitchell and all the team at

Jerry Mitchell Productions; Kim Poster and the team at Stanhope Productions Ltd; Nicola Seed and all the team at Triumph Entertainment; Fiona Clark, Lee Connolly, Phil Ewell and all the team at ITV Studios and Sunday Night at the Palladium; Karl Sydow; Annie Reilly, Sam Hodges and the team at Nuffield; Robyn Hardy, Becky Paris and all the team at Hampstead Theatre; Nicole James, Sally Hoskins, Roger Penhale, Rhian Thomas, Marina Zain, Gregory Doran, Philippa Harland, Emma Welch, Olivia Farrant, Ben Tyreman and all the team at Royal Shakespeare Company; Amy Powell Yeates, Sam Sargant, Georgia Gatti, Lucy Osborn, Georgina Rae, Amy Michaels, Matthew Byam Shaw, Nia Janis, Nick Salmon and all the team at Playful Productions; Julian Stoneman and all the team at Julian Stoneman Associates; Emily Vaughan Barratt, Sarah Gimblett, Zareen Walker, Charlotte Longstaff and all the team at Ambassador Theatre Group; Martyn Hayes, Kezia Lock and the team at Kenny Wax; Tom Powis, Eleanor Lloyd and the team at Eleanor Lloyd Productions; Richard Clayton; Jenefer Tait; Oli Bagwell-Purefoy; Elaine De Saulles; John Caswell; Ben Delfont; Dan Gammon; Heather Bull; Katie Bazell; Keith Hayes; Steve Grant; James Boston; Jacqueline Morgan; Emma Banwell-Knight; Richard Fitch; Howard Jepson; Becca Ridley; Rosie Gilbert; Kirsty Nixon; Panny Elrington; Claire Sibley; Jo Miles; Mike Mansfield; Jason Golbourn; Jasper Fox; Anna Cole;

Alex Constantin; Jess Banks; Sian Wiggins; Wyn Williams; Rory Neal; Lynsey Hall; Lizzie Chapman; Olivia Ward; John Power; Izzy Perrin; Matthew Cullum; Marina Kilby; Heidi Lennard; Nicholas Bromley; Gaz Wall; Maria Baker; Alison Rankin; Xenia Lewis; Martin Hope; David Marsland; Davin Patrick; Matthew North; Sally Hughes; Mary O'Hanlon; Natalie Wood; Penny Foxley; Chloe Pritchard-Gordon, Hannah Clapham, Sara Sherwood, Theo Bosanquet and all the team at The Corner Shop PR; Georgie Robinson and the team at Emma Holland PR; Jo Allan PR; Premier PR; Kate Morley PR; Alan Snell – for his stellar work on creating our logo and setting our brand out on the right path; Ethan Kennedy – for his stunning, intuitive and insightful design work that set the tone for the book; Annabel Wright, John Bond, Molly Powell and all the team at Whitefox for believing in our book and making it a reality; Laura Marchant – for her super-organised and calm project management; Amanda Scope – for her beautiful, efficient and rapid design work; David Brimble and his expertise in printing; Printer Trento; Dawkins Colour Ltd; Kaye Moors, Kate Fernie, Stewart Fowler, Jaz Kilmister, Stephen Boulter, Lucy Regan and all the team at Drum Studios; Swan Press; Luke Westland; Will Taylor and his team; and anyone else we have inadvertently forgotten.